# Studies in Revelation

# Studies in Revelation

## An Expositional Commentary

by

W. Leon Tucker

KREGEL PUBLICATIONS
Grand Rapids, Mi. 49501

**Library of Congress Cataloging in Publication Data**

Tucker, Walter Leon, 1871-1934.
Studies in Revelation.

(Kregel Bible Study Classics)
Reprint of the ed. published by J. Young, Binghamton, N.Y.
1. Bible. N.T. Revelation—Commentaries.
I. Title. II. Series.
BS2825.T77 1980 228'.07 80-16206
ISBN 0-8254-3826-8

*Printed in the United States of America*

# CONTENTS

*Foreword* ... 7
*Structure of the Book* ... 17

| | | |
|---|---|---|
| Revelation 1:4-20 | The Voice and the Vision | 30 |
| Revelation 2-3 | God's People on Earth | 75 |
| Revelation 4 | A Throne: The Beginning of Judgment | 91 |
| Revelation 5 | A Kinsman in Heaven | 117 |

*Pre-Millenial Judgments Revelation 6-19*

| | | |
|---|---|---|
| Revelation 6:1-8 | Four Horses in Succession | 144 |
| Revelation 6:9-11 | The Fifth Seal | 158 |
| Revelation 6:12-17 | The Sixth Seal | 162 |
| Revelation 7 | Sixth and Seventh Seals | 170 |
| Revelation 8:1-14:20 | Seventh Seal, Silence, Seven Angels, Seven Trumpets | 185 |
| Revelation 8:7-14:20 | The Seven Trumpets | 193 |
| Revelation 11 | Two Witnesses | 233 |
| Revelation 12 | Man-child and the Dragon | 255 |
| Revelation 13 | Marine and Mundane Beasts | 275 |
| Revelation 14:1-5 | One Hundred and Forty-four Thousand | 297 |
| Revelation 14:6-20 | Six Angels and Son of Man | 301 |
| Revelation 14:14 | God's Wrath and His Winepress | 307 |
| Revelation 15 | Seven Angels, Golden Vials and Plagues | 311 |
| Revelation 16 | The Great Day of His Wrath | 317 |
| Revelation 17 | The Harlot Woman and the Beast | 336 |
| Revelation 18 | Fall of Babylon | 349 |
| Revelation 19:1-10 | Voices in Heaven | 353 |

*Millenial and Post-Millenial Events Revelation 20-22*

| | | |
|---|---|---|
| Revelation 19:11-20:6 | A King on Earth | 358 |
| Revelation 20:7-15 | A Throne: The End of Judgments | 366 |
| Revelation 21-22 | Post-Millenial Order | 370 |
| Revelation 22:6-21 | Conclusion | 383 |

Suggestive and Significant Notes ... 388

# FOREWORD

As one who attempts to climb challenging heights appreciating the magnificent beauty of mountain splendor, so is he who attempts to grasp, gain and give the supernatural truths of God's Word.

The earnest, disciplined climber finds inexpressible glory and fulfillment when he reaches the paramount peak. Likewise the believer who reads, receives and researches Christ's own testimony, The Revelation, finds God's Person, plan and prospect with glory that is immeasurable in magnitude.

*Studies in Revelation* by W. Leon Tucker is one of the most well-structured commentaries on the book of the Revelation that has ever been published. The author's grasp of The Scriptures shines forth in every chapter like the brightness of a noonday sun on snow-crowned peaks. The text in each chapter is superbly correlated with relevant Scripture verses in other books of the Bible. Author Tucker has explained the text in such an excellent fashion that not only can the beginning student understand the revelation of prophecy, but also the maturing mind is challenged with yet unopened portals of truth.

Focusing upon the occurrence of the word "throne" (some 37 times in the Book of the Revelation), the author presents the Book of Revelation as the "Throne Room" of the Bible. In a most useful manner, Tucker uses alliteration providing, for a student of The Scriptures, a very helpful means to get a handle on prophetic truths that are generally not so easily grasped. He also employs the method of reiteration of significant points so as to implant truths that are often glossed over or eroded by verbage.

Pastors and Christian teachers will be grateful that both the outline of *Studies in Revelation* and the terms are clearly expressed, enumerated, and explained. The orderliness and organization of this book easily commend this excellent outline as a reference for a pastor teaching his flock or as a textbook for the teacher offering a course covering the Book of the Revelation.

Mr. Tucker firmly holds to the premillennial, prophetic view of scripture. With conviction, he clearly supports his position. He presents this view not in a preachy or offensive manner but very forthrightly and with scholarly taste. The often overlooked and woefully-neglected subject of the *Justice of God* is also tastefully presented.

This is not a volume given to absurd speculation. The author is more concerned with the communication of Divine revelation. It is very evident, even from a superficial reading, that this book has been very prayerfully and carefully written. Lesson forty-five which covers *The Two Witnesses* is a classic. It demonstrates how tactfully accurate the author tried to be in his treatment of God's inerrant, infallible sacred Word. His *Suggestive and Significant Notes* found at the end of the book contain a gold mine of handy and rare information for the inquisitive student of the Revelation.

The Book of Revelation begins with a beatitude of blessing. The reader of *Studies in Revelation* will also receive much blessing. This commentary does not attempt in any way to add to or take away from or even to distract from the sacred majestic splendor of the Revelation of our Lord and Savior, Jesus Christ.

J. Arnold Fair

# STUDIES IN REVELATION

Lesson One

## INTRODUCTION

Divine prophecy followed human sin and prophecy will run its course when human sin has gone its length.

Prophecy which reveals God's plan of restoration follows closely the channel of human ruin.

The **last Book** of the Bible witnesses the **consummation** of prophecy as the **first Book** of the Bible records the commencement of prophecy.

The **Book of Revelation** is the final and finishing touch to the prophetic picture. Prophecy remains unfilled and unfinished until the Book of Revelation brings it to fulfillment.

The Book of Revelation is the **last word** of the Holy Ghost and reveals the **last work** of a Holy God.

The Book of Revelation not only bears testimony to Moses, the Psalms and the Prophets of the Old Testament, but also to the Evangelists and the Epistles of the New Testament.

They all run with straight course into the Book of Revelation and there receive finality and finish. The Bible is one Book from the first to the last Book.

The first Book of the Bible, Genesis, is completed only by the last Book of the Bible, Revelation. The Book of Revelation is not an **independent** contribution to the Scriptures, but is **dependent** upon the sixty-five Books preceding it.

The seemingly tangled threads of Bible history all come straight in the Book of Revelation.

The Book of Revelation produces all they promised. Said Jesus: "Not one jot or tittle shall fail till all be fulfilled." The Book of Revelation witnesses to the fact of His eternal truth. When Revelation is finished not one jot or tittle has failed but **all is fulfilled.**

The Book of Revelation is a consummation of the anticipation of the other Books of the Bible. Whatever is the fruit of Revelation is from the root of the Books which came before it.

O that men would study the **trend of prophecy** in the former writings, and look for the **end of prophecy** in this the final writing!

The four rivers which rise and run early in Genesis run into the sea in Revelation. When all these rivers run into the sea, then the sea is full.

Many have written much on the Book of Revelation, perhaps God will be pleased if others write more. For many years we have refrained from writing on this Book, lest we should entangle rather than impart. There are so many helpful writings on this great Book, it seems but little, if any be required. In our wide ministry about America many who have heard our lectures have insisted that we write. We shall. We trust to be suggestive as we cannot be exhaustive. May God use us to help the student and to provoke a more serious and sober consideration of this last great Book of prophecy.

**We shall avoid all controversy.** We shall seek to be constructive. We gratefully acknowledge help received from others and hope to be of some help to others. What we do not know we shall frankly acknowledge. We shall not enter into speculation, there has been too much of this. We shall write for the English student.

### The Title of the Book

It is the Book of **Revelation**—not **Revelations.** There are many visions but one **Revelation.** Its revelation is one and its visions many. It is a Book of **Revelation.** A Book of things **revealed.** A thing **revealed** is not a thing **concealed,** nor is a thing **concealed** a thing **revealed.** Surely this is sensible and simple.

R-E-V-E-L-A-T-I-O-N is the name of the Book. Its name indicates **what it is.** It is not a puzzle picture, **it** is a **revelation.** It is not a dark saying, it is a **revelation.** It is not an enigma, it is a **revelation.** It is so necessary to impress this on the minds of many who have been told this Book was **concealed** in **mystery.** No, it is **a** Book which is **revealed** and will one day be fulfilled in **history.**

"The secret things belong unto the Lord our God, but those things which are revealed belong unto us and our children forever" (Deut. 29:29).

We do not intrude into the secret things of God. They belong to Him. But **revealed** things are ours and therefore, the **Book of Revelation.** Many pastors have never encouraged their people to study this Book, indeed they have discouraged them. We have in mind a pastor in a large church in a great American city who, when asked by some of his flock to teach them this Book of Revelation, gave them what he said was "all he learned in the seminary" concerning this Book. He gave the inquirers the following:

1. **"I don't know anything about the Book of Revelation."**
2. **"You don't know anything about the Book of Revelation."**
3. **"Nobody knows anything about the Book of Revelation."**

A pastor **should** know something about the Book of Revelation, many of his people **do know** if he does not, and it is **not true** that "nobody knows anything about the Book of Revelation." It is a BOOK OF REVELATION and all believers may know much about this Book. The Holy Spirit delights to communicate what God has revealed.

It is the Book of unveiling. It is the Book of the open door. It is a simple Book when studied after the manner indicated in the Scripture. In this we shall seek to induct the student.

The Book of Revelation is much needed by the church today. The false philosophy of **human advance** has taken the place of the hope of the **Divine advent**; man's reason has supplanted **Divine revelation,** therefore the great need for this Book.

Throughout these studies we shall observe a few fundamental principles of interpretation as follows:

I. The Scriptures are self-explanatory, otherwise they would be **incomplete.** God's Word is sufficient for the interpretation of God's Word.

II. Nothing will be admitted as a **symbol** or as **figurative,** without the sanction of the Book itself. All will be understood as **literal** if not declared otherwise by the text.

III. We shall not attempt to reconcile to human **reason** things within the realm of Divine **revelation,** not subject to the **test** of the **natural** that which is **supernatural.** We shall accept by **faith** what we cannot understand in **fact.**

IV. We shall not spend time in **speculation** but in the study of the Book of Revelation. We shall seek not to go beyond what is written but to abide by and within what is written.

Lesson Two

## INTRODUCTION (continued)

The Book of Revelation in character and contact is summed up in one statement in the Second Epistle of Peter.

Says Peter: "The **power** and **coming** of our Lord Jesus Christ" (II Peter 1:16). Revelation is the Book of the **Power** (chap. 1—19) and the **Coming** (chap. 19; 20) of our Lord Jesus Christ.

The Book of Revelation is the answer to the prayer Jesus taught the twelve when at the first advent He came to offer unto "His own" the "kingdom of heaven." **"Thy kingdom come"** is the first petition. In the Book of Revelation, the **"kingdom comes."** "Thy will be done on **earth** as it is in heaven." The Book of Revelation brings the kingdom rule of heaven to the earth, which rule is known in the Scriptures as "the **kingdom of** heaven."

At the close of this prayer which Jesus gave unto the twelve, we read the words, "For Thine is the **kingdom** and the **power** and the **glory."** In the Book of Revelation indeed "Thine is the kingdom." See chapters 12:10; 11:15. In the Book of Revelation His is the **power.** See Revelation 2:26; 4:11; 5:13; 7:12; 12:10; 19:1. What a display of power in these verses. "Now is the 'power' of His Christ come" (12:10). Hallelujah!

The Book of Revelation is the Book in which all **"glory"** is given unto Him. See 5:12, "Thou art worthy to receive **glory."** See also 4:12; 7:12. The Book of Revelation is the Book of His **"kingdom," "power"** and **"glory."** It is the Book of the **"power"** and **"coming"** of our Lord Jesus Christ.

In the First Epistle of Peter there is also an indication

of the scope of the Book and the judgments therein. Says Peter:

"For the time is come that judgment must begin at the **house of God**: and if it begin at us what shall the end be of them that obey not the Gospel of God?" (I Peter 4:17).

In the Book of Revelation judgment **begins at the house of God** (chap. 2;3), the "end of them that obey not the Gospel of God" is seen in chapters 6—19 and a terrible end it is indeed!

Further says Peter, "If the righteous (the seven Churches of chapters 2 and 3), are scarcely saved, where shall the ungodly (antichrist) and the sinner, (the allies of antichrist and all others) appear?"

Where they shall appear is answered by **chapters 6—19** of the Book of Revelation.

The historical divisions of the Book of Revelation may be understood as follows:—

PREMILLENNIAL (chap. 1—20).

MILLENNIAL (chap. 20).

POSTMILLENNIAL (20:7—22:6).

In other words the first nineteen chapters record events prior to the advent.

In the first part of chapter 20 we have the record of things in times **millennial**—during the thousand years Christ reigns upon the earth. From the 7th verse of chapter 20 to the 6th verse of chapter 22 we have the record of things **postmillennial**—that is after the thousand-year reign of Christ.

Objection is often strongly urged against the teaching that Christ is to reign upon the earth a thousand years, upon the ground that it is mentioned in but one passage of Scripture and that one passage Revelation 20:4-6. This objection is indeed objectionable. It reveals great ignorance of both Old and New Testament Scriptures. If there were but one statement in the Bible that Christ would return and reign upon the earth this would be quite satisfactory and conclusive beyond controversy.

God is not as man who must repeat to impress. The Bible is not a Book of superfluities and excesses. God says **what He means** and He **means what He says.** The fact of the reign of a thousand years is six times repeated in the 20th chapter of Revelation alone. The student will do well to read vss. 1-7 of this chapter marking "thousand years" each time it is mentioned.

Surely these words are plain. If not another reference to the thousand years was anywhere to be found, this should be sufficient. But the thousand years was a well-known subject to Moses, to psalmists and prophets as well as unto New Testament writers. In subsequent studies we will discover that there are many Old Testament **words** and **phrases** which are the equivalent and indeed are the **very words** for a thousand years, or an age of millennial duration.

The great subjects of the Bible are in the Book of Revelation brought to consummation. There are **seven** great subjects in the Book of Revelation which must be considered and must not be overlooked in the study of the Book. These subjects may be tabulated as follows:

1. **The Confirmation of the Covenants.**
2. **The Preservation of National Israel.**
3. **The Tribulation Predicted by the Prophets.**
4. **The Destination of the Nations.**
5. **The Manifestation of Messiah.**
6. **The Subjugation of the Earth.**
7. **The Termination of the Dispensations and Consummation of Divine Revelation.**

The student will discover that the seven above mentioned subjects have been carefully chosen, and if these things are sought after in the study of this Book **there will be no disappointment.**

There are many covenants in the Scriptures, they are all confirmed and the terms thereof fulfilled in this last Book of the Bible.

The preservation of Israel as a nation comes to its full in this last Book of the Bible.

The terrible tribulation period predicted throughout the Scriptures, in the last Book of the Bible reaches the time of its fury in the furnace of Jehovah.

The destiny of the nations of the earth, is in this last Book of the Bible traced to triumph on the new earth.

The manifestation or the period of Messiah in power and great glory, is accomplished in this last Book of the Bible.

The subjugation of the earth to the rule of the last Adam who rules with a rod of iron, is also one of the victories of this last Book of the Bible.

The termination of a series of dispensations through which God in His eternal purpose had made Himself known, are brought in this Book to a consummation, thus completing Divine Revelation.

It can be seen that the Book of Revelation is dealing with the ponderous subjects of the Bible. In this Book all scattered things are gathered together.

Lesson Three

## STRUCTURE OF THE BOOK

In the study of the Book of Revelation the student should distinguish the INTRODUCTION and the CONCLUSION of the Book. They should not be read into the **main body of the prophecy.** The INTRODUCTION to the Book of Revelation is contained in the **first three verses of chapter 1.** The CONCLUSION of the Book of Revelation will be found in **chapter 22, verse 6 to the close.**

The unfolding of the prophecy of the Book begins at chapter 1:4, and the end of the prophecy of the Book ends at chapter 22:5. It would be well for the student to make notation in the margin of Bible at 1:1-3, **"Introduction,"** and at 22:6-21, **"Conclusion."** Do not hesitate to preserve the result of study on the margin of Bible.

The Book of Revelation, it will be seen, opens with a BEATITUDE: **"Blessed** is he that readeth and they that hear the words of this prophecy and keep those things which are written therein; for the time is at hand" (vs. 3).

The Book of Revelation not only opens with a BEATITUDE but it closes with a BENEDICTION: "The grace of our Lord Jesus Christ be with you all. Amen" (22:21). Thus we see the Book of Revelation is bounded by a **beatitude** and a **benediction.**

While the Book opens with a "beatitude," it ends with a "burden." A **blessing** is promised for those who read and receive, and a curse is pronounced upon those who **"take from"** or **"add unto."** There is no place in prophecy for **addition** or **subtraction.** Prophecy is **full** and **final** and **finished** when this Book comes to its close. It is

"Ne-plus-ultra"—no more beyond. There is blessing upon those who read and receive, **burdens** upon those who reject! **Promise** for the reader but plagues for the rejecter!

There is no place in prophecy for **addition** for God has spoken finally and fully—there is nothing lacking. He has said all He wanted said, nothing further is required. The body of prophecy is **completed** and **consummated** at the close of the Book of Revelation. There has been **no authoritative or valid prophecy uttered since the close of the Book of Revelation.**

All prophecy since this Book has been, has been **false prophecy** and all prophets have been **false prophets.** Why should there be yet other prophecy? The things which **were then** and are now and will be hereafter are all told and foretold in this Book, therefore no other prophet or prophecy is necessary. The perfection of prophecy forbids of addition. **Mathematics can not enter into a completed and perfected whole.** The Spirit of God is the Author of prophecy and all other writings are less than prophecy for they are apart from Him (Rev. 1:4, 11; II Peter 1:20, 21).

The Scriptures are built upon mathematical precision and cannot by mathematics be brought to confusion. Nor is there place in prophecy for **subtraction.** Nothing can be taken from prophecy. The body of prophecy can not be broken into fractions. Its unity forbids it. No prophecy of olden time came by "private interpretation" (II Peter 1:20). Prophecy is as finished and as final as the work of Christ on the cross—nothing can be **added to it** or nothing **taken from it!** Not one jot or one tittle will fail till **"all be fulfilled"** (Matt. 5:18). Man by taking thought can not add one cubit to the stature of prophecy, nor can he take away from it so much as the smallest Hebrew punctuation mark or point.

There are many things in the body of prophetic writings which evil man would gladly remove but they are unremovable! Man dislikes the prophetic future so far as he is concerned, for it is to him humbling and not honoring. Its purpose is to abase him and exalt the Lord, and that is not the mind of natural man (Is. 2:11, 12, 17, 22).

If man attempts to **add**—God adds. If man attempts to **subtract**—God subtracts. Hear! Here is the condemnation of the critics:

"If any man **add** unto these things, **God shall add** unto him the plagues written in this Book. If any man **shall take away** from the words of the Book of this prophecy **God shall take away** his part out of the Book of Life, and out of the Holy City and from the things which are written in this Book" (22:18, 19).

**Addition** and **subtraction** are awful things in the power of a **holy and angry God!**

It is thus a Book which opens in a blessed beatitude of **benediction,** ends with a **malediction,** just preceding its final **valediction.**

The next thing to be considered in the INTRODUCTION (1:1-3), and the CONCLUSION (22:6-21), of the Book of Revelation is the

## ORIGIN AND ORDER OF THE REVELATION

From whence came this Book and the vision thereof? This is answered in both the **"introduction"** and the **"conclusion."** The **introduction affirms** it. The **conclusion confirms** it. The descent of the Book is as follows:

**GOD**
CHRIST
ANGEL
JOHN
SERVANTS

**God** gave it to **Christ. Christ** gave it to an **angel.** An **angel** gave it unto **John.** John gave it unto his **"servants"** (1:1). The "genealogy" of the Book reveals its origin with God and its descent down to man. This revelation may be traced from **God** to **"His servants."** As in the incarnation, so here in the Revelation, the **initiative** is with God and the **issue** for man.

At the **conclusion** of the Book we see **John** at the feet of the **angel** to whom **Christ** has given it from **God** (*22*:8). "The **Lord God** of the holy prophets sent His angel to show unto **His servants** the things which must shortly be done" (*22*:6).

At the CONCLUSION as at the INTRODUCTION, we behold the Book of Revelation coming from:

**GOD**
CHRIST
ANGEL
JOHN
SERVANTS

The **origin and order** of the Book is of much importance and vital to its understanding. It has been said, "John borrowed the visions of this Book." It has been declared that these visions were "heathen visions Christianized." This Book is not a patchwork of heathen folklore. It is **from God** as is all of the Bible from Genesis to the Revelation.

## JOHN'S TESTIMONY

The testimony of John is also a subject of both the **introduction** and **conclusion** of this Book of Revelation.

Says the **introduction:**

"His servant John who bare record of the Word of God and of the testimony of Jesus Christ and **of all the things that he saw"** (1:1, 2).

At the **conclusion** we also read:

"And I John, **saw these things** and **heard them** and when I had **heard and seen,** * * I worshipped" (22:8, 9).

We receive and believe the testimony of John. He was not a visionary; he **saw these visions.** He got them from an **angel** as the angel got them from **Christ,** who received them from **God.**

The Book of Revelation is from God, let us so receive it! Who will therefore assume and presume that the Book of Revelation is from other source than is here plainly and particularly stated in both the **introduction** and the **conclusion** of the Book? We bow to the authority of Holy Writings. We have no controversy. We have confidence and worship before the God of Revelation.

## Lesson Four

# STRUCTURE OF THE BOOK (continued)

In the further consideration of the **Introduction** (1:1-3), and the **Conclusion** (22:6-21), of the Book of Revelation attention is called to the manner in which both the Introductory and Concluding portions attest the true character of the Book. Notice the emphasized or italicized words in the two verses presented:

"Blessed is he that readeth, and they that hear the words of **this prophecy**, and keep those things which are written therein; for the time is at hand" (1:3).

"And if any man shall take away from the words of the Book of **this prophecy**, God shall take away his part out of the Book of Life and out of the Holy City and from the things which are written in this Book" (22:19).

At the opening of the Book of Revelation, in the Introduction, this Book is declared to be a Book of "**prophecy.**" At the close of the Book in the Conclusion, it is declared to be a Book of "**prophecy.**" The Book of "**this prophecy.**"

The Book of Revelation is a Book of PROPHECY. It must be classified with the Books of prophecy. It is not a Book of **history** as for instance, is the Book of Acts—it is a Book of **prophecy.**

**Seven times** the Book of Revelation is stamped with the seal of prophecy. See 1:3, 11:6; 19:10; 22:7, 10, 18, 19.

Chapter 1:3 says, "**This prophecy.**" In 22:7, "The prophecy of this Book." At 22:10, "**The prophecy** of this Book." Again 22:18 says, "The words of **the prophecy** of this Book," and finally at 22:19 we read: "The Book of **this prophecy.**"

In the Introduction it is proclaimed a Book of "**prophecy.**" **Four times** in the Conclusion, it is affirmed to be a Book of "**prophecy.**"

This Book, as all other prophecy, came not by the

"will of man," nor was it of "private" or independent "interpretation" (II Peter 1:20, 21). The Book of Revelation is not apart from other Books of prophecy. It deals with the same subjects with all other Books of prophecy.

The Book of Revelation does not introduce a discordant note into the harmony of the prophetic writings. It brings out of the roots of prophecy, the full fruit of prophecy. Whatever was the subject of prophecy anywhere in the Scripture, is the subject of prophecy in the Book of Revelation. Prophecy had for its great subject the person of Christ. Christ is seen throughout prophecy in two aspects, viz.: His **"suffering"** and His **"glory."** While the former prophecies were forecast prior to His "sufferings," they deal with the two aspects, that is, with both the "suffering" and the "glory." Inasmuch as the prophecies of the Book of Revelation were given unto John after His "suffering," therefore the burden of the Book of Revelation is the **"glory that should follow."**

In the Book of Revelation it is:

"Worthy is the Lamb that **was slain** to receive power, and riches, and wisdom and strength and honour and **glory** and blessing" (5:12).

In the Book of Revelation we see the "glory" of which the slain Lamb is worthy.

The nation Israel and the Gentile nations are also the subject of prophecy and the only subject of prophecy, therefore in the Book of Revelation, Israel and the nations are before us.

The Book of Revelation is not a Book historically fulfilled, but a Book which is yet to be fulfilled.

May God hasten it in His time!

## THE TESTIMONY OF JOHN

In the **Introductory** portion of the Book we read:

"John * * who bare record of the Word of God, and of the testimony of Jesus Christ, and of all things that he saw" (1:1, 2).

In the concluding portion of the Book we read:

"And I John saw these things and **heard** them. And when I had **heard** and **seen** I fell down to worship before the feet of the angel which **shewed** me these things" (22:8).

The testimony of John is that he both **"heard"** and **"saw."** He heard the voices and saw the visions of this Book. His testimony is true. The **Introduction** and the **Conclusion** both bear record of this fact.

That the sayings of this Book are **"faithful and true."** See 19:9; 21:5; 22:6. It is a threefold affirmation.

## THE SALUTATION AND THE SUPPLICATION

The Book also opens with a **Salutation** and ends with a **Supplication.**

### THE SALUTATION

"John to the seven Churches which are in Asia: Grace **be** unto you, and peace, from Him which is, and which was, and which is to come; and from the seven Spirits which are before His throne; and from Jesus Christ, **who is** the Faithful Witness, **and** the First Begotten of the dead, and the Prince of the kings of the earth. Unto Him that loved us, and washed us from our sins in His own Blood. And hath made us kings and priests unto God and His Father; to Him **be** glory and dominion for ever and ever. Amen. Behold, He cometh with clouds; and every eye shall see Him, and they **also** which pierced Him: and all kindreds of the earth shall wail because of Him. Even so, Amen. I am Alpha and Omega, the Beginning and the Ending, saith the Lord, which is, and which was, and which is to come, the Almighty" (Rev. 1:4-8).

### THE SUPPLICATION

"He which testifieth these things saith, Surely I come quickly. Amen. EVEN so, COME, LORD JESUS."

In the **Salutation** John says: **"Behold He cometh"** (1:7).

In the **Supplication** the cry is: **"Even so, come, Lord Jesus."**

This is all very beautiful and as it should be. In **Salutation** the Lord declares He is coming and in **Supplication** His people bid Him come on. "I am coming," saith the Lord. "Come on," saith His waiting people.

At the opening of the Revelation the Lord announces His coming, and at the close, the **"Spirit,"** the **"Bride,"** and **"him that heareth,"** all say, **"Come."** See 22:17.

At the opening there is **announcement,** at the close there is **answer.** The Revealer at the opening, and the **Response** at the close. How blessed! Salutation and Supplication!

At the opening of the Book He says, "I come quickly" (3:11). At the close of the Book He says, "Surely I come quickly" (22:7, 20). Amen. "Even so, come."

**Six times** in the Book there is word of "quick" and speedy coming. See 2:5; 2:16; 3:11; 22:7, 12, 20.

The Conclusion of the Book three times promises this hasty coming (22:7, 12, 20).

It is **"I John"** who speaks at the opening of the Book announcing the advent of his Lord (1:4, 9).

It is **"I Jesus,"** who announces His own advent at the close of the Book (22:16).

**"Even so, Amen,"** opens the Book (1:7). **"Even so, Amen,"** closes the Book (22:20).

The **"Coming One"** is declared to be "Alpha and Omega, the Beginning and the Ending," at the opening of the Book (1:8), and the same is confirmed at the close of the Book: "I am Alpha and Omega, the Beginning and the End, the First and the Last" (22:13).

**John** testifies at the opening of the Book, **Jesus** testifies at the close of the Book. See 1:2 and 22:16.

At the opening of the Book, John **fell as dead** at the feet of the "One like unto the Son of man" (1:17).

At the close of the Book he **fell down** to worship before the feet of the angel (22:8).

At the opening of the Book an Angel is sent to **signify** and at the close an Angel is sent to **testify** (1:1; 22:16).

At the opening of the Book there is instruction to send what was seen and heard to the seven Churches or Assemblies. At the conclusion of the Book this is again mentioned (1:4, 11; 22:16).

Between the opening and the closing portions of the Book of Revelation there is a **comparison** and a **correspondence** which is indeed interesting, and is also a testimony to Divine inspiration. The study may continue on this with much pleasure and profit.

Lesson Five

## STRUCTURE OF THE BOOK (continued)

Having considered the **Introduction** and the **Conclusion** of the Book of Revelation we shall now look upon the broad framework of the Book and trust we shall be enabled to see something of the design purposed by the Divine Architect in its structure. The Book of Revelation, as all other Books of Holy Scripture, is framed fitly after a perfect pattern.

In order to arrive at the unity and continuity of the Book, the structure or framework is of great value and may be viewed most advantageously by the comparison of the extremes until the center is reached—or in other words from the **circumference** to the center.

The Book of Revelation is bounded by the **Introduction** and the **Conclusion** and the visions of the Book lie between. Beginning at the outer divisions we shall move to the center where we shall find the main division of the Book. The major portion of the Book is concerned with a period of time lying between the **rapture** and the **return.** It is a period of judgment—of judgments upon Israel and the nations. And upon all evil in whatever manifestation, and from wherever sphere or source, in any part of the universe, it may arise.

The student may arrive at the scope and the structure of this Book by alternating with numbers of the outline.

When a number is reached, as for instance 1, 2, or 3, look below for the corresponding 1, 2, or 3. By this method development and design may be discovered and with much delight and priceless profit.

It will be well to preserve this outline as it will be the subject of reference throughout the studies which are, if Jesus tarry, to follow.

## DIVISIONAL DISPLAY OF THE BOOK OF REVELATION

I. INTRODUCTION (1:1-3).

II. THE VOICE AND THE VISION (1:4-20).

THE VISION OF THE ASCENDED CHRIST.
(Christ in Heaven).

III. THE PEOPLE OF GOD ON PRESENT EARTH (chap. 2—3).

PREMILLENNIAL PREPARATION

IV. A THRONE—THE BEGINNING OF JUDGMENT (chap. 4).

THE JUDGMENT OF THE WICKED LIVING

V. A KINSMAN IN HEAVEN (chap. 5).

**THE PREMILLENNIAL PROPHETIC JUDGMENTS—THE SEVENTIETH WEEK OF DANIEL'S PROPHETIC CHRONOLOGY—THE TIME OF JACOB'S TROUBLES (chap. 6-19).**

V. A KING ON EARTH (chap. 19:11—20:6).

IV. A THRONE—THE END OF JUDGMENT (chap. 20: 7-15).

THE JUDGMENT OF THE WICKED DEAD

III. THE PEOPLE OF GOD ON THE NEW EARTH (chap. 21:1-8).

POSTMILLENNIAL BLESSINGS

II. THE VOICE AND THE VISION (chap. 21:9—22:5).

THE VISION OF THE DESCENDING CITY
(God on Earth).

I. CONCLUSION (chap. 22:6-21).

With this outline we are somewhat prepared to consider the subject matter of the Book of Revelation. We believe and receive what is written. We are confident we have here a revealing and not a concealing. It is not a "dark saying," but a Divine seeing. We are not here before a Book enshrouded in mystery, but a Book unfolded in simplicity. We again acknowledge our own ignorance, and gladly accept the revelation which is freely given unto us. We are rejoiced to confess that we believe what is written to be what God desired us to know. Our chief boast is that we do not know enough to question God's Word, but trust enough to receive His Word. We urge our readers to carefully read the Book again and again.

## Lesson Six

# THE VOICE AND THE VISION (Rev.1:4-20) Part 1

We shall now consider each member of the **Divisional Display** of the **Book of Revelation** as presented in **Lesson Number five.** The introduction and conclusion having been the subject of former lessons, we pass to Division II which is designated as—

II. THE VOICE AND THE VISION (1:4-20).

THE VISION OF THE ASCENDED CHRIST
(Christ in Heaven).

John (vs. 4), the person by whom came the communication of this revelation. A **special revelation** was committed unto Paul (Eph. 3:2-9), for which cause he was a prisoner (Eph. 3:1; 4:1), and this **final revelation** was communicated through John who was also, perhaps, a prisoner (Rev. 1:9).

The revelation committed to Paul was **unknown** to the prophets, while that communicated to John was **well known** to all the prophets. Paul's revelation was peculiar to this **dispensation;** John's revelation has to do with the **consummation.**

To the seven churches which are in Asia, hereafter designated as:

1. **Ephesus** (1:11; 2:1) meaning "desirable" or "throwing" or "casting down."

2. **Smyrna** (1:11; 2:8) which signifies "myrrh," "bitter but fragrant."

3. **Pergamos** (1:11; 2:12) which may signify either "elevation," "lifted up" or "actual marriage."

4. **Thyatira** (1:11; 2:18) which may signify either "perfumed, bruised, or from thuo, to sacrifice, and tiero, to tear away—the perfume from persecution."

5. **Sardis** (1:11; 3:1) which means "things remaining" to which there may be an allusion in verse 2.

6. **Philadelphia** (1:11; 3:7) signifying "brotherly love."

7. **Laodicea** (1:11; 3:14) which may mean "righteous people."

Because these names of Churches may have spiritual signification, it does not intimate or imply that they were not of **actual location.** Says John, "To the Seven Church which are in Asia."

### GRACE BE UNTO YOU AND PEACE

This is the Divine order—first "grace" and then "peace." The Prophet Isaiah however, seemed to understand the Divine order by which "peace" should result. It was to follow the work of "righteousness," and in this Book of Revelation it is the order. A period of righteous retribution is followed by peace. "The work of righteousness," said the prophet "shall be peace and the effect of righteousness will be quietness and assurance forever" (Is. 32:17). The judgments (chap. 6—19) which constitute the major portion of this Book will be "cut short in righteousness" because a **"short work will the Lord make upon the earth"** (Rom. 9:27, 28). Their **severity** accounts for their **shortness.** "Except they be shortened," said Jesus. After the judgments of this Book **peace** and **quietness** on the earth, but **never till then.**

### FROM HIM WHICH IS, AND WHICH WAS, AND WHICH IS TO COME

This is the first of a series of Divine titles following through to verse 8.

1. Him which is, and which was, and which is to come (vs. 4).

2. Seven Spirits before the throne (vs. 4).
3. Jesus Christ (vs. 5).
4. The Faithful Witness (vs. 5).
5. The First-Begotten of the dead (vs. 5).
6. The Prince of the kings of the earth (vs. 5).
7. God and His Father (vs. 6).
8. Alpha and Omega, the Beginning and the Ending.
9. The Lord, which is, which was, and which is to come.
10. The Almighty.

Thus it will be seen that this passage which begins with the word **"John"** and continues until again the word **"John"** occurs (vss. 4-8), opens and closes with what we call the **"Jehovah titles."**

**"Him which is and which was, and which is to come,"** ascribes to God as containing in Himself **past, present** and **future.** It is the unspeakable and incommunicable name of God. This word has had the form of the **past,** in its final letter—the **present** in its participle and the **future** in the commencing letter.

Attention has also been called to the fact that the letters occur in the reversed order—the future first, and the past last of the series of this union of time can not be expressed any other way in Hebrew.

That the name Jehovah should practically preface this Book and all its titles, is in full keeping with the character and contents of the Book, for it was Jehovah who was revealed and made known to Israel, with whom this Book is largely concerned.

This occurs in 1:4, 8, in 4:8 and in 11:17, and is the Greek translation of the Hebrew title—**Jehovah.** It combines the past and future in one word. The word occurs 7,000 times in the Hebrew Scriptures, but only so translated about seven times in the Authorized Version.

The "I AM" who came down at the opening of the Exodus is at the opening of the Book of Revelation about to come down again.

**AND FROM THE SEVEN SPIRITS WHICH ARE BEFORE HIS THRONE**

"**Before** His throne," not **on** His throne. "Before His throne"—the place of **servants.** "Seven spirits"—angels are called "spirits" (Heb. 1:7, 14). Psalm 104:4: **"He maketh His angels spirits."** As servants they await before His throne to do His will (I Kings 10:8).

In Revelation 3:1 they are joined with the seven stars.

In Revelation 5:6 they are "sent forth unto all the earth."

At the opening of the Book of Revelation the "end of the age" is at hand, so also are the angel servants as Jesus had foretold—**"The Son of Man shall send forth His angels." "At the end of the age the angels shall come forth"** (Matt. 13:41, 49).

The **seven** here mentioned are seen at Revelation 8:20. **"And I saw the seven angels which stood before God."** This is not the only place angels are mentioned with God and the Lord Jesus Christ. See First Timothy 5:21: **"God, the Lord Jesus and the elect angels,"** the same as in the passage at the opening of the Revelation. God, the Lord Jesus and the elect angels constitute the Supreme High Court of heaven about ready to execute judgments on the earth.

The Book of Revelation is a Book of "angels." Each chapter save three (chap. 4; 6; 13), has many references to angels who are active throughout the Book. There are about **seventy** references to angels in this Book. Watch "angels" in the Book of the Revelation. Angels may be traced through the Revelation at the following places: 1:1, 20; 2:1, 8, 12, 18; 3:1, 5, 7, 14; 5:2, 11; 7:1, 2, 11; 8:2-8, 10, 12, 13; 9:1, 11, 13-15; 10:1, 5, 7-

10; 11:1, 15; 12:7, 9; 14:6, 8-10, 15, 18, 19; 15:1, 6-8; 16:1, 3, 5, 17; 17:1, 7; 18:1, 21; 19:17; 20:1; 21:9, 12, 17; 22:6, 8, 16.

### AND FROM JESUS CHRIST

**Jesus,** the name of His humiliation at the incarnation, first, then, **Christ,** the name of His exaltation. See Philippians 2:5-11. The name **"Jesus"** occurs in the Book of Revelation **nine** times and in **combination with Christ, five** times. See 1:1, 2, 5, 9; 12:17. **"Christ"** occurs in this Book **four times** (11:15; 13:10; [His] 20:4, 6), and always with the definite article in the Greek—**"The Christ."**

### WHO IS THE FAITHFUL WITNESS

Christ is two times called a **"Witness"** in this Book. Faithful Witness (1:5). Faithful and True Witness 3:14). Isaiah was first to confer upon Him this title, **"Behold I have given Him for a Witness to the people** * *" (Is. 55:4). Christ Himself said: "I came into the world that I should **bear witness"** (John 18:37), and this was spoken unto a **Gentile ruler.** It will be well to look into the Scripture, Isaiah 55:4, where first the title **"Witness"** occurs. In Isaiah 55:3 we have the "Jew first"—**"I will make an everlasting covenant with you even the sure mercies of David."**

At verse 4 we have **"the Gentile"—"Behold I have made Him a Witness to the Gentiles, a Ruler and a Governor to the nations."** See A. V., R. V., Lowth's and LXX translations.

This **"Witness"** is given to the Gentiles and is to be **Governor** and **Ruler** of the nations (peoples), and the appearance of this title at the opening of the Book of Revelation is in common concord with the Book itself in which we see the Gentile nations brought first under the judgment of God and ultimately under the **rod** and **rule** of Christ. To the "overcomers" of the assembly at

Thyatira, there is a promise given for "power over the nations" (Gentiles) and "He shall rule them with a rod of iron; as the vessels of a potter shall they be broken to shivers; even as I received of My Father" (Rev. 2:26, 27). In chapter 19 Christ goes forth to "smite the nations" (Gentiles) and to "rule them with a rod of iron" (Rev. 19:15). This is also the prophecy of Psalm 2:8, 9. As "Witness" He is related to the "Gentiles" or "nations" or "peoples," and at the threshold of a Book which deals with "Israel" and the "nations" it is the natural thing that this title should be mentioned. The word **"Witness"** is never used in connection with **Israel** but with the **Gentiles** who, before this Book has concluded, come under Messiah's rule. He will be Governor of the nations. When God raised His Joseph-Jesus to the throne, He forgot not the Gentiles, either in judgment or mercy.

### AND THE FIRST-BEGOTTEN OF THE DEAD

Christ is called "First-born" or "First-Begotten" five times in the New Testament (Rom. 8:29; Col. 1:15, 18; Heb. 1:6; Rev. 1:5). Christ arose from the dead not only first in point of **time** but also in **rank.** This is a reference to **rank.** See Psalm 89:27. It was the **"declared decree"** (Ps. 2). "Thou art My Son, this day have I begotten Thee" (Ps. 2:7; Heb. 1:5; Acts 13:33).

A brief review of Paul's sermon at Antioch as recorded in Acts 13 may be of help in the understanding of the title, "First-Begotten from the dead."

### THE OLD TESTAMENT HISTORY OF ISRAEL

### Acts 13:17-22

**The Choice of National Israel** vs. 17—Gen. 12.

**Their Sojourn in the Land of Egypt** vs. 17—Gen. 46 to Exod. 12.

**Their Deliverance Out of Egypt** vs. 17—Exod. 13 to 15.

**Their Wilderness Wanderings** vs. 18—Exod. to Deut.
**The Possession and Division of the Land** vs. 19—Josh.
**The Period of the Judges** vs. 20—Judg.
**The Period of Samuel the Seer** vs. 20—I Sam.
**The Period of King Saul** vs. 21—I Sam.
**The Period of King David** vs. 22—I and II Sam.

### THE NEW TESTAMENT HISTORY OF ISRAEL
### Acts 13:23-37

**The Birth of Christ** vs. 23—Matt. 1.
**The Ministry of John** vs. 25—Matt. 3.
**The Presentation of Christ to Israel** vs. 25—Matt. 3; 4.
**Salvation Sent to Israel** vs. 26—Matt. 5 to 12.
**Israel's Rejection of Christ** vs. 27—Matt. 12 to 26.
**The Trial before Pilate** vs. 28—Matt. 26; 27.
**His Death on Cross and Burial in Tomb** vs. 29—Matt. 26 to 28.

### BUT GOD

**Raised Up from the Dead** vs. 30—Matt. 28.
**The Post-Resurrection Ministry** vs. 31—Matt. 28; Acts 1:1-8.
**The Preaching of the Resurrection** vs. 32—Acts.

"God hath **fulfilled** the same unto us (Israel) their children, in that He hath raised up Jesus again; as it is also written in the second Psalm, **Thou art My Son, this day have I begotten Thee.**"

"And as concerning that He **raised Him up from the dead,** now no more to return to corruption, He said on this wise, **I will give you the sure mercies of David"** (vss. 33, 34).

So here at the opening of the Book of Revelation is the One whom **"God raised up,"** the **"First-Begotten from the dead,"** in whom the oath God swore unto David is certain and secure. The death of Christ, David's Son and Heir, did not result in the overthrow of the Davidic Dynasty. David's throne shall be occupied by David's greater Son. God raised Him up for this purpose and in the resurrection of the "First-Begotten from the dead," "the sure mercies of David" (Is. 55:3) are guaranteed.

The "Sign of Jonah" the prophet is at the threshold of this Book—One "begotten from the dead" on the **"third day."** He has been raised up to sit on David's throne. It was the decree and **it can not fail.** He **shall sit** on David's throne on Zion's Holy Hill in the Holy City in the Holy Land! The "nations will rage" in this Book of Revelation, the "people" (Israel) will "imagine a vain thing" (image the antichrist), but by power of the resurrection Christ shall yet sit as "King" upon **"My Holy Hill of Zion."**

Lesson Seven

## THE VOICE AND THE VISION (Rev.1:4-20) Part 2

We shall further consider the Divine titles which were before us in **Lesson Number Six.**

**AND THE PRINCE OF THE KINGS OF THE EARTH (vs. 5).**

**"Prince of the Kings of the Earth,"** is one of the **triology of titles** occuring here and which are a reference to Psalm 89 where **all three of these titles appear.**

| **PSALM 89** | **REVELATION 5** |
|---|---|
| "Also will I make Him my First-born, | "The Firstbegotten from the dead" (Rev. 1:5). |
| * * * | * * * |
| higher than the kings of the earth" (Ps. 89:27). | "Prince of the Kings of the Earth" (Rev. 1:5). |
| * * * | * * * |
| "And as a Faithful Witness in heaven" (Ps. 89:37). | "Who is the Faithful Witness" (Rev. 1:5). |

That these three titles from Psalm 89 should be recalled here at the opening of the Book of Revelation, is in full harmony with the prophetic Word. Psalm 89 is a **recital** of, and a **rejoicing** in the covenant sworn unto David.

David is three times mentioned by name in this Psalm.

1. I have **sworn** unto David My servant (vs. 3).
2. I have **found** and **anointed** David My servant (vs. 20).
3. Thou **swarest** unto David in Thy Truth (vs. 49).

The portrait of this Psalm is too full to fit David, nor does he fill it in. It is the greater Son of David which is before us here. It is **"Jesus Christ the Son of David"** (Matt. 1:1). It is "His Son, Jesus Christ our Lord, which was made of the seed of David according to the flesh" (Rom. 1:3). He, Christ, is the "First-born," the **"Prince of the Kings of the Earth"** and the **"Faithful Witness."**

David's Son and Heir, in this triology of Psalm titles, is introduced at the opening of this Book of Revelation for He will be required.

One must early be found to have the **kinsman's rights** of David's people to take the **kingdom reign** of David's throne. When such is demanded, there will be One discovered and disclosed who is the **"Lion of Judah's** tribe" (royal rights) and of the **root of David** (kinsman ties) to take the Book and open the seals thereof, put in motion the judgments which will ultimately issue in the ejection of the usurper and the restoration and restitution of the disponed possession to the rightful heirs and legal claimants (Rev. 5:5).

He is the "Prince of the Kings of the Earth" and is here placed in comparison with them. This title takes on great significance when viewed in the light of the second Psalm where not only the words **"kings of the earth"** occur, but where also is found the preceding title, "The Firstbegotten from the Dead." See Revelation 1:5; Psalm 2:2, 7.

At the opening of Psalm 2, the "heathen" or **Gentiles** are "raging" (reference is to the sons of Japheth [Gen. 10:15]) and **"the people"** (Israel) are imagining a vain thing. There is a confederation of governments, both kingdoms and other forms as is indicated by the terms **"kings"** and **"rulers,"** for in the days of the coming confederation **all rulers will not be kings,** for in foretelling the political character of these days, Daniel, the prophet, describes them as "iron and clay mixed." See Daniel 2:41-44. Monarchy and democracy will mix and mingle but with no more coherence than **"iron with clay."**

"Rulers" as used here may even include the "rulers

of this world's darkness" or spiritual hosts of darkness, and doubtless it does.

These "kings" and "rulers" are in a "confederation," they have "set themselves" and have "taken counsel" against the Lord and against His **"Anointed"** (Ps. 2:2). Among these **"kings of the earth"** are kings particularly designated and described by Daniel in chapter 7 of his prophecy. The **"fourth beast"** had **"ten horns."** Says Daniel, "These **ten horns** are **ten kings** that shall arise" (Dan. 7:24). These **"ten horns"** are seen again in Revelation and it is written, **"The ten horns which thou seest are ten kings"** (Rev. 17:12-18).

From the mouth of the **dragon** (Satan) the mouth of the **beast** and of the **false prophet** came forth evil spirits (Rev. 16:13) which go forth unto the **"Kings of the Earth"** and of the **whole world,** and this results in the confederation and commanding of them to the "battle of the great day of God Almighty" and the place to which they are gathered as in the "Hebrew tongue called Armageddon." See Revelation 16:14-16.

The wicked confederates are saying, "Let us break the bands asunder and cast away their cords from us." The tie between Christ and His people Israel, is described in these very words, **"I drew them with the cords of a man with bands of love"** (Hos. 11:4). ("Unto Him that loved us" [Rev. 1:5]) This **cord** of a Man cannot be **broken** for the Man is in heaven ready to save and succor (Heb. 4:14-18; Rev. 5:5), and the **bands** of love cannot be severed for says the Scriptures of His love for Israel, "Yea, I have loved thee with an everlasting love: therefore with lovingkindness have I **drawn** thee" (Jer. 31:3; Deut. 7:6-8).

With these things in mind, see with what significance the title, **"Prince (or Ruler) of the Kings of the Earth,"** appears here. Over the kings of the earth in their raging is One who **rules** and will soon **reign.** He will speak to them in the **"day of His wrath"** (Ps. 2:5; Rev. 6:17). "Vex them in His sore displeasure" (Ps. 2:5). The nations will be "His possession" and "He shall rule them with a rod of iron."

The second Psalm opens with **The Confederation of the Nations against Messiah** and ends with **The Subjugation of the Nations unto Messiah.** See Psalm 2:1, 9. This is the scope of Revelation also; see Revelation 19:15 which is a quotation from Psalm 2.

He is the **"Prince of the Kings of the Earth,"** and is it any wonder that the second Psalm speaks unto these **"kings of the earth"** in an exhortation:

> "Be wise now therefore, **O ye kings:** be instructed, ye **judges** (rulers)"?

The confederation existed at the first advent of Christ (see Acts 4:25-27), but is yet to be fulfilled in the full and final terms of the prophecy. Psalm 110 speaks also of the judgment work of the "Prince of the Kings of the Earth:"

> "The Lord at thy right hand shall **strike through kings** in the **day of His wrath"** (Ps. 110:5).

### "UNTO HIM THAT LOVED US AND WASHED US FROM OUR SINS IN HIS OWN BLOOD"

The R. V. reads "loveth us," the **present** and not **past** (John 13:1; Jer. 31:3; Deut. 7:6-8). The **love** is **present,** the **washing** is **past.** The **washing** is a result of the **love.** It was done with "His **own Blood."** Israel was accustomed to washings and purifyings through the blood of lambs and bullocks, but this was His **"own Blood"** of a new covenant. His **own Blood.** The "new covenant" His **own Blood.** The "new covenant" is about to be made with the house of Israel and "His own Blood" secures it. See Hebrews 8:6-13.

The meats and drinks and sacrifices of the Mosaic ritual were "imposed on them till the time of reformation" (Heb. 9:10), but Christ took not the blood of goats and calves, but by **His own Blood** He entered in (Heb. 10:12). The washing with blood which we have here at the opening of Revelation is not under the law but of that which brought an end to the law. He sanctified the people with **"His own Blood."** See Hebrews 13:12.

When Christ was first presented to Israel He was to "save His people from their sins" (Matt. 1:21). He will so deal with "His people."

This washing is required because they are

## "KINGS AND PRIESTS UNTO GOD AND HIS FATHER"

Peter reminds the circumcision of their relation to God. Says he, "Ye are a **royal** priesthood, an holy nation, a peculiar people" (I Peter 2:9). This quotation is from Exodus 19:5, 6, spoken by God at the time of their constitution as a nation. Saith He, "Ye shall be unto Me a kingdom of priests and a holy nation."

There was a "washing" which was for "priests." It was appointed by God for the washing of Aaron and his sons, therefore the use of it here (see Exod. 29:4); but the washing and the purifying is by His **own** Blood.

**Israel** was the **priestly** nation (Is. 61:6; I Peter 2:5).

Israel was the **kingly** nation (Dan. 7:22, 27).

How full these words, "And He made us to be a **kingdom** and **priests."**

## UNTO GOD AND HIS FATHER

This was the post-resurrection word of the Risen One. Said He to Mary: "I ascend to **My God** * * and to **My Father."** Mary was also commanded to "go to **My brethren** and say unto them, I ascend to **My Father** * * and **My God."** See John 20:17, 18. The proclamation of God's name to **"His brethren"** was according to a prophecy found in the **twenty-second Psalm,** the Psalm of both His suffering and His glory.

"I will declare Thy name unto My brethren, in the midst of the congregation (assembly) will I praise Thee" (Ps. 22:22). "My praise shall be of Thee in the great congregation" (Ps. 22:25).

At the opening of the Revelation the One who was saved from the "lions' mouth" and heard from the "horns of the unicorn" (Ps. 22:21); who "was dead" but "alive for evermore" (Rev. 1:18), is about to appear to His own brethren in the midst of the congregations or assemblies (Rev. 1:4, 11), therefore the use of this name—**"His God and Father"** which is again, in final fulfillment proclaimed unto them.

### TO HIM BE GLORY AND DOMINION FOR EVER AND FOR EVER. AMEN

This concluding ascription of praise and the Amen, reminds us much of the conclusion of the prayer of the disciples in Matthew 6:9-13.

Indeed it is in full harmony, for that prayer commonly called the **"Lord's Prayer"** is a kingdom prayer in the Book of the King and the kingdom, for such is Matthew's Gospel. This Book of Revelation is also a kingdom Book and these words occur so often throughout the Book. We shall consider this and kindred ascriptions, **when chapter 5:13 is reached.** Follow these references through the Revelation: 1:6; 4:9, 11; 5:12, 13; 7:12; 14:7; 19:1.

Lesson Eight

## THE VOICE AND THE VISION (Rev.1:4-20) Part 3

"Behold, He cometh with clouds, and every eye shall see Him, and they also which pierced Him; and all kindreds of the earth shall wail because of Him. Even so, Amen" (vs. 7).

The passage in consideration may be displayed as follows and then followed as displayed.

| | |
|---|---|
| **Announcement:** | **"Behold"** |
| **Advent:** | "He cometh" |
| **Revelation:** | "With clouds" |
| **Manifestation:** | "And every eye shall see Him, and they also which pierced Him" |
| **Tribulation:** | "All kindreds of the earth shall wail because of Him" |
| **Acquiescence:** | "Even so" |
| **Amen:** | **"Amen."** |

The word "Behold!" stands as a sentinel at the threshold of this passage. It is a figure of vital force in the Scriptures. See Isaiah 7:14; Matthew 1:23; John 1:29; I Corinthians 15:51; I John 3:1. The word "behold" is used as an exclamation as here, in the Book of Revelation, **about eighteen times.**

Then follows the advent announcement—**"He cometh."** The prophetic word is near the goal of fulfillment, therefore this final advent notice. **History produces** all that **prophecy promises.** The **first** advent is the guarantee of the **second.** The Primal Prophetic Proto-evangel in Eden (Gen. 3:15) proclaimed this advent, and the First Prophet of the Pre-patriarchal Period, Enoch, predicted this advent (Jude 1:14, 15), and the Patriarchs and Prophets following after promised this advent (I Peter 1:11). Christ by both Parable and Prophecy (Matt. 13

and 24), published it, and the Book of Revelation in His person, **performs** and **perfects it.** Amen.

**The Revelation** is in "clouds." Clouds appear hereafter in the Book of Revelation at the following places and with much significance. (1) "He cometh with clouds" (1:7). (2) An angel "clothed with a cloud" (10:1). (3) Two witnesses ascend "up to heaven in a cloud" (11:12). (4) "A white cloud, and upon the cloud, * * One * * like unto the Son of Man" (14:14). (5) "Crying with a loud voice to Him that sat on the cloud" (14:15). (6) "He that sat on the cloud thrust in His sickle on the earth" (14:16).

It will be found that in the Scriptures, clouds are associated with the **ascent, descent,** and **advent** of the Lord.

A cloud is associated with Him in His **ascent.** See Acts 1:9. Also with the resurrection and rapture of the dead in Christ (I Thess. 4:17). The two witnesses ascended to heaven in a cloud (Rev. 11:12).

In Old Testament times the Lord made **descent** in clouds. See Exodus 16:10; 19:9; 34:5; Leviticus 16:2; Numbers 11:25.

"The Lord rideth upon a swift cloud" (Is. 19:1). A cloud is His chariot (Ps. 18:11; 104:3).

His **advent** will also be in clouds. The following passages are synchronous and are in prophetic compliment and concord: Daniel 7:13, 14; Matthew 24:30; 26:64; Mark 13:26 and Revelation 1:7. He comes **"in clouds."** This is the united testimony of **Daniel, Jesus** and **John.** He went in a **cloud,** He comes with **clouds.** A cloud associated with His **transfiguration** (Matt. 17:5), a cloud at His **exaltation** (Acts 1:9), and a cloud at His **revelation** (Rev. 1:7).

**The Manifestation** at the revelation is described in the words: **"Every eye shall see Him"**—the universality of His revelation and manifestation. Every eye on earth shall see Him. The communication will be as lightning shineth from the **east** unto the **west** (Matt. 24:27). The angel that rolled away the stone of His sepulcher (Matt. 28:3) had countenance like lightning. **What then will be the Lord's?** His countenance "was as the sun shineth in his strength." What a universal manifestation is a noonday sun! The Psalmist in speaking of the sun says, "His going forth is from the end of the heaven, and his circuit unto the ends of it: and **nothing is hid from the heat thereof"** (Ps. 19:6). So universal will be the manifestation of the **"Son of Righteousness,"** that nothing shall be hid from Him, "Every eye shall see Him" whose countenance is as the sun shining in its strength, for be it known that at present the sun is much dimmed and is not now shining in strength. In coming days the light of the moon shall be equal to that of the sun now, and the light of the sun shall be **sevenfold,** that is, increased to the volume of **seven days in one.** See Isaiah 30:26. The mouth of the Lord hath spoken it. With a countenance as the sun when full length, His presence will be known in all the world, and to the under-world as well as upper-world. Even the blind know when the sun shines. It can not be hid, it penetrates and pervades, so also shall His presence!

"As the lightning cometh out of the east, and shineth even unto the west; so shall also the coming of the Son of Man be." Universality of manifestation will be the revelation of the Lord from heaven. See Matthew 24:27.

**"And they also which pierced Him."**

They who pierced Him have looked upon Him once, but not when He was coming in clouds, but when hanging on the cross. Says John: "One of the soldiers with a spear pierced His side." The result of the piercing was the issue of **blood** and water (John 19:34-37). He also declares it was a fulfilling of Scripture (John 19:37).

The Scripture referred to is Zechariah 12:10: "They shall look upon Me whom they have pierced." That the looking upon Him not only as He hung upon the cross, but as He comes in clouds, is required to fill full this prophecy is established by a study of the 12th chapter of Zechariah.

Zechariah says, **"In that day."** Many times in the chapter occur these words. See Zechariah 12:3, 4, 6, 8, 11. It is the day when the nations are come against Jerusalem and the Lord is in readiness for return—it is then He says they shall "look upon Me whom they have pierced." See Zechariah 12. The 53d chapter of Isaiah will on this day be on their lips and take on its deep meaning. The people who clamored for His death will say, as they see to their surprise:

We hid our faces from Him, surely He did bear our griefs and carry our sorrows, we esteemed Him as smitten under a judgment of God, but surely it was our judgment laid on Him. He **was** wounded for our transgressions, we see now that He was bruised for our inquities and with His stripes there was healing. See Isaiah 53.

It will be a day of **revelation** indeed to Israel when they see One coming in clouds whom they saw last on a cross—a cursed tree.

**"And all the kindreds of the earth shall wail because of Him."**

As the statement concerning the piercing, carried us back to Zechariah 12, so this one keeps us there. Undoubtedly the "kindreds of the earth" should read, **"tribes of the land."** This is established by the best manuscripts and translations. Zechariah has this mourning of "the tribes of the land" following immediately after the beholding of the One they had pierced. This also John does. See Zechariah 12:10 to 14 where this mourning is described. God pours upon them this spirit of desire for grace in supplication (12:10). God gave His only Son and **gave Him unto Israel** and now they mourn as a man **"mourneth for his only son"** (vs. 10). God gave Israel His "Firstborn." He is the First-born from the dead (Rev. 1:5), now their bitterness for Him is as the bitterness for a first-born (vs. 10). This great mourning is in **Jerusalem.** Zechariah 12:11 to 14 describes it in detail. Every family or tribe will mourn apart. It will be a day of sorrow, humiliation and repentance.

Jesus also speaks of this event in connection with His advent (Matt. 24:30).

"Then shall all the tribes of the earth mourn, and they shall see the Son of Man coming in the clouds of heaven with power and great glory."

Behold He cometh! Even so, Amen.

Lesson Nine

# THE VOICE AND THE VISION (Rev.1:4-20) Part 4

"I am Alpha and Omega, the Beginning and the Ending, saith the Lord, which is, and which was, and which is to come, the Almighty" (vs. 8).

**"I am"** (vs. 8), **"I am"** (vs. 11), **"I am"** (22:13), and in each occurrence connected with **"Alpha and Omega,"** "Beginning and Ending," and "the First and the Last."

This is the "I Am" mentioned first in Exodus 3:14. It is Jehovah—the self- and ever-existing One. It is used only of God, for unto God it belongs. Christ is God in **name** and **nature.** He is the **"I Am."**

## "ALPHA AND OMEGA"

Alpha is the first of the Greek letters corresponding in name and order to the first Hebrew letter **"Aleph."** Being the first letter in the alphabet, it is applied to what is first whether in point of **time** or **rank.** Christ is **"Alpha"** in both **time** and **rank.** "He is before all things." "In the beginning was the Word" (Col. 1:17; John 1:1). "I was set up from everlasting or ever the earth was." "When no depths"—no fountains—"before mountains" —"before hills"—"before earth"—I was there. See Proverbs 8. He is before all things, He is first in time who was ever in eternity.

He is "Alpha" in **rank.** He is the "Heir," the "Firstborn." "He is the firstborn of every creation" (Col. 1:15). This use of "firstborn" is not a reference to His **person** but to His **position.** Officially He is the "firstborn" or the Head of the household. He is the responsible One for all things. He is Omega—the last letter of the alphabet. He is before all things and He will be after all things. "Which was," (Alpha), "which is" (all the letters lying between), and "which is to come" (Omega).

Before Him—no one, apart from Him—no thing, and beyond Him—no one or no thing. In this title we have His eternity and His finality fully set forth.

Letters form words and words are the medium of **thought, wisdom** and **will.** Christ is the "Word" and the alphabet from which all words are created.

This title "Alpha and Omega" as used here is in harmony with the purpose of the Book. He was the **Author** of the purpose and program for Israel and the nations. He will be also the **Finisher.** This is the Book where things of which He was the Author come to a finish.

As Alpha and Omega, He is the Guarantor of all prophecy and its verbal fulfillment.

### "WHO IS TO COME" OR THE "COMING ONE"

This title occurs sixteen times in the Gospels and Acts with Hebrews 10:37 also. It is three times in the Book of Revelation.

John was in the **"isle that is called Patmos"** (vs. 9). Daniel was carried away unto Babylon and then saw the visions of the prophecy bearing his name. Paul went into Arabia to receive the revelation which was vouchsafed unto him (Gal. 1:15-17). John was in Patmos. Patmos was a locality actually on the map and is not to be taken spiritually but literally, and so also is every other place hereinafter mentioned, unless plainly and unmistakably declared otherwise.

Patmos was indeed a suitable situation for the revelation. Rome, the city of the "seven hills" was at the west, Palestine, Euphrates and Babylon were at the east. Amid such geographical surroundings were the apocalyptical visions revealed, with each of the places mentioned figuring prominently.

"I was in the Spirit on the Lord's Day, and heard behind me a great voice, as of a trumpet" (vs. 10).

We are now ready for the **"Voice and the Vision."** First the **"Voice,"** then the **"Vision."**

The word for Spirit here is the Holy Spirit. This is the first mention of the Holy Spirit in the Book. We see Him as the inspirer of the Prophetic Word and the revealer of things to come.

**He is the Author of prophecy.** See II Peter 1:21; Acts 28:25. He testified through the Old Testament prophets of the suffering of Christ and of the coming glory (I Peter 1:11).

**He is the Vouchsafer of vision.** John, as Paul, came "to visions and revelations of the Lord" (II Cor. 12:1). They were of the Holy Spirit of God. Ezekiel had also experienced the impartation of visions of the future by the same Spirit.

"The Spirit took me up, and brought me in a vision by the Spirit of God into Chaldea, to them of the captivity. * * Then I spake unto them of the captivity all the things that the Lord had shewed me" (Ezek. 11:24, 25). See also Ezekiel 1:1; 8:3, 4.

Some prophets spake particularly of the earthly life of Messiah and His sufferings in vicarious atonement, some spake particularly of the coming glory of Christ and the millennial kingdom, and some spake of the age lying beyond the Sabbatic or Kingdom age, and some spake of all of them and often in one portion of prophecy. Unto John, however, it was given to foretell visions of events which are to take place in a period of time known in the Prophetic Word as the **"Day of the Lord."** Into the events of this "day" the Spirit gave him vision and preview.

This day in detail, constitutes the major portion of his visions. He could well be called **"the prophet of the Day of the Lord."**

It is true, he was given vision into the state of things prior to the "Day of the Lord" and also vision of things lying beyond this day. He saw beyond the judgment period, beyond the reign of Christ as David's Son and Heir for a thousand years, beyond the revolutionary revolt at the close of the thousand years (see Rev. 20:21-23), beyond the throne of white and its universal judgments, beyond the new heavens and the new earth and the accompanying glory, beyond the new and heavenly city and unto the eternity to come, but chiefly his vision consisted of the events of the **"Day of the Lord."**

Of the other things mentioned he, John, speaks not in detail—the Old Testament prophets have done this—but it is given unto him to speak in detail of the judgments which begin at the "House of the Lord" and continue until the sinner and the Ungodly One have been finally dealt with in the full sentence of the Holy God in His Holy Word.

The present day is **"man's day"** (I Cor. 4:3). Man wills and works to the limit of the Divine permission. "Man's day" will be brought to its conclusion by the **"Day of the Lord."**

Joseph Seiss, the most popularly read author on the Book of Revelation, says:

"What is meant by the Lord's Day? Some answer Sunday, the first day of the week; but I am not satisfied with this explanation. Sunday belongs indeed to the Lord, but the Scriptures no where call it 'the Lord's Day.' None of the Christians writing for one hundred years after Christ ever call it 'the Lord's Day.' But there is a **'day of the Lord'** largely treated of by the prophets, Apostles and fathers, the meaning of which is abundantly clear and settled" (Vol. I, page 20, 21).

This "day" is first mentioned by Isaiah (2:10-22). In this passage is found a complete summary of the Book of Revelation from 4 to 19.

In verse 6, we see the divination and fornication in the land.

In verse 7 is the accumulated wealth, the land full of horses or militarism.

In verse 8, the idolatry characterizing these days upon which judgment must certainly fall.

Verse 10, the glory of the Lord's majesty is about to be revealed.

Verses 12-22 may be placed parallel with chapter 6 and the correspondence will be found most remarkable. It is the day of the Lord of Hosts. It is the day which the Spirit of God showed unto John. What John saw he wrote in a book at the Divine command, and what he wrote, we have in the Book of Revelation. Precious Book!

The Spirit of God knows "things to come" and it was His ministry to make them known.

> "He will shew you things to come."
> "He shall glorify Me."
> "He shall take of Mine, and shew it unto you" (John 16:13, 14, 15).

These things the Holy Spirit does in the Book of Revelation. "Things to come" are on display here and in the lamp of this prophecy none need be in ignorance of the trend of the present or the end of the age.

The Day of the Lord cometh! A day fraught with fear and terror! John saw it. He looked upon the most terrible judgments this present world and the human race have ever known. What Daniel and the other prophets saw in general, he describes in detail. This is the Book of the Day of the Lord.

Lesson Ten

## THE VOICE AND THE VISION (Rev.1:4-20) Part 5

"I was in the Spirit on the Lord's Day (Day of the Lord), and heard behind me a great voice, as of a trumpet" (vs. 10).

We are considering the **"Voice"** afterward the **"Vision."** The revelator declares this to be a **"great voice,"** as "of a trumpet."

Inasmuch as the "Day of the Lord" is about to begin, it is not strange this **"great voice"** should be heard. Says the Prophet Zephaniah:

"The great day of the Lord is near, * * and hasteth greatly, even the

**Voice of the Day of the Lord:**

* * that day is a day of wrath, a day of trouble and distress, a day of wasteness and desolation, a day of darkness and gloominess, a day of clouds and thick darkness,

**A day of the trumpet**

and alarm against the fenced cities, and against the high towers" (Eph. 1:14-16).

Here we have both the **"voice"** and the "trumpet" of the "Day of the Lord."

What the Prophet Zephaniah declares ushers in the Day of the Lord, is just what John also hears—a **"great voice"** as of **"a trumpet."**

Many events in the history of national Israel were connected with the blowing of the trumpet.

1. At Sinai with the revelation of God in the giving of the law, there was the "voice of the **trumpet** exceeding loud" (Exod. 19:16).

2. It is said when the Temple services began in the morning and the door was opened, it was with the sound of a **trumpet.** (Edersheim).

3. The **"year of jubilee"** was ushered in by the sounding of a silver **trumpet** (Lev. 25:9).

4. The **trumpet** was used to assemble the children of

Israel (Num. 10:2), to call them to the Tabernacle (Num. 10:3), and to "call the heads of the thousands of Israel" (Num. 10:4), and for the blowing of the alarm to gather the tribes from the four quarters of the camp (Num. 10:5, 6, 7). The trumpets were blown when they went out to war (Num. 10:9), they were blown also in "days of gladness" and at "solemn feasts" and other days, at the "beginning of months," over "burnt offerings" and before "peace sacrifices" (Num. 10:9, 10). These trumpets were for an ordinance **throughout the generations** of Israel (Num. 10:8), and were to be a memorial before God (Num. 10:10).

In a Book which deals with Israel and the nations, is it strange that the "voice of the loud trumpet" should here be heard? No. At the opening of the Book of Revelation the time has come when God is again to reveal Himself; not as at Sinai, in law, or as at Bethlehem or Calvary, in incarnation to make expiation, but in wrath and in judgments, so why not the "great voice of the trumpet"?

In Revelation, the Temple services begin again. The Temple at Jerusalem has been rebuilt by the Jews in their unbelief. This Temple has been desecrated by the Man of Sin and then, also the Millennial Temple, as seen by Ezekiel, is to be reared upon the ruins of this former Temple, therefore with the Temple thus at hand, is the sounding of the trumpet out of harmony with the tenor and truth of prophecy? By no means! May God hasten the day when trumpets will not only announce the opening of the gates of the Temple of the days of desecration and tribulation, but also of the days of millennial gladness and joy!

The Book of Revelation is the Book which introduces the events preceding the "year of jubilee" and the "Kinsman Redeemer" who is to redeem without a challenge from heaven, earth, or the under-earth (chap. 5), therefore is it strange that the trumpet should here be introduced? Certainly not. The children of Israel will be assembled again, they will be called to their Temple and land, the heads of the thousands will be summoned to again appear before God, therefore the deep significance of the loud voice of the trumpet at the opening of the Book.

The scattered tribes of Israel are to be regathered and recalled from the four corners of the earth and here is the trumpet. The alarm for war is yet to be sounded when the nations come yet again against Jerusalem in an allied exhibition of anti-Semitism, and the trumpet is the summons of warfare.

With these things in mind the significance of the "voice and the trumpet" will be readily discovered.

The Book of Revelation is the Book of the **"Voice."** In the A. V. the word **"voice"** occurs nearly fifty times and in the R. V. over sixty times. It is interesting to trace the word "voice" through the Book of Revelation. Surely, "The Lord shall roar out of Zion, and utter His **voice** from Jerusalem; and the heavens and earth shall shake: but the Lord will be the hope of His people, and the strength of the children of Israel" (Joel 3:16).

"What thou seest, write in a book, and send it unto the seven Churches which are in Asia; unto Ephesus, and unto Smyrna, and unto Pergamos, and unto Thyatira, and unto Sardis, and unto Philadelphia, and unto Laodicea" (vs. 11).

**"What thou seest"**—till then John had seen nothing, so the command is prospective (Van Someren). **"Write in a book."** What he saw, is in this Book of Revelation, for John "bare record of the Word of God, and of the testimony of Jesus Christ, **and of all the things that he saw"** (1:2). "What thou seest," includes all that he should see. **The present tense is here used.**

In speaking of the Scriptures as a whole, Joseph

Parker once remarked, "**God in order to make revelation, accepted the limitations of a Book.**" This "Revelation" is to be written in a "**book;**" not as several separate Epistles, but one Book, not a separate Epistle sent to each Church, concerning itself alone, but **the whole Book to each Church.**

The seven places here mentioned are **actual places.** They are not **symbolical,** they are **historical.** If they are symbolical so also is **Patmos.** Patmos is a place, so also each of these.

These seven Assemblies actually existed in Asia Minor and when this Book was given, it was sent for them to read and to keep in mind.

As members of the Church, the Body of Christ, in whom we are raised and seated in heavenly places, these letters and this Book has an application and these things are for us, though not about us, who are neither Jews nor Gentiles in Christ Jesus, but one Body.

The marks of spiritual deterioration and decay are always applicable to God's people whether it be Israel in the wilderness, Israel in the land, or the Church of this time or of any time. The application of these seven Epistles to the Church of this dispensation may be freely made so long as the interpretation does not interfere with or contradict the position of the believer in Christ as revealed in the Pauline Epistles.

It is our growing conviction, as also that of many throughout the land, that these seven assemblies have not only an historical past and a spiritual present but also a **literal future.** This is not a modern or a new view, but rather an old one reviewed and renewed.

Perhaps it will not be found incredible or unscriptural that these seven assemblies will exist in the days after the Church of this present dispensation has been removed from the judgments through which the Church is not destined to pass. To these seven assemblies or synagogues, these letters will have specific and timely meaning and will come to final fulfillment. It is well to have an open mind for the things of God. There is the **near** and the **far** horizon on the Word of God, and we should not fail to see either. There is a danger with all Bible students in that some see so much in the future they can not see things present and there are those who see so much in the present they can not see the things of the future. This should not be the case with either. Things future often interpret things present and things present throw light upon things future. How ignorant are we, but O the inspiration of the Holy Ghost!

Having heard the **Voice,** we now turn to the **Vision** (vss. 12-20).

## THE VISION

It is with fear and trembling we begin to write on this Vision. If a view of this glorious Person took away the strength of John and laid him prostrate until assurance was necessary for his strengthening, what humiliation shall be ours as we behold the adorable and glorious Lord of this Vision? Praise the Lord!

"And I turned to see the voice that spake to me. And being turned, I saw seven golden candlesticks" (vs. 12).

Candlesticks remind us of the Tabernacle or the Temple, and inasmuch as the Tabernacle was made after the pattern of things in the heavens (Heb. 8:2, 5; 9:23), we need not be surprised to find things in heaven the pattern of the Tabernacle on the earth.

To every Israelite the golden candlestick was a familiar piece of furniture in the Tabernacle or Temple. This is a reference to the lampstand in the Tabernacle, the description of which will be found in Exodus 25:31, 32, 37, and 37:23, also Hebrews 9:2. Zechariah describes also a "candlestick all of gold, with a bowl upon the top of it, and his seven lamps thereon, and seven pipes to the seven lamps, which are upon the tops thereof." (Zech. 4:2).

"And in the midst of the seven candlesticks one like unto the Son of Man, clothed with a garment down to the foot, and girt about the paps with a golden girdle" (vs. 13).

It was also a familiar figure to the Hebrews of one walking among the candlesticks, for this was the daily work of the priest, and the Book of Revelation finds Christ **just where the Book of Hebrews leaves Him.** In Hebrews Christ has gone into heaven and is in the Tabernacle of which the Tabernacle was the figure (Heb. 8:1, 2).

"We have an High Priest, who is set on the right hand of the throne of the Majesty in the heavens; a minister * * of the true Tabernacle, which the Lord pitched, and not man." His more excellent ministry demanded the higher Tabernacle, and here we see Him in the ministry of the upper or heavenly Tabernacle as He walks amidst the candlesticks.

The Hebrew letter shows us Christ in heaven, and here the Book of Revelation confirms what the Hebrew Epistle declares. Christ is in heaven—John saw Him—saw Him in the priestly garments and as he saw Him, so is His description.

Lesson Eleven

## THE VOICE AND THE VISION (Rev.1:4-20) Part 6

**"One like unto the Son of Man"** (vs. 13).

There is a vast difference between the past humiliation of the Son of Man and the present exaltation. Speaking of Himself in the days of His flesh, He said,

"Foxes have holes, and the birds of the air have nests; but the Son of Man hath not where to lay His head" (Luke 9:58).

This is all changed in the Apocalypse for here we see the glorious One of God.

In the days of His humiliation. He was hung amidst malefactors; **here** He walks amidst the golden candlesticks (vs. 13).

**Then** He was unclothed and displayed in nakedness, while His garments were left to the gamblers' chance, but **now** He hath His "garments" and they reach "down to His feet." **Then,** His head was encircled with a crown of thorns. **Now** His paps are girt about with a golden girdle. There was no place to lay His head, now that head white like wool, white as snow in radiance (vs. 14).

Then His eyes were sob-swollen, but here in John's vision they are "as a flame of fire" (vs. 14).

Then His feet were nail-pierced, but here as fine brass burnished in a furnace (vs. 15).

In the days of His flesh His voice was heard as He "offered up prayers and supplications with strong crying and tears unto Him that was able to save Him from death" (Heb. 5:7), but now His voice is as the sound of many waters (vs. 15).

On the cross He had naught in His right hand save a spike, **now** "in His right hand seven stars" (vs. 16). **Then**

His mouth was full and choked with cryings, **now** a sharp twoedged sword goeth forth, and instead of a "visage marred more than any man" (Is. 52:14), His countenance is "as the sun shineth in his strength" (vs. 16).

He was crucified in weakness but He lives by the power of God!

The One John sees from the Patmos Island, Daniel also saw at the Hiddekel River. See Daniel 10:5. Daniel had vision of One clothed in linen and loins girded with fine gold of Uphaz. This Son of Man is to come with the clouds of heaven in the prophecy of Daniel and also in the Apocalypse of John. See Daniel 7:13, 14 and Revelation 19:11-15.

Let us now look briefly at the details of His person and His apparel. Let us see Him as He is in the robes which indicate His official power and prerogatives.

Let us remember we not only look here upon a **Priest,** but upon a **Judge,** and also a **King,** and the garments He wears and the personal qualities He possesses, are in relation to the official position He occupies.

We expected to find Christ a priest in heaven, for on earth He could not exercise that office. He was not of the tribe of which Moses spake concerning the priesthood. For this cause His priesthood must be exercised in heaven for He had none on earth.

The garment of linen and the girdle of gold are priestly garments. The "holy garments" of the high priest were of linen (Lev. 16:32).

Joshua, the high priest, was seen standing before the Angel of the Lord. He was resisted by an adversary. Joshua was clothed in filthy garments. The Lord said, I will clothe thee with a change of raiment and the word translated "poderes," is the word used in Revelation 1:13 and means a garment down to the foot.

The girdle, which was of gold, was also a portion of the priestly paraphernalia. See Exodus 28:4; Leviticus 8:7, 13; 16:14.

Christ is in heaven awaiting the hour to begin judicial prosecution of His enemies, for He is there until His enemies are made His footstool (Ps. 110:1; Heb. 1:13).

The time is near when the Judge must appear. In chapter 4 we see the thrones set, and here the Judge in garments befitting His official right to sit as judge upon a throne.

"His head and His hairs were white like wool, as white as snow; and His eyes were as a flame of fire" (vs. 14).

This Judge is here seen in the garments and characteristics befitting the tribunal. Was thus seen also by Daniel (Dan. 7:9). White hair signifies seniority, superiority, and its accompanying sobriety. He is the "Ancient of Days." He arises to judge. In the Book of James, which is itself an Epistle addressed to the days of tribulation, "the Judge standeth before the door" (James 5:9). Here is the Judge with His eyes of flame—piercing, penetrating, perceiving, consuming, commending and condemning. Eyes before which heaven and earth, at a later period, "fled away" (Rev. 20:11). This Judge is presented in full length portrait in Isaiah 11.

He is "quick of understanding" (vs. 2), judges not after the sight of His eyes but has inward vision and penetration (vs. 3), "smites the earth with the rod of His mouth" (vs. 4), and with the "breath of His lips slays the wicked" (vs. 4), and "righteousness is the girdle of His loins" (vs. 5).

Isaiah and John are writing of the same Person, and paralleling the two passages will bring wonderful results.

"And His feet like unto fine brass, as if they burned in a furnace; and His voice as the sound of many waters" (vs. 15).

One of the "four living ones" of Ezekiel, had "feet that sparkled like the colour of burnished brass" (Ezek. 1:7), and here the "Living One," Christ, had feet like unto polished brass. Brass is a symbol of judgment throughout Scripture, and here the Judge is seen with feet of brass ready for the tread and triumph of judgment.

The altar of offering at the door of the Tabernacle was of brass where judgment fell and wrath was appeased and guilt expiated. Christ has been to the altar of brass and has expiated sin. Upon Him fell the judgment of sin, and now from Him is to come the judgment on sinners. He has borne the holy wrath of God and is qualified to execute wrath upon the unholy. When Moses was blessing the tribes of Israel it was unto Asher he said, "Thy shoes shall be of iron and **brass,**" but here are **feet** of brass.

It is said that brass in a state of white-heatedness is "almost insufferable to human gaze." When the day of the Lamb's wrath is come, who will be able to abide?

His voice as the sound of many waters is a forceful figure and statement. This seems to be a reverberation of Psalm 29 in which we read:

"The voice of Jehovah is upon the waters; the God of glory thundereth, even Jehovah upon many (great) waters. The voice of Jehovah is powerful; the voice of Jehovah is full of majesty."

"Jehovah sat as king at the flood; yea, Jehovah sitteth as king forever."

In Ezekiel is a reference also to this voice; and as here, it is in relation to His Second Advent and the return of the departed glory.

"And, behold, the glory of the God of Israel came from the way of the east: and **His voice was like the sound of many waters:** and the earth shined with His glory" (Ezek. 43:2).

The voice of the Almighty is again likened to "many waters" in Ezekiel 1:24—"like the noise of great waters, as the voice of the Almighty."

At Revelation 1:8, Christ calls Himself **"The Al-**

**mighty,"** and here is the voice as sound of waters—the voice of the Almighty.

"Many waters," roar. See Psalm 46:3; Isaiah 55:15; Jeremiah 6:23; 51:55; I Chronicles 16:32; Psalm 96:11; 98:7.

The Lord also "roars." "The Lord shall roar out of Zion" (Joel 3:16). "The Lord will roar out of Zion and utter His voice from Jerusalem" (Amos 1:2). At the opening of the Book of Revelation the time is at hand to fulfill these prophecies and for the roaring of the Lord's voice in Zion and as the voice of many waters will He "roar" in His judgments. The Book of Revelation is the Book of the Lord's "voice." "Voice" occurs many times in the Book.

Lesson Twelve

## THE VOICE AND THE VISION (Rev.1:4-20) Part 7

The Book of Revelation is a Book of **Judgments.** This is its super-message. When the Book of Revelation is finished, all judgment for all time is past. The Judge is seen in His official judicial garments in verses 13 to 16 of the 1st chapter. In the former lecture we considered His garments, girdle, hair, head, eyes, feet and voice. In each we found the qualifications of a Judge. He is at the door. Soon judgment will begin. In chapter 4 the thrones will be set, or "cast down" as Daniel states it. Let us further the study in the portrait of the Judge, as John saw Him.

"He had in His right hand seven stars: and out of His mouth went a sharp twoedged sword: and His countenance was as the sun shineth in his strength" (vs. 16).

His right hand is the hand of authority and power. All power for judgment was committed unto Him, He is about to take it and reign.

Two things are here mentioned—The **Sword of His mouth** and the **Shining of His countenance.**

These have to do with His advent judgment. The sharp two-edged sword He will use for the consuming and condemning of the Wicked One.

Says Paul to the Thessalonians: "Whom the Lord shall consume with the **spirit of His mouth."** His Word of judgment in the work of judgment is the sharp two-edged sword (II Thess. 2:8). There is a time when the Word of His mouth is full of grace, but not now. His tongue is now as a **sharp sword.** In Isaiah 11:4 we have Divine and human characteristics of the Judge described. Many are His attributes which distinguish Him from all others.

He is quick of understanding (Is. 11:2).

He does not judge after the sight of His eyes (11:3).

He does not reprove after the hearing of His ears (11:3).

He judges the poor righteously (11:4).

He reproves with equity for the meek of the earth (11:4).

He shall smite the earth **with the rod of His mouth,** and

He shall with **His breath slay the wicked** (Wicked One) (11:4).

This is the prophet's portrait of Christ and when compared with John's vision in the Revelation they are identified as the same Person.

Isaiah, Paul and John, are speaking of the same Person and of the same act of judgment, at the same advent.

Isaiah says: "Smite the earth with the **rod of His mouth,** and with the breath of His lips slay the **Wicked One**" (Is. 11:4).

Paul says: "And then shall that Wicked One be revealed, whom the Lord shall **consume** with the **spirit of His mouth**" (II Thess. 2:8).

John says: "Out of His mouth went a sharp twoedged sword" (Rev. 1:16). "And out of His mouth goeth a sharp twoedged sword, that with it He should smite the nations" (Rev. 19:15).

Christ shall indeed send a sword in the earth; but no sword of human making or of earthly metal, it will be the sharp two-edged sword of His mouth! "The Word of God is quick and powerful and sharper than any two-edged sword," and when He is seen coming He was clothed in a vesture dipped in blood and His name is called the **"Word of God."**

But not only the **Sword of His Mouth** is here mentioned but also the **Shining of His Countenance,** for we read:

"And His countenance was as the sun shineth in his strength" (vs. 16).

Paul declares that this coming One will come in "flaming fire" (II Thess. 1:8). He also states that the One who consumes with **"the spirit of His mouth"** shall also destroy with the **"brightness of His coming"** (II Thess. 2:8).

John says the coming One has a countenance as the **sun shining in its strength.** They are speaking of the same manifestation.

Christ is coming, says Malachi, the **Sun** of Righteousness. The last Old Testament Book promise is to be fulfilled in the last Book of the New Testament.

At the Transfiguration "His face did shine as the sun." What will His face radiate at the coming advent when it is as the sun shineth in his strength?

We do not know the strength of the sun, nor have we ever seen it so shine. Sin's disorder, like a robe over the face of nature, obscures the strength of sun, moon and stars. In the days of the Son of Man the physical changes in the solar and lunar heavens will be remarkable.

"Moreover the light of the **moon** shall be as the light of the **sun,** and the light of the **sun** shall be sevenfold, as the light of seven days, in the day that the Lord bindeth up the breach of His people, and healeth the stroke of their wound" (Is. 30:26).

We have considered the personal appearance of Jesus. **Two** points concerning His clothing and **seven** connected with His person, viz.: (1) His head, (2) eyes, (3) feet, (4) voice, (5) hand, (6) mouth, (7) countenance.

Having seen Him whom John saw we shall now hear Him.

"And when I saw Him, I fell at His feet as dead. And He laid His right hand upon me, saying unto me, Fear not; I am the First and the Last: I am He that liveth, and was dead; and, behold, I am alive for evermore, Amen; and have the keys of hell and of death" (vss. 17, 18).

Man's body must be rebuilt and recovered by the resurrection process, before it can stand erect in the presence of Divine Majesty. Sin brought alienation from God, and man was excluded and driven out from the presence of God. Fear of God has held sway in the bosom of man since then.

Through grace and the work of the Holy Spirit in the new creation, the believer is a child of God. John says, "Now are we the sons of God." This is a present fact. "It doth not yet appear what we shall be." God is withholding this. In our present mortal state of humiliation and weakness we have no intimation of our future glorification. "When He shall appear we shall be like Him." Ah, this is our expectation ("He shall appear") and anticipation ("we shall be like Him"). When we are **"like Him"** then we shall **"see Him** as He is," but not until then. Until then we **"fall at His feet as dead."**

Again, as in verse 7, and 11, He takes to Himself the title of the **"First and the Last."** This is His Jehovistic title—the self-existing and eternal One.

"None created Him, He is the First. He exists forever, He is the Last. He upholds all things through that endless interval."—Govet.

In the first cycle of prophecies of the second half of Isaiah, chapters 40 to 48, this title occurs **four** times. See Isaiah 41:4; 43:10; 44:6 and 48:11, 12.

What a person is here! He is the absolute Ego, without limitations on His freedom. He is the being who is imminent in history and at the same time transcending history. He is the eternal and all-conditioning One, who is Himself unconditional. It is Jehovah-Jesus.

He speaks next of His humiliation which came to Him as a result of the incarnation. **"And was dead."** The Gospel consists of the death, burial and resurrection of Christ (I Cor. 15:3, 4). I "was dead, I am alive forever more." He affirms unto John two facts—the fact of **His death** and the fact of **His resurrection from the dead.**

The Book of Revelation is the Book of the "sign of Jonah." The major portion of the Bock of Revelation has to do with Israel, and unto this nation there will be no sign given, though they sought for signs, save the **sign of the Prophet Jonas** (Matt. 12:39, 40). A Christ Messiah who was dead and raised again on the third day, confronts the Jewish nation and there is no salvation for them till He is received by them. Romans 10, which deals especially with Israel, the brethren of the Apostle after the flesh, also confirms this. See Romans 10:9, 10. The One God raised from the dead is now standing at the threshold of this Book and a greater than Jonah is here.

**Jonah** was three days and three nights in the belly of the fish. **Christ** was three days and three nights in the bowels of the earth.

**Jonah** was delivered on the third day, so also was **Christ.** Jonah prayed a remarkable prayer, quoting from many of the Psalms (Ps. 120; 130; 61; 34; 88; 42; 31; 69; 16; 18 and 50).

THE PRAYER OF JONAH

"Out of the belly of Sheol cried I, and Thou heardest my voice. For Thou didst cast me into the depth, in the heart of the seas; the flood was round about me; all Thy waves and Thy billows passed over me. And I said, I am cast out of Thy sight, yet I will look again toward Thy holy Temple. The waters compassed me about to the **soul;** * * the earth with her bars closed upon me forever, I went down to the **bottom of the mountains;** * * yet hast Thou brought up my life from corruption, O Lord my God" (Jon. 2:3-6).

Jonah mentions his burial in the **heart of the sea,** his imprisonment in the belly of Sheol, down at the bottom of the mountains, and his **deliverance from corruption.**

Peter at Pentecost uses also the language used by Jonah in his experience and declares its fulfillment in the resurrection of Christ from the dead.

Says Peter, "For David speaketh concerning Him, * * therefore did My heart rejoice, and My tongue was glad; moreover also My flesh shall rest in hope; because Thou wilt not leave My **soul in Hades,** neither wilt Thou suffer

Thine Holy One to see corruption. * * He seeing this before spake of the **resurrection of Christ,** that His soul was not left in Hades, neither His flesh did see corruption" (Acts 2:25-31).

Hades is the Divine Scriptural equivalent of Sheol. Sheol is found sixty-five times in the Old Testament, and ten times in the New Testament in its Greek equivalent Hades.

Now behold the greater than Jonah, of whom the Apostle Paul declares that after His resurrection He ascended on high, as Psalm 68:18 declared He would, leading with Him a company of captives, the fruit of His visit to the abode of the dead—but **prior** to His ascension, He descended first, into the **lower parts of the earth.** See Ephesians 4:8-10 and compare with Psalm 68:18.

The **"lower parts of the earth,"** which is the same as Jonah locates at the **"bottom of the mountains."** Jesus Himself names it and locates it, as "the heart of the earth" (Matt. 12:40).

John says Jesus, "I was dead, I was not left in Sheol, My flesh saw no corruption, lo, I have with Me as the trophy of My triumph in and over the underworld of the dead, the **'key of Hades (Sheol) and the grave.'** I went down to the lower parts of the earth, I led captive captivity. I am alive forever more! The keys are in My hands and before the prophecies of the visions of this Book vouchsafed unto you, are fulfilled, I will open the underworld and the dead shall stand before God."

O Thou greater than Jonah! Thou art here! Thou hast been down to the underworld and abode of the dead. Thou hast the keys on Thy girdle! From the keepers of the underworld He wrested the keys. The very "gates of Hades" cannot prevail against Him nor against His people. He, the great Samson, has carried away the gates. His work will be done and the Sea, Death, and Hades must yet give up their dead. They and all that are in them, are due to stand before the Great White Throne assize and **there is no escape** (Rev. 20: 13).

"I was dead—I am alive forever more—I have the keys of Hades and of death."

"I am the Jesus Jonah, I was dead but My soul was not left in Hades, I saw no corruption, I delivered captives and I will, I have the keys on My girdle." Amen. Hallelujah!

Lesson Thirteen

## THE VOICE AND THE VISION (Rev.1:4-20) Part 8

At the close of Lesson Twelve we beheld the **Key-bearer** and the Keys. John had seen the **Vision** and heard the **Voice.** The "vision" had laid him prostrate. He had fallen as one dead. John who had rested on the bosom of the Lord in the days of His humiliation in the flesh, was now at His feet. He had laid upon him the hand of the risen One and was commanded to write.

"Write the things which thou hast seen, and the things which are, and the things which shall be hereafter; the mystery of the seven stars which thou sawest in My right hand, and the seven golden candlesticks" (vss. 19, 20).

We have here:

First: **The Scope of the Writing:** "Things which thou hast seen, things which are, and the things which shall be hereafter."

Second: **The Subject of the Writing:** "The mystery of the **seven stars** which thou sawest in My right hand, and the **seven golden candlesticks."**

Third: **The Secret Symbol of the Writing:** "The seven stars are the angels of the seven Churches; the seven candlesticks * * are the seven Churches."

The **scope** of the Book of Revelation reaches unto the consummation of the ages. When the Book of Revelation has come to its fulfillment time periods and ages are full and things eternal have come into reality. There will be no prophecy to fulfill—all will be history. "God will be all and in all."

The scope of the Vision vouchsafed unto John includes not only the Risen One, in His official and judicial garments, but also the Seven Churches of Asia Minor, the events connected with the judgment period preceding the thousand years, the events during the thousand years, the events following the thousand years. John truly saw the "**things which shall be hereafter.**" The scope of the Book of Revelation is plainly stated in this verse.

1. **John Saw and Wrote to Testify of the Resurrection of Christ from the Dead, with the Prerogatives and Power of Resurrection and Judgment as the Sign of Jonah—The Solitary Sign for a Wicked and Adulterous Generation** (1:4-18).

2. **John Saw the Visions of This Book and Wrote Them unto the Seven Churches of Asia Minor Where the Judgment Was to Begin** (I Peter 4:17, 18) (chapters 2 and 3).

3. **John Saw and Wrote Concerning the Placing of the Throne and of the Seating Judge** (chapters 4 and 5), **and the Judgments in Their Succession of Seals, Trumpets, and Vials** (chapters 6 to 19).

4. **John Saw and Wrote of the Advent of Christ to David's Throne; the Events Attending and the Reign of the Thousand Years Following** (chapters 19:11 to 20:6).

5. **John Saw and Wrote of the Events Following the Thousand Years and of the Eternal State, Thus Closing the Book of Divine Revelation** (chapter 20:7 to close).

What tremendous subjects are here before us, in our next division! Every symbol and every sign of the Book of Revelation is fully interpreted **within** the Book. This **absolutely** prevails throughout the Book. Everything in this Book is to be **taken literally** except when distinctly stated in the text. This is carefully guarded throughout. It is a Book of revelation not a Book of confusion.

We are now ready to behold the One "that holdeth the seven stars in His right hand, who walketh in the midst of the seven golden candlesticks" as He addresses the seven Churches of Asia Minor. We have with this lecture brought to a finish our observations on the **Introduction of the Book** (1:1-3), and the first main division **"The Voice and the Vision"** (1:4-20). We shall look unto Him who hath helped to help. Amen.

In the Second Series of Lessons of the Book these things came before us.
When John saw Him, He was

1. "Walking in the midst of the seven candlesticks" (vs. 13).
2. "He had in His right hand seven stars" (vs. 16).

These two things are of particular mention and the Holy Spirit is so occupied with them that the interpretation is advanced.

When first we read of the "seven stars in His right hand" a desire for understanding took hold upon us. We are supplied with the interpretation.

"The seven stars **are the angels** of the seven Churches."

"The seven candlesticks are the **seven Churches.**"

Lesson Fourteen

## GOD'S PEOPLE ON EARTH (Rev.2 and 3) Part 1

We have seen Christ in Heaven. We shall now see His people on the earth. They are seen in **Seven Assemblies** and the record of these **Seven Assemblies** is found in chapters 2 and 3.

This division may be known as the Premillennial Preparation. It must be remembered that all events this side of the close of chap. 19 and the opening of chap. 20 are **premillennial,** or events that precede the one thousand years' reign of Christ.

Inasmuch as judgment must begin at the "house of God" and from thence move out to the "sinner and the ungodly" (see I Pet. 4:17) (Ps. 1:4-6), so here the judgment begins in program order—judgment on the "house of God."

These seven Churches are to receive from John a record of the things **"he saw"**—the condition within them **—"the things which are,"** and the things which follow **"which shall come to pass hereafter."**

This threefold division (1) "the things which thou sawest;" (2) "The things which are," and (3) "the things which shall come to pass hereafter," is seen in all these seven Epistles to the seven assemblies. Each one of these seven Epistles is of **three fold division.**

(1) **The Introduction**—in which we see the things thou sawest.

(2) **The Body of the Epistle** in which we see the things that are.

(3) **The Promise**—in which we see the things which shall be after these.

In the **introduction** to each Epistle there will be found

a reference to Christ as revealed in the former vision (1:13-19).

I. **Ephesus**—"Seven stars in right hand in midst of seven golden candlesticks" (2:1).

Former Vision—"Midst of the candlesticks" "in His right hand seven stars" (1:13, 16).

II. **Smyrna**—"These things saith the First and Last, who was dead and lived again" (2:8).

Former Vision—"I was dead, am alive forever more" (1:18).

III. **Pergamos**—"These things saith He that hath the sharp two-edged sword" (2:12).

Former Vision—"Out of His mouth proceeded a sharp two-edged sword" (1:16).

IV. **Thyatira** "Who hath eyes like a flame of fire and feet like burnished brass" (2:18).

Former Vision—"His eyes were as a flame of fire: His feet like unto burnished brass" (1:14, 15).

V. **Sardis**—"These things saith He that hath the seven Spirits of God, the seven stars (3:1).

Former Vision—"He had in his right hand seven Stars" (1:16). "Stars" are angels, 1:20. Angels are calling "ministering spirits" (Heb. 1:14).

VI. **Philadelphia**—"These things saith He that is holy and true, He that hath the key of David" (3:7).

Former Vision—"I have the keys of death and Hades" (1:18).

VII. **Laodicea**—"These things saith the Amen, the faithful and true witness" (3:14).

Former Vision—"From Jesus Christ the faithful witness" (1:5).

The person described in the former vision in the first chapter, is the one who is speaking unto these Seven Churches. A characteristic of the former vision is recalled in each of the Epistles. This should be firmly fixed in the mind of the student.

The description of Jesus in this former vision (1:4-20) consists of **seven parts.**

1. Head and Hair
2. Eyes
3. Feet
4. Voice
5. Hand
6. Mouth
7. Countenance.

In the Epistle to **Ephesus** the title given unto Jesus is taken from the description given prior to the mention of parts of His body. Number five of the above is also mentioned.

**Smyrna** uses the titles used by Jesus in His consolation of John when he was terrified by the vision.

**Pergamos** refers to the number **six,** His mouth.

**Thyatira,** to the parts mentioned **second** and **third.**

**Sardis** refers to His hand on the **fifth. Philadelphia,** is taken from the consolation of John after the vision (1:18). In **Smyrna and Philadelphia** there are false Jews and the titles used by Jesus are Jewish.

The hair, the voice, and the countenance of Jesus are not mentioned in any of the seven.

The promises to the **overcomers** are of the priestly and kingly character. NOTE: **Paradise, No Second Death, Manna, Power, White Robes, Pillar, Supper, Throne.** Think on these things. They are not without deep significance and will come to our consideration in future studies.

Satan is found in **four** of the Churches and in each assembly is seen the germ of evil which is seen in full development in the chapters following.

This is most interesting, and is a matter of vital importance to true interpretation. Each sin charged and corrected in these seven Epistles is fully developed in the judgment portion of the Book.

If the first letters of the cities in which the Churches are formed, be taken in the Hebrew they form two words. The first of three letters, the second of four reading **"I gather, thou shalt be humbled."**

In pointing out wherein these Epistles are alike and wherein they differ, it will be well to notice in each of them it is said—**"I know."**

1. **Ephesus**—"I know thy **works**" (2:2).
2. **Smyrna,** "I know thy tribulation" (2:9).
3. **Pergamos,** "I know where thou dwellest" (2:13).
4. **Thyatira,** "I know thy **works**" (2:19).
5. **Sardis,** "I know thy **works**" (3:1).
6. **Philadelphia,** "I know thy **works**" (3:8).
7. **Laodicea,** "I know thy **works**" (3:15).

We have purposely emphasized the word **"works"** which occurs in **five** of the **seven** Epistles. This will be the matter of comment in future studies.

In each Epistle there is the admonition: **"He that hath an ear let him hear what the Spirit saith unto the Churches."** (See 2:7, 11, 17, 29; 3:6, 13, 22). In three of the Epistles (the three former) this admonition immediately **precedes** the promise to the overcomer, while in the four remaining Epistles the admonition immediately **succeeds** the promise of the overcomer.

In two of the Epistles there is also the exhortation—**"remember"** (see 2:5; 3:3).

In two Churches thus exhorted are the **first** and the **fifth**—Ephesus and Sardis.

The significant word **"repent,"** occurs in each of the Epistles. They are the Epistles of Repentance, reproof, rebuke, reprehension and reward. The word **"repent"** appears at the following places: 2:5, 16, 21, 22; 3:3, 19. In two of the epistles, to Ephesus and Thyatira, the word **repent** is used two times.

**Three** Old Testament persons who are enemies and

traitors to Israel. These three persons well shadow forth three enemies of Israel yet to come and of whom the latter portion of the Book of Revelation gives faithful record. These three records are **Balak, Baalam** and **Jezebel.** Two of them are in the Epistle to Pergamos and third a **woman** in the Epistle to Thyatira.

The name of David appears in the Philadelphia Epistle.

These things may appear to be of minor importance to some but we assure the student such is not the case. As our study in these Epistles continues the wisdom of careful study in these things will be apparent. There is not a word or a phrase of the seven Epistles that is not deeply rooted in the Old Testament Books.

Lesson Fifteen

## GOD'S PEOPLE ON EARTH (Rev.2 and 3) Part 2

There is a remarkable uniformity and unity in the plan, pattern, structure, and scope of each of the seven Epistles of Revelation 2 and 3. The student will do well to become familiar with the **construction** and the **contents** of these Epistles. The following order maintains in each Epistle of the seven:

1. **THE REVELATOR** (His Person)—**"Saith He that holdeth the seven stars in His hand,"** or the six other personal representations, whichever they may be. See 2:1; 2:8; 2:12; 2:18; 3:1; 3:7; 3:14.

II. **REVIEW AND RECOGNITION—"I know thy works, and thy labors."** Occurring at 2:2; 2:9; 2:13; 2:19; 3:1; 3:8; 3:15.

III. **REPREHENSION—"Nevertheless I have a few things against thee"** etc., etc. (as found in each Epistle).

IV. **REPRIMAND AND REPROOF—"Remember and repent, or else I will"** (as the case may be in the different Epistles).

V. **THE REWARD** (His Promise)—**"To him that overcometh I will."** See 2:7; 2:11; 2:17; 2:26; 3:5; 3:12; 3:21.

In each of these Epistles learn to look for the order above mentioned.

FIRST—The **Revelator** Himself and some aspect of His **person** and **power** as the authoritative Judge.

SECOND—A **review** of each Church with **recognition** on His part of both the **pleasing** and **displeasing.**

THIRD—A **reprehensory word** of the **"somewhat I have against thee"** character.

FOURTH—A severe **reprimand** of **reproof** and **rebuke** (with the exception of the Epistle to Philadelphia) followed by advice for correction.

FIFTH—The **reward** is promised by the One who is **faithful to perform.** Every promise of God **yea** and **amen** in Him.

Thus we see that in each of the Epistles He **commends, censures, corrects** and **consoles** each Church. He is the supreme authority in the "House of God." He rebukes or rewards at will. Indeed, it is difficult to pass a Censor, "whose eyes are as a flame of fire."

There will be found in these Seven Churches, the near and the far horizon, which is often true of Scripture. There is the event **at the time,** and the event of a **time to come,** and the two may be fashioned after an event **of the past.**

The **past** and the **present** and the **future** in Scripture are marvelously harmonized. The **present** may look back to the **past** and on to the **future,** and **mirror them both.**

**"Out of Egypt have I called My Son"** was true in the **past** when Israel was called out of Egypt: **"When Israel was a child, then I loved him, and called My son out of Egypt"** (Hos. 11:1).

But not only was this Scripture related to the nation Israel, but also to the Son of Abraham, the King of Israel, for we read:

"The angel of the Lord appeareth to Joseph in a dream, saying, Arise, and take the young child and His mother, and flee into Egypt; and be thou there until I bring thee word: for Herod will seek the young child to destroy Him.

"When he arose, he took the young child and His mother by night, and departed into Egypt;

"And was there until the death of Herod: that it might be fulfilled which was spoken of the Lord by the prophet, saying, Out of Egypt have I called My Son."

Here we see the **past event of history** enlarge into a **fulfillment of the event at hand.**

A footnote in the "Scofield Bible" referring to this quotation of Hosea 11:1 in Matthew 2:15, says:

"The words quoted are in Hosea 11:1, the passage illustrates the truth that prophetic utterances often have a LATENT AND DEEPER MEANING than at first appears. Israel, nationally, was a 'son' (Exod. 4:22) but Christ was the greater 'Son.' See Romans 9:4, 5; Isaiah 41:8 with Isaiah 42:1-4; 52:13, 14, where the servant nation and the Servant-Son are both in view."

These two events may also foreshadow another deliverance from Egypt at a **future time.** Isaiah tells of a day when the Lord will recover and return His people. It is not an event of past history but of future, for the prophet declares, the "Lord shall set **His hand again the second time** to recover the remnant of His people (Israel), which shall be left, from Assyria, and **from Egypt,"** etc., etc.

The prophet affirms that the "Lord shall utterly destroy the tongue of the **Egyptian** sea; and with His mighty wind shall He shake His hand over the river, and He shall smite it in seven streams, and make men go over dryshod."

He further declares that event will be "like as it was to Israel in the **day that he came up out of the land of Egypt."**

This passage takes one back to Exodus 14 and to verses 21 and 22, in particular. It also takes one forward to the events connected with the advent when God shall again gather His persecuted and oppressed people, Israel. Says Micah: **"According to the days of thy coming out of the land of Egypt will I shew unto him marvellous things."**

It will readily be seen that prophecy often covers the past, present, and the future. Prophecy is as the One of whom it speaks; "which **was,** which **is** and which **is to come."** "Prophecy is an intermingling of the near and the far." This principle, as exemplified in Israel in Egypt as above illustrated, will often be found throughout the prophecies.

These Seven Epistles to the Seven Churches may also demonstrate the selfsame fact. They may not only show the **trend** and **end** of the present church period in seven epochs, but also seven stages of **Israel's past history** as well as seven assemblies of the remnant of Israel in days yet to come, after the church of the present period has been taken away from the coming judgments which are scheduled to fall upon Jew and Gentile in their distinctive national capacity.

Thomas Newberry, author of the Englishman's Bible, an invaluable publication, sees in the Seven Churches a spiritual review of stages of Israel's past history. Says Mr. Newberry:

**"The course of the Seven Churches corresponds with certain stages in the history of the Kings of Judah and Israel."**

Mr. Newberry has shown this correspondence in the manner which is summarized below:

1. **The Church at Ephesus** first planted and in its prime, corresponds with the kingdom of Solomon in its first fair glory.

2. **The Church at Smyrna** "has its historic type in the reign of Rehoboam (I Kings 12)." "What a contrast," says Mr. Newberry, "between the bright reign of Solomon, and the turbulent reign cf his son."

3. **The Church at Pergamos** "answers to kingdom of Israel in the reign of Jeroboam with his house of high places and imitation ritual (I Kings 12:26-33)."

4. **The Church at Thyatira** "is foreshadowed by the reign of Ahab and the wife of Ahab, Jezebel, who stirred him up (see Rev. 2:20; I Kings 18, etc.)."

5. **The Church at Sardis** "is typically foreshadowed by the reign of Jehu (II Kings 9 and 10)."

6. **The Church in Philadelphia** "represents a work of the Spirit of God of deep and spiritual character, fore-

shadowed by the reign of Hezekiah and Josia (II Chron. 29; 31; 34; 35)."

7. **The Church at Laodicea.** "The historical types are Manasseh and Zedekiah (II Chron. 33 and 36)."

There is in Mr. Newberry's suggestion much to be highly esteemed and more seriously studied. The author of the Companion Bible (Oxford Press) sees in these Seven Churches a review and a calling to remembrance, the past history of Israel and Judah in the following correspondences:

1. **EPHESUS: The Day of Israel's Espousals** (Exodus).

2. **SMYRNA: The Period of Israel's Wanderings** (Numbers).

3. **PERGAMOS: The Wilderness Period** (Numbers).

4. **THYATIRA: The Period of Israel's Kings** (I and II Kings).

5. **SARDIS: The Period of Israel's Removal** (I and II Chronicles).

6. **PHILADELPHIA: The Period of Judah's Kings** (II Chronicles).

7. **LAODICEA: The Period of Judah's Removal** (Minor Prophets).

The author says: "It is a remarkable fact that the seven past phases of Israel's history are referred to in these Epistles; and the **literary** order in Revelation corresponds with and answers to, the **historical order of** the Old Testament.

Having taken the backward look to past history we now look upon the present. The Seven Churches of Revelation shadow forth the decline, degeneration and deterioration of the Church of the present time, with remarkable likeness. The marks of spiritual declension are ever the same, whether it be in Israel in the Wilderness, Israel in the Land, or the Church of this present dispensation. The application of these Seven Churches to the seven epochs of ecclesiastical history is interesting and instructing and informative.

Many teachers have arranged the history of the Church into seven divisions corresponding with the Seven Churches of Revelation 2 and 3. A majority of the best known teachers have steadfastly held to this correspondence. Their conclusions are generally well known and accepted by the students of this last Book of the Bible.

Dr. Scofield in the "Oxford Bible" known as the Scofield Reference Bible compares and corresponds the Seven Epistles to the Seven Churches with seven divisions of the history of the Church as follows:

1. **THE MESSAGE TO EPHESUS:** "The Church at the end of the Apostolic age; first love left."

2. **THE MESSAGE TO SMYRNA:** "Period of the great persecutions to A. D. 316."

3. **THE MESSAGE TO PERGAMOS:** "The Church after imperial favor, settled in the world. A. D. 316 to the end."

4. **THE MESSAGE TO THYATIRA:** "A. D. 500 to 1500; the triumph of Balaamism and Nicolaitanism; a believing remnant (vss. 24-28)."

5. **THE MESSAGE TO SARDIS:** "The period of the Reformation; a believing remnant (vss. 4, 5)."

6. **THE MESSAGE TO PHILADELPHIA:** "The true Church in the professing church."

7. **THE MESSAGE TO LAODICEA:** "The final state of apostasy." The church at the end of the age with Christ without.

Those who are familiar with church history, though there is no "Thus saith the Lord," identifying and confirming these various events, may see a remarkable correspondence in the characteristics of history in comparison with these Seven Churches.

While the Church, the Body of Christ, is not an earthly body, but called into the heavenlies and is viewed as in Christ before God, yet its service and testimony has been upon the earth. The calling of the Church is to the heavenlies, the conduct of the Church is on earth. The standing of the Church is before God in Christ in the heavenlies, but the service of the Church is on earth and limited to a dispensation committed to its particular and peculiar ministry.

Lesson Sixteen

## GOD'S PEOPLE ON EARTH (Rev.2 and 3) Part 3

In our former lesson we discussed a law which maintains in prophecy—a law of **past, present** and **future** fulfillment. We found prophecy to be very full and fruitful and not so easily exhausted. Its meaning often comprehends the events of the past and the events of the present and forecasts the events yet to come. The fulfillment of many prophecies is at first **partial** and then **final** and **full.**

Take for instance the day of Pentecost. Much that Joel spoke of that day was fulfilled in the early chapters of Acts, but **not all** of which Joel spoke. There is yet to be a fulfillment which shall **fully fill all** that was spoken by the mouth of that prophet. There was an arrest of prophecy in the **Acts,** as there was also in the **Gospels.** The events which began fulfillment were **arrested,** and are **held over** for fulfillment. The following events will yet be fulfilled to an extent transcending the record of the Acts.

1. The Holy Spirit poured out on all flesh.
2. Sons and daughters prophesy.
3. Young men see visions; old men dream dreams.
4. Spirit's outpouring on handmaidens and servants.
5. Wonders in heaven above; signs on earth beneath.
6. Blood, fire and vapor of smoke.
7. Sun turned into darkness.
8. The moon turned into blood.
9. The notable day of the Lord come.
10. Universal call upon the Lord.

See Joel 2:28-32 and compare with Acts 2:17 to 21.

The complete and final fulfillment of these things is

seen in the Book of Revelation, as the Book of Acts did not exhaust the prophecy. Take another instance; The disciples "being let go" by their persecutors in the first persecution, lifted their voice in one accord to prayer, in which prayer they quoted the **Second Psalm** as follows:

"Who by the mouth of Thy servant David has said, Why did the heathen rage, and the people imagine vain things?

"The kings of the earth stood up, and the rulers were gathered together against the Lord, and against His Christ.

"For of a truth against Thy Holy Child Jesus, whom Thou hast anointed both Herod, and Pontius Pilate, with the Gentiles, and the people of Israel, were gathered together, for to do whatsoever Thy hand and Thy counsel determined before to be done" (Acts 4:23-28).

The things above mentioned occurred at the crucifixion of Christ. There was a confederation of kings, rulers, Israel and Gentiles, and for the very purpose mentioned. But the prophetic horizon of the **Second Psalm** was not removed. There will yet be a confederation of nations under kings and rulers. At that time there will be the declaration of a decree which will ultimately issue in the actual seating of Christ the Messiah on the **throne of David** on the **Hill of Zion.** It will be a day of seven judgments when He shall "break them with a rod of iron" and "dash them in pieces like a potter's vessel." See Psalm 2. This is unmistakably the coming advent. See Revelation 19:15.

Just as the wonders in heaven, signs on earth, blood, fire, vapor, smoke, the sun darkened and moon bloody, in the prophecy of Joel, enlarge the fulfillment beyond Peter's words, so also does the Second Psalm demand a second advent for a complete fulfillment.

This is a characteristic of prophecy. It has what some one has called the **"near and the far horizon."**

We are not to be confined in the study of prophecy. There are lines laid to far distances. There are prophetic points often lying beyond the vision. We are prone to "pack" and "telescope." We are near-sighted and cannot see afar off. Doubtless many Scriptures and their fulfillment are crowded into the millennial age, when they belong to an age or ages lying beyond. We are so anxious and are so longing for earth's "Sabbath" age, that we see all our hopes therein, little realizing that God has plan and purpose beyond the coming age even unto the ages of the ages and to an eternal state.

There are extremists on the study of the Book of Revelation. These are often valuable, in that attention is often called by extremes. Goethe, the poet and dramatist, spoke soberly when he said: **"Between two extremes the truth is often found."**

There are some who believe the letters to the Seven Churches of Revelation 2 and 3, have been fulfilled in the past, and that now, historically, the Church is far down in the seal, trumpet and vial judgments. They place everything in the past.

Others see in these chapters, the Church of the present. Indeed, we never read the message to the Church at Laodicea that we do not see the declension and spiritual decay of the present church in bold relief. Unquestionably the Seven Churches are applicable to the Church of the present dispensation, featuring seven epochs of its spiritual history. We are more and more inclined to believe that not only as with Thomas Newberry, do these Seven Churches recall epochs of the past national history of Israel, and the seven stages of the present Church dispensation, as do the majority of students; but also that they will have final fulfillment in seven assemblies and synagogues yet to be located in Asia Minor after the Church of this present dispensation is gone. It does not seem wise to either place these Churches wholly in the **past,** in the present, or in the future. These Seven Churches not only show the things which have been, and the things which are, but the things also which shall be hereafter. Tc read the record of these seven assemblies in the light of the coming tribulation days is equally as interesting as is the reading of them in the light of the events of the present Church age. There is no violation of the law which has prevailed throughout prophecy in this view point. There is among many students a growing conviction that the present age does not fully exhaust the prophetic meaning of these Seven Churches.

There will be a believing remnant of Israel in the tribulation days. They will be searched, sealed and secured in those days. They will be reprimanded, rebuked, and rewarded. They could well read the message to the Seven Churches and find therein vital words for their victory in the dark hour of tribulation so intense but for its shortening, no flesh could expect salvage. If this prophecy should be extended to include them and to succor and sustain them who would desire to withhold the comfort and consolation? If unto this suffering remnant these letters may contain a particular message in a perilous hour, who would desire to take from a timeless book comfort for a testing hour? How wonderful would be the meaning of the promises tc the overcomers if they were the sealed ones of Revelation. If the Church, which is destined to escape the judgments which are coming upon the earth, found consolation and hope in these messages, would any be envious that if unto others in days yet to come these words be found full of meaning and timely for triumph?

Lesson Seventeen

## A THRONE: THE BEGINNING OF JUDGMENT (Rev.4) Part 1

Romans has been called the **"Court Room"** of the Books of the Bible. In the Roman Epistle legal questions are raised and **eternally settled,** as also is the guilty sinner, who accepts the judicial work of Christ in his behalf, **eternally secured.** If Romans is the "Court Room" of the Bible then the Book of Revelation is the **"Throne Room"** of the Bible. The word "throne" occurs at least 37 times in the Book. The Book opens with a **"throne"** and closes with a **"throne."** See 1:4 and 22:3. At chapter 4 we enter the "Throne Room." The door to the throne is "open."

"After this I looked, ar d, behold, a door was opened in heaven: and the first voice which I heard was as it were of a trumpet talking with me; which said, Come up hither, and I will shew thee things which must be hereafter. And immediately I was in the spirit; and, BEHOLD, A THRONE WAS SET IN HEAVEN, and One sat on the throne."

Here is both a **throne** and a **throne sitter.** This throne indicates the hour of judgment. This throne is preparatory tc the judgments which begin at chapter 6 and end at chapter 19. A reference to the divisions of the Book as presented in Lesson Number One, will show that the Book of Revelation is bounded by judgment thrones. In chapter 4 there is **"A Throne for the Beginning of Judgment"** and at chapter 20, **"A Throne for the End of Judgment."** The former is a **"Five-colored Throne"** and the latter a **"Great White Throne."** The first is set for the **"Judgment of the Wicked Living"** and the last, for the **"Judgment of the Wicked Dead."**

He shall judge the **"quick** (living) and the **dead."** When the Book of Revelation, which is a Book of judgment, is finished, there is no more judgment for with this

Book all judgment is forever at an end, for all are judged. We are now ready to enter the throne room. At chapter 1 we beheld the Judge with judicial garments down to the feet, girt about the paps with a golden girdle, His head and hair white like wool as white as snow, eyes as a flame of fire, feet like unto fine brass and His voice as the sound of many waters, holding seven stars in His right hand, out of His mouth a sharp two-edged sword and His countenance as the sun shining in his strength. It was the Judge.

Daniel saw also this same Person and also this throne and its establishment for this same period of judgment.

"I beheld till the thrones were cast down, and the Ancient of days did sit, whose garment was white as snow, and the hair of his head like the pure wool: His throne was like the fiery flame, and His wheels as burning fire. A fiery stream issued and came forth from before Him; Thousand thousands ministered unto Him, and ten thousand times ten thousand stood before Him; the judgment was set, and the Books were opened" (Dan. 7:9, 10).

This is not the throne of grace of which we read in Hebrews. This Book is not a Book of grace. The events in this Book occur after the dispensation of the grace of God has come to its close.

This throne is a throne of **Judgment** and of **Justice.** These are days of retribution and revelation. The slumbering judgment of God is now awakening. The Second Psalm declares, "**Then** shall He speak unto them in His wrath, and vex them in His sore displeasure."

The time for Him to speak has now come and the judicial arrangements are disclosed in this vision.

A **throne** in heaven! How comforting, when soon there will be a reign of lawlessness on the earth. A throne in **heaven!** There is rule and righteousness above all and over all.

Says the Psalmist, "He hath prepared His throne for judgment" (Ps. 9:7). "The Lord hath prepared His throne in the heavens" (Ps. 103:19).

How wonderful! A throne and One sitting on that throne! Soon the earth will be invaded by a white horse, a red horse, black horse, and a pale horse. Soon the earth quaking and the heavens shaking! Soon hail, fire, and blood and mountains moving into the sea with waters turned into blood! Soon the falling of great stars, and disturbance of sun, moon and stars above, and the opening of a great pit beneath and the underworld of wicked spirits in hordes moving forth! Soon the drying of the river Euphrates and the dragon cast out of heaven and into the earth with the beast and the false prophet! Then grievous sores, seas and rivers of blood with the scorching sun and the seat of the beast! Soon Babylon and its terrible judgments and—what else?

Time fails, pen is inadequate—but—over all and above all, is a **THRONE! SEALS, TRUMPETS** and **VIALS,** but **over all and above all,** a **THRONE** and God on that throne and Christ, the Executor! Praise be to the Lamb that sitteth on the Throne! His Throne is in the heavens! God has committed all judgments unto the Son and now the hour for the commencement of that judgment committed, has come!

**"A door opened in heaven."** Let us prepare ourselves for scenes of **justice,** for scenes of **judgment,** for **battle,** for **war,** for **retribution,** for **wrath** and for the **overthrow** of all enemies! There will be no rest or no arrest, till justice be established in the earth and the rebellious put down.

**"I heard as it were the sound of a trumpet talking with me."**

The **TRUMPET** is associated with the throne and with judgments. The word **TRUMPET** occurs at least six times in this Book. See 1:10; 4:1; 8:2; 8:6; 8:13; 9:14. An alarm was blown with a trumpet (Num. 10:9). It gives warning and excites fear. **"Shall a trumpet be blown in the city, and the people not be afraid?"** (Amos 3:6).

Everything indicates the preparation for judgment, both the throne, and the trumpet's voice. There is preparation for both assize and assembly. It is a solemn hour and an august Presence and Person! But not only does the throne and the trumpet speak of judgment, but also the "rainbow round the throne, in sight like unto an emerald" (vs. 3).

The appearance of the rainbow followed a former judgment of God upon the earth, when He condemned it with **water,** but here the rainbow precedes the judgment by the **fire.** See Genesis 9:12 to 16; Revelation 4:3. God has said unto Noah:

"And it shall come to pass, when I bring a cloud over the earth, that the bow shall be seen in the cloud; And I will remember My Covenant" (Gen. 9:14, 15).

A cloud is about to come over the earth at Revelation 4—**a dark cloud of judgment.** The gathering storm is ready to break. Lo, here is the bow! He keeps His covenant with every living creature, and in chapter 5, they all sing His praise.

"The rainbow," says Thomas Newberry, "is the Divinely constituted sign of covenant mercy founded on accepted sacrifice (Gen. 8). In the rainbow the three primitive colors are blended and harmonized, beginning with the blue and ending with the red, with the yellow in the center, and in their beauteous combinations completing the perfect seven. So in God's covenant-keeping goodness, every Divine perfection is harmonized and displayed." The earth which was once judged with water, is now to suffer a judgment of fire. The bow, with its prevailing tint of green, perhaps referring to the earth, is here seen encircling the throne. God has yet wonderful plans for the earth and it shall not perish or be moved.

"While the earth remaineth," saith God, "seed time and harvest, and cold and heat, and summer and winter, and day and night shall not cease" (Gen. 8:22).

This earth shall not always remain. There shall be a new heaven and a new earth. This present earth shall not ultimately survive the fire. See II Peter 3:7. But no judgments will interfere with the earth until the Word of God for this present earth is fulfilled. The bow about the throne is the assurance of not only the covenant made with Noah, but every covenant of God respecting the earth and His people and all people.

The **throne,** the **trumpet,** and the **bow,** each speaks of judgment, but each are also a guarantee of earth's blessing as promised to the patriarchs and to the prophets.

There is but one statement concerning the One on the throne. It is—**"And He that sat was to look upon like a jasper and a sardine stone."**

We do not know what this means and why the appearance was to look upon as rare stones or gems—jasper and sardine or sardius. Precious stones in Scripture are often used as emblematic of various excellencies of character and perfections. Why these two stones—we know not, God knows, perhaps some day we shall also know.

Lesson Eighteen

## A THRONE: THE BEGINNING OF JUDGMENT (Rev.4) Part 2

Having taken a look through the "open door" at the "Throne," who was **on** it, and what was **around** it, we shall now consider who was **before** it and in the **midst** of it.

There are **seven** conspicuous things connected with this throne and the student should ponder and consider them.

1. **ON THE THRONE—One Seated.**
2. **ROUND THE THRONE—A Rainbow.**
3. **ROUND THE THRONE—Twenty-four Thrones.**
4. **OUT OF THE THRONE—Thunders.**
5. **BEFORE THE THRONE—Seven Lamps of Fire.**
6. **BEFORE THE THRONE—Sea Like unto Glass.**
7. **AMIDST AND ROUND THE THRONE—Four Beasts or "Zoa."**

Let us concern ourselves with a few of the above orderly detail. The dealing of God with the earth is ready to begin, hence the rainbow, speaking of His covenant, for He remembers His covenant.

This judgment is not to be a water judgment, but a fire judgment. There are many plagues coming upon the earth—plague upon plague—but no inundation to devastate the earth. God will keep His word unto Noah, but will fulfill His Word spoken by the lips of the Prophet Malachi—

> "For, behold, the day cometh, that shall burn as an oven; and all the proud, yea, and all that do wickedly, shall be stubble; and the day that cometh shall burn them up, saith the Lord of Hosts, that it shall leave them neither root nor branch" (Mal. 4:1).

There is a baptism of fire due. John baptized with

water. Christ baptized with the Holy Spirit. But there is yet another baptism awaiting. It awaits His second coming at which time He will baptize with fire (Matt. 3:11, 12).

"Whose fan is in His hand, and He will throughly purge His floor, and gather His wheat into the garner; but He will burn up the chaff with unquenchable fire."

This throne is not a throne of **mercy**—it is a throne of **justice.** It is not a throne of **grace** but of **judgment.**

It is more like a Sinai. It is a place of thunder. Both lightnings and thunders proceeded from it. See verse 5. There was also a voice. The scene reminds one much of Sinai and the giving of the law.

"And it came to pass on the third day in the morning, that there were THUNDERS and LIGHTNINGS, and a thick cloud upon the mount, and the VOICE of the TRUMPET exceeding loud; so that all the people * * trembled" (Exod. 19:16)

So here we read:

"And OUT OF the throne proceeded LIGHTNINGS and THUNDERINGS and VOICES" (vs. 5).

Sinai was the place where God, by means of the law, made revelation of the **sin of man.** By the law was the knowledge of sin. It put man's evil nature to a full manifestation.

This throne in Revelation is established that ultimately retribution may fall upon the **Man of Sin.**

The **sin of man** will come to its fullness and its climax in the **Man of Sin.**

The character of this throne is indicated by those things which proceed out of it—**thunder, lightning** and **voices.**

Let us remember, however, the words of Habakkuk the Prophet—"In **wrath** remember **mercy**" (Hab. 3:2). The **throne** is first seen, then the **rainbow.** Judgment first and then the peaceful reign of David's Son and Lord. "First the sea and then the Cherubim" says Govet. Yes, in wrath God remembers **mercy.** He will be "merciful" to **"His people."**

Moses, in his Valedictory Song, Deuteronomy 32, after describing the judgment and vengeance of God upon Israel cried:

"Rejoice, O ye nations, with His people; for He will avenge the blood of His servants, and will render vengeance to His adversaries, and will be MERCIFUL unto His land, and to His people" (Deut. 32:43).

The thunder, lightning and voice, guarantees the vengeance upon the enemies, and the rainbow, the **mercy** upon His people and the remembrance of His covenant.

The throne was **red or fire color** (see vs. 3); the rainbow was "like unto emerald." The sea of glass seemed to make a circle of the rainbow rather than a half arch. Surely this throne and its surroundings speak not only of the character of God but also of His covenants.

Around this throne were twenty-four seats with an Elder for each seat (vs. 4). Their garments were of white and upon their heads were crowns of gold. These thrones were subordinate and associate. The Elders are of the governmental order. They appear to be both kingly and priestly. In verse 10 they fall down before the Throne Sitter and cast their crowns before the throne. In 5:2 one of the Elders speaks. In 5:8 the four and twenty Elders with the four beasts fall down before the Lamb.

They appear to be the head of an angelic priesthood. They are the chief priests of the heavenly courses. They are chief officers associated with the throne. They doubtless rule over angels and through them over the earth. A Hebrew could well understand these twenty-four Elders and their activities.

**They had white garments.**

A white linen dress was the priests' ordinary attire. There were garments for special attire but the white for the ordinary and the routine. Read Exodus 28:42; Leviticus 6:10 and 16:4.

**They have harps, songs and golden bowls.**

This was also a priestly employment. A Jew could well understand this. It was quite orderly and after the Temple service, and the Tabernacle and Temple were after a pattern of things in the heavens.

See I Chronicles 25:3-6, where the harp and the cymbal and praise is for the service of the priests.

In II Chronicles wherein is recorded the celebration of the location of the ark in the Temple under Solomon, one can almost see the heavenly vision in Revelation 4 enacted in the Temple in the time of Solomon. See the remarkable likeness. Read II Chron. 5:11-13.

The division of the priests in the earthly Temple was into **twenty-four courses** as in the heavenly sanctuary. I Chronicles 24 and 25 show us this division. The **"Scofield Bible,"** makes this division very clear.

When Eli and his sons are set aside, the king is promised, as about to take rule above the priest. When David is king he divides and distributes the priests into twenty-four courses (I Chron. 24:3-5). This order continued until the days of the Lord. See Luke 1:5.

**Twenty-four** thousand Levites were to serve in the House of the Lord (I Chron. 23:3, 4).

The prophets who were to praise God with instruments of songs were also **twenty-four** in number. See I Chron. 25:31.

There were **twenty-four** porters, sons of Levi appointed for the Temple (I Chron. 26:17-19).

Why should there be attempt to interpret these **twenty-four Elders** apart from things revealed in the Word of God? Why speculation and fanciful interpretation to confuse what is plainly written? The Word of God is the best commentary on the Word of God. Why not accept the Scriptures as a help in studying the Scriptures? "Comparing spiritual things with spiritual things," is God's order.

Lesson Nineteen

## A THRONE: THE BEGINNING OF JUDGMENT (Rev.4) Part 3

In the former lecture we found the kingly and priestly Elders, in the heavenly scenes as in the days of the Temple and its services—**twenty-four** in number. As in the Temple, so in the sanctuary above, they were clothed with white garments and employed songs and harps. As in the Temple of David and Solomon so in the Temple above.

The law of the earthly temple was a shadow of things above. Some would have us think this heavenly order was **borrowed from the earthly.** The truth is **exactly the opposite.** The Lord gave David to **"understand."** He committed to him the pattern.

"Then David gave to Solomon his son the pattern of the porch, and of the houses thereof, and * * of the inner parlours thereof, and of the place of the mercy seat, and the pattern of **all that he had by the Spirit,** of the courts of the House of the Lord, and of all the chambers round about, of the treasuries of the House of God, and of the treasuries of the dedicated things: **also for the courses of the priests and the Levite,** and for all the work of the service of the House of the Lord, and for all the vessels of service in the House of the Lord" (I Chron. 28:11-13).

"**ALL THIS,** said David, have I been made to understand in writing from the hand of Jehovah, even all the **works of this pattern**" (I Chron. 28:19).

Thus we are permitted in this chapter to see the "true" and the "heavenly" after which the earthly was patterned. These "Elders" the heads of angelic priesthood were in number twenty-four, and sat in priestly service and governmental rule.

**Elders** associated with the government of Israel from the beginning was not a new thing.

**Abraham** had in his house a servant, an Elder that **"ruled over all that he had"** (Gen. 24:2).

**Moses** was surrounded by Elders who were associated with him in judgment. "Go, and gather the **elders of**

**Israel together,** and say unto them, The Lord God of your fathers * * appeared unto me" (Exod. 3:16). They were together with Moses when he called on Pharaoh to let Israel go (Exod. 3:18; 4:29).

And here again another Moses is ready to lead Israel from bondage. Another Pharaoh (the Man of Sin) is about to receive the judgment stroke and is it strange the Elders are round about Him as He lifts His voice to cry, "Come," and order forth the apocalyptic judgments upon the Beast, the false prophet and the devil? **At Sinai** when the covenant is laid before the people, Moses called for the **Elders of the people.** Seventy of them were called up to a feast with God. They with Moses, Aaron, Nadab and Abihu saw the God of Israel, the Record says (Exod. 24:9). And they saw the God of Israel; and there was under His feet as it were a paved work of sapphire stone and as it were the very heaven for clearness. They beheld God and did eat and drink.

So here in the Revelation are Elders again before His face. They are the true kingdom of priests unto God. The shadow of God's plan is seen here. These Elders were afterwards associated with Moses in the government, as these of Revelation 4 are with the Lamb. See Numbers 11:16. Moses put some of the same spirit that was on him on them.

**In Samuel's day** when the people request a king the elders make the request: "Then all the Elders of Israel gathered themselves together, and came to Samuel" (I Sam. 8:4).

At Revelation 4, the earth is in need of a king, and the Elders are present not to make a **request** but to witness the **conquest.** Even Saul requests Samuel to honor him before the Elders (I Sam. 15:30). But here the Faithful Witness and Israel's true King receives honor from the elders.

**David and his association with the Elders** is interesting and illuminating. They are next to the king and his councillors. So are they next to the king in Revelation 4. David sends them spoil when the throne is vacant by the death of Saul.

So will Jesus the greater Son of David share His spoil with the "strong ones," for one of these days the satanic Saul, "the head of many countries," will receive the death stroke (Ps. 110:6) and a vacant throne shall be declared.

The Elders were present at the anointing of David in fact, they do the anointing. Here when the time is near when the rejected King as was David, is to be enthroned, the Elders are crying the proclamation and enter into the jubilation.

David chided the slowness of the Elders in failing to take the lead to bring back the king to Jerusalem after his flight from Absalom. See II Samuel 19:11. With these Elders, there is no slowness but swiftness. They are not asked, "Why are ye the last to bring back the king to his house?" They cast their crowns before Him who is the King of all the kings and the Lord of all the lords.

At the dedication of the Temple they are next to the king. See I Kings 8:1-3.

With these Scriptures before us why should there be speculation concerning the twenty-four Elders in the heavenly order? The Bible is never confusing. It is not what we read **in** the Bible that confuses; it is what we read **into** the Bible that causes the confusion.

Beyond this we shall not further consider the four and twenty Elders. It is plainly evident they are of the official order of "things in the heavens."

The very number, **twenty-four** is associated with heavenly government and worship. **Twelve** seems to be the governmental number for the earth, but **twice twelve** for the heavens.

In our next study we shall consider the four living creatures or the "cherubim." Our subject is not an easy one as much speculation has made difficult interpretation. We will come short of what is written, but we shall attempt with the help cf God not to go **beyond what is written.**

Lesson Twenty

# A THRONE: THE BEGINNING OF JUDGMENT (Rev.4) Part 4

"And in the midst of the throne and around the throne were four living creatures full of eyes before and behind. And the first living creature was like a lion, and the second creature (or beast, A. V.) like a **calf,** and the third living creature had a face as a **man,** and the fourth living creature was like a flying **eagle.**

And the four living creatures had each of them six wings about him, and they were full of eyes within: and they rest not night and day saying, Holy, Holy, Holy, Lord God Almighty, which was and is and is to come."

We now approach the subject of the Cherubim. We must remember again that the book we are now studying is the Book of **Revelation** and not a book of speculation. Many have speculated here. May we be content to believe the Bible means what it says and says what it means, and to receive it in its plain and literal meaning except it be there is a direct claim to figurative speech.

They are called the "Cherubim" on the first occasion of their being named. They are not called Cherubims, but Cherubim. There is no article before Cherubim in the first mention of the name, either in the Hebrew or the Greek.

Their **form** is twice given in the Scriptures. Once by John as above quoted and by (Ezekiel 1:5-14). Read.

This form was **not given** when they were first named and they are first named at Genesis 3:24. It is **not given** when Moses is directed to make them. From Moses we but learn that they had **faces** and **wings.** Moses saw the originals on the mount.

There is some difference in detail as to their form between Ezekiel and John. There is no doubt they are the same beings. Ezekiel identifies the living creatures which he saw with the Cherubim. Says he:

"This is the **living creature** which I saw under the God of Israel by the river of Chebar; and **I knew that they were Cherubim** (Ezek. 10:20) And again:

"The **Cherubim** were lifted up: this is the **living creature** that I saw by the river Chebar" (Ezek. 10:15). Compare also Ezekiel 1:22; 10:11.

Are the cherubim **"who"** or **"what"?** Are they persons or principles? Do they stand before God as creatures or do they stand as figures for representation? These are vital interrogations, the answers of which, **seriously effect interpretation.**

There is a theory that the Cherubim "were emblematical of the ever-blessed Trinity in covenant to redeem man, by writing the human nature to the Second Person, which union is signified by the union of the faces of the lion and man in the Cherubic exhibition" (Parkhurst and Hutchinson).

We cannot receive this view as reverent as it is on the ground that God forbade any likeness of Himself to be made and commanded against all visible representation and appearance of Himself. This was done that Israel might not be led into idolatry (Deut. 4:15, 16).

In the Book of Romans where God is making known the distance and depravity of man from God, He reckons the insult of an attempt of a likeness unto God or to comparison with any living being.

"Professing themselves to be wise they **became fools,** and changed the glory of the incorruptible God into an image made like to corruptible **man** to birds and four-footed **beats** and "creeping things" (Rom. 1:22, 23).

The **calf** was made in Horeb in a molten image and God was displeased. Says the psalmist: "They changed their glory into the similitude of an ox that eateth grass."

With these in mind and with the four living creatures or Cherubim with faces **lion, calf, man** and **eagle,** we can not take them to stand for and represent by visible manifestation the adorable Trinity or God head.

The God head is presented here the **same time** with the Cherubim. They are used at His seat. They are the basis of His throne. He dwells between them. The Cherubim were either **two** in number as on the **ark** or **four** as in Ezekiel, never Three as in **Trinity.** They are never **worshipped** nor are they the subjects of adoration. Indeed they offer worship. This should be sufficient. See Isaiah 6, and Revelation, chapters 4 and 5.

Many excellent students believe them to be emblematic or representative of the **Four Gospels.** Those who hold this view are not in accord with each other as to which of the Four Gospels answers to each one of the living creatures respectively.

We cannot accept this viewpoint as much as we respect those that do. Our reasons are as follows:

They are members of **justice** and **wrath.** They call for the plagues on the earth and they give the bowls of wrath to God's ministers (Rev. 6; 15:7). This would be strange action for the Four Gospels which are heralds of **mercy,** not justice and wrath. They are **not books** but actual and living creatures worshipping God.

They appear before Christ as seen and praise God for **Creation.**

Some think they are emblematic of angels. We never find anywhere the ministration of angels connected with the Cherubim. They are never confounded or connected with angels in the Scriptures. First the "zoa" or living creatures worship God, **then** the angels worship God (Rev. 5:8, 11). Angels would not be twice represented in the same verse as worshippers, first spoken of emblematically and then literally. Scripture does not so confuse.

There is always identification of difference. One of the **living creatures** gives the seven books to the **angels.** The living creatures are **never** dismissed on any mission or with any message as the angels are. They remain **attached** to the throne of God.

The Cherubim or living creatures are not emblems of angels.

There are others who take them as symbolic of the **Ministers of the Gospel.**

This can only be done by the most general application. The lion they say, denotes their **boldness,** the ox their patient service, the eagle their affections, the man their prudence.

This not worthy of any serious attention and in refutation of this attempt at interpretation one has but to ask such questions as—Why did they appear in Eden? Why are they so conspicuous in the **Mosaic covenant?** The living creatures it must be insisted upon, are ministers of justice connected with the throne of judgment which is seen set for judgment, not ministers of a Gospel of mercy and of grace. They were not seen or heard of in any of the seven Churches of Revelation 2 and 3.

If there was such a ministration would they not be seen with the Churches?

It is not possible to so wrest the Scriptures.

Lesson Twenty-one

## A THRONE: THE BEGINNING OF JUDGMENT (Rev.4) Part 5

We sought to understand in the former lesson who the Cherubim **were not.** In this lesson we shall seek to discover from the Scriptures who they are.

The division of the Book of Revelation which we are now studying is **"A Throne for the Beginning of Judgment."**—(Division Number Four) and everything is associated with that throne. The Cherubim are seen attached to and connected with the throne of God and **are never seen apart from it.** Let this be remembered by the student.

Opinions differ as to the derivation of the word "Cherubim." The view which favors the meaning to be derived from two Hebrew words signifying, "As—the great ones" or "As—multitude," appears and appeals, as most correct.

The Cherubim are not **emblems,** or are they **symbols,** they are representatives.

It is well to remember that the **symbols** of Revelation 4 and 5 are expounded and explained unto the student. The torches the horns and eyes of the Lamb, and the odours which the elders present to God and to Christ are explained for they are symbols. See 4:5 and 6:8. But the elders and the "zoa" or the living creatures are not explained for they **are not symbols nor emblems.**

The Cherubim are the **representatives** of the animal creation of the world.

Their number is **four.** Four is the number of **creation** and of the **world.**

Where the divisions of the inhabitants of the earth are mentioned, it is in a **fourfold** division—viz: **"tribe,**

**tongue, people, nation."** See 5:9; 7:9; 10:11; 11:9; 13:7; 14:6; 17:15.

The great divisions of the creation are **four—heaven, earth, under world, sea.** See 5:14, 14:7.

When God would send judgment on the creation, it is by **four score** judgments. These may be seen in Ezekiel 14:21:

1. The Sword
2. The Famine
3. The Noisome Beast
4. The Pestilence

In Psalm 148, a Psalm which is for the instruction of praising the Lord in the days of millennial gladness, there are four times four parties and in **particular** four kinds of living creatures. See verse 10. In Ezekiel these living creatures have **four** faces and **four wings.** Ezek. 1:6).

The camps of Israel were **four** toward the cardinal points. The great empires of the earth are **four.** See Daniel 2 and 7.

These four living creatures are specified as the heads of their tribes and divisions.

1. The **Lion** is the head of the **wild beasts** (Prov. 30:30).
2. The **Ox** is the chief of **cattle.**
3. The **Eagle** is the chief of **birds.**
4. **Man** is the head of all **creation.**

This is the division of living creatures which is recognized in the Scriptures. Let us consider. God creates.

First: **"Birds"** out of the waters (Gen. 1:20).

Out of the earth He caused

Second: **"Cattle."**

Third: **"Creeping things."**

Fourth: **Wild beast** to arise. Lastly, He creates **Man.** See again at the time of the flood; (1) every wild beast; (2) each kind of cattle; (3) of creeping things, and

(4) the birds enter the ark (Gen. 7:14). These four kinds were also cut off by the flood. (Gen. 7:21).

There are however, two classes who have no representative among the Cherubim—the **fish** and **reptiles** or "creeping things."

There is a reason for this. The first may be omitted because there is no sea in the new earth. See Revelation 21.

The reptiles have no representative with these living creatures and the reason is not hard to find. It was the serpent that introduced sin into the world and was condemned to his place among the creeping things.

Out of the **five** animal tribes of the earth God enters into covenant with but **three** only.

"And, I behold, I establish My covenant with you, and with your seed after you; and with every living creature that is with you, of the **fowl**, of the **cattle**, and of every (wild) **beast** of the earth, with you; from all that go out of the ark, to every beast of the earth." (Gen. 9:9, 10).

In conjunction with man, only these **three** appear in the Cherubim. When other Creatures are in amity and reconciliation the marks of humiliation and of judgment are still upon the serpent or the "creeping things." "Dust shall be the serpent's meat." The coming age promises nothing for the serpent. But the **eagle,** the servant's foe, is one of the four of the Cherubim. This is the Book which has much to do with the Serpent, "that old Devil" the great enemy of Christ.

It is interesting also to classify the "zoa" or four living creatures and the relations among themselves.

Of the **four**, two are unclean by the **law,** the **lion** and the **eagle.**

**Two** are **clean**—the **ox** and the **man.** But here are all cleansed and seem to stand as a pledge and a prophecy of the final cleansing of creation. Peter's vision in Acts 10:6 was a glimpse into millennial state now withheld for a season.

Two are creatures that, now by nature, while yet the curse is on the earth prey on each other—the lion and the eagle. The ox is sometimes the victim of the lion and man is sometimes the destroyer of them all.

But here is pacification, domestication and amity. There is no strife in the presence of God and what a prophecy when creation is delivered and the disorder of Adam's sin has been remedied and a great reconciliation and concordance has taken place. God be thanked, the creatures nor the creation will always be at variance!

Isaiah saw in the very nature of things, what is set before us in the four living creatures—

"The **calf** and the young **lion** and the fatling together and a **little child** shall lead them."

Here are three of the Cherubic figures. "The **lion** shall eat straw like the **ox.**"

So, as the twenty-four elders are the heads of the angels, so are the four living creatures heads of the tribes of the earth.

Here are the attendants of His throne and with them appears Jesus as the Lamb slain. When he takes the book, the **whole creation** utters a note of joy, led by the zoa or living creatures around the throne. Earth is soon to come into view as the living creatures call "the four horses of the Apocalypse" to come forth. See chapter 6. They are says R. Govet "the fitting supplement of the **rainbow** and the **sea,** which all speak of the covenant with Noah. For they are described under this **four-fold** division in the history of the flood, and in the covenant which followed thereon. "And all flesh died that moved upon the earth, both of **fowl** and of **cattle** and of **beast** and of creeping things that creepeth upon the earth and every **man.**" (Gen. 7:21).

"And behold, I will establish My covenant with **you** and with your **seed after you,** and with every living creature that is with you, of the fowl and of the cattle, and of every beast of the earth with you" (Gen. 9:9, 10).

**Man** is not the only one in the covenant with Noah; living creatures have a claim upon God and His covenant. It includes fowl, cattle, and beasts. Not a bird that flies through the air but is the object of the covenant following the flood. The cattle on the hills have a covenant claim on Him and His Word, and the wild beasts as well, roam jungles on **His covenant.** He made it to **include them.** While the old earth remains so do the living creatures.

They appear no longer after the earth is destroyed and are not mentioned in relation with new heavens and the new earth.

Let us remember that the redemption of creation as well as man is God's decreed and declared purpose.

Read what Paul says in Rom. 8:19-23. This is the key note of the subject, and much of the Book of Revelation has to do with this very thing. The Book of Revelation is the consummation of all things. Here all things in a seeming tangle unravel and clear up. The creation fell with Adam. It was not his own choice. It was subjected and became a slave. At the deliverance of redeemed men from their graves, creation itself will come in for a deliverance which is to be wonderful and glorious indeed.

Since the world began the prophets have spoken of a "restoration" (Acts 3:21). God will keep His word and creation will not be forgotten and the sin-imposed burden and bondage lifted. O praise Him!

Lesson Twenty-two

# A THRONE: THE BEGINNING OF JUDGMENT (Rev.4) Part 6

The Cherubim are mentioned first in Genesis 3:24. The sin of man had brought the culprit to judgment. The devil has introduced sin by means of the animal creation and every vegetable creation is also involved. God presses sentence upon the serpent. Says He, "Because thou hast done this thou art cursed above all cattle and above every wild beast of the field."

The way of the tree of life is still open and as yet man is not driven out. If man in his fallen nature had partaken of the tree of life he would have been immortal in his guilt and fixed in nature and destiny.

The record says:

"So He drove out the man, and He placed at the east of the Garden of Eden Cherubims, and a flaming sword which turned every way, to keep the way of the tree of life." (Gen. 3:24).

Kitto says that the word rendered by the translators "placed" signifies properly—**"to place in a tabernacle."** He thinks there was a local tabernacle in which the Divine presence was manifested and it was to this tabernacle Cain and Abel repaired with their sacrifices. This explains the words of God to Cain—"A sin-offering lieth at the door" (Gen. 4:7, Heb.) and the words of Cain—"From **Thy face** I shall be hid." "And Cain went out from the **presence of the Lord."**

The Cherubim are first seen as **sentinels** and **guards.** "Full of eyes" as they were and in possession of a flaming sword turning every way they stood against all or any who would intrude to eat the fruit. The word signifies to **guard.** It is used in other places.

The Levites were to keep a guard over the Tabernacle

and had power to kill any intruder (Num. 1:51-53). **"The stranger that cometh nigh shall be put to death."** David stood guard over Saul. See II Samuel 26:15. The word to **"keep"** is manifestly **guard.**

Thus do the sleepless Cherubim guard. The representatives of the animal creation are set a sentinel to guard the way back. If any approach they must pass the sword and suffer death. There was One, the Mighty Deliverer who did this. He was slain in so doing but arose from the dead, reached the Tree of Life and brought the fruit out to the children. The sword was awakened against "one that was My fellow," and because He was **fellow with God** He arose from the dead and opened the way back to God. "Thou **wast slain** and hast redeemed us to God."

Thus we behold the Cherubim associated with the throne and presence of God in His justice and His judgments. It is possible the Cherubim retained their position till the earth was deluged. Perhaps after the flood images were made of them and were kept in houses and worshipped under the name of Teraphim which is possibly a corruption of Seraphim or "burning and shining one."

Rachel stole the Teraphim from Laban and Laban complained because of the theft of his **gods.** See Genesis 31:19, 31-35. Micah made a house of God and a Teraphim perhaps a representation of the Garden of Eden (Judg. 17:5). The children of Dan carry them off (Judg. 18). Michal with the image of the Teraphim deceived the messengers sent to slay David (II Sam. 19:13, 16).

Next is, the Flood in the days of Noah. Adam's race has so corrupted the earth it must be cleaned of its corruption and cleared of its demons. God would keep secure the line of "the woman's seed" and the source and spring of all nations in **Ham, Japeth,** and **Shem.**

Noah prepares the vessel for the saving of the remnant of the earth. But man is not alone in God's plan for preservation but His creatures also. The ark is to hold them as well as Noah and his family for they were cursed with man and are now cared for with man. See Gen. 7:13-15.

God was not unmindful of animal creation and they went in from the old earth with Noah and came out with Noah to the new earth.

Noah then offers a sacrifice unto God which is pleasing to God. The Lord smelled its sweet flavor and odor of **"rest"** says the margin. The offering consisted of every clean **bird** and **beast.** He then utters His blessing on **man** and **beast.** Jehovah then publishes His covenant, the terms and time thereof and the parties concerned.

"And I behold, I establish My covenant with you, and with your seed after you; and with every living creature that is with you, of the fowl, of the cattle, and of every beast of the earth (wild) that is with you, from all that go out of the ark, to every beast of the earth." (Gen. 9:9, 10).

These four are represented in the Cherubim, the fowl **—eagle,** the cattle—the **ox;** the wild beast—the **lion,** and **man.**

Then the bow in the cloud and its covenant character is next seen.

The extent of its token is "between **Me** and **you** and **every living creature** of all flesh."

Whenever the Cherubim are seen in the future it is with the bow of God. See Ezekiel 1:20 and Revelation 4.

There are two things which we must not fail to see at the flood. First. The creatures suffered with man at the flood. Second—Creatures are also secured with man through the flood.

When God delivers Israel from Egypt He forgets not man and beast (Exod. 12:12, 29). He smote the cattle of the Egyptians. When Israel went through the Red Sea their flocks and herds came along with them.

Then by Divine instruction we behold the construction of the Tabernacle, or as Govett calls it **"His Royal Tent."** It was God's dwelling place, and it was His seat.

The first piece of furniture was the **Ark.** On this ark again we behold the Cherubim. Out of the gold on the mercy-seat were the Cherubim to be made. See Exodus 25:17-22.

Now in the tabernacle, Eden is removed to the wilderness. Man could not get back into Eden but Eden could go along with man. Once again God is dwelling in the midst of the people with one chosen man to enter His presence in behalf of the people. Eden had entered the desert and went wherever God and His people went. Eden was not lost. It was journeying on to a land of rest.

And here we see with this Eden the Cherubim but in another attitude. There is a mistake made in not connecting always the Tabernacle and the Temple with Garden where first we see God dwelling. There will be a time when there will be no Temple or Tabernacle for God Himself will tabernacle with men."

Lesson Twenty-three

## A KINSMAN IN HEAVEN (Rev. 5) Part 1

In chapter 4, we have seen the throne and its surroundings and servants. Surely, "He hath established His throne in heaven." There is readiness and preparation for a great assize. "The Judge is at the door." The dispensation of the grace of God is at its **close** and a dispensation of the judgments of God, is about to **commence.**

Too much importance can not be attached to this chapter of the Book. It is the climax and the crisis of human history. It may be understood only in the institutions of the nation Israel. It is the larger fulfillment of a calendar event in the history of Israel.

We must remember that the Church, the Body of Christ, is gone, and the judgments which are now in preparation, are to fall upon the **earth** and the dwellers thereof which, are of necessity, the Jew and the Gentile —the Jews as a **nation** and the Gentiles as **nations.**

There was a year in the calendar of Israel known as the "year of jubilee." See Lev. 25:8-11.

The fiftieth year was the year of jubilee—the year of restoration, restitution, reparation and liberation. It was on the year after seven Sabbaths of years. It followed the **forty-ninth.** It was the beginning of new **series of sevens.** Seven times seven equaled **forty-nine** and then jubilee year.

It was the year of liberty. All slaves were freed. All property returned and restored. Usurpers were ejected and squatters cast out and the rightful heirs possessed their property. It was the year of jubilation and emancipation! (See Lev. 25).

On this day the judge took his throne which was

established for justice and judgment. The title deeds were brought from the archives of the nations. They had been sealed and secured awaiting this day of restitution and restoration.

The property would be restored to those from whom it had been wrested or confiscated, if there was some one who was of nearest kin to appear for the estate in behalf of the heirs.

The record says: **"One of his brethren may redeem him."** (Lev. 25:48).

If any appear to claim the title deed to break the seals thereof and institute the prosecutions for the ejection of the usurper and the restoration of the possession, who could not **prove the claim** of a kinsman, they would be challenged, contested, and declared impostors. They must be a kinsman, with the kinsman's **rights of redemption.**

At this point in the Book of Revelation the year of jubilee is about to be proclaimed.

The throne of justice is set. The Judge we saw in the 4th chapter as well as the throne.

The proclaimer is ready as at all tribunals for legal procedure. The rolls, books, or scrolls are ready. Says John:

"And I saw in the right hand of him that sat on the throne a Book written within and on the back side sealed with seven seals" (5:1).

This is a familiar scene enacted each year of jubilee, which took place after **49 years,** on the **fiftieth.** Prophetically it is exactly jubilee year when these judgments of the Book of Revelation begin to fall.

Said Daniel the prophet, speaking with authority from heaven:

"Seventy weeks are determined upon thy people and upon thy holy city, to finish the transgression, and to make an end of sins, and to make reconciliation for iniquity, and to bring in everlasting righteousness and to seal up the vision and prophecy and to anoint the Holy" (Dan. 9:24).

The "Seventy Weeks" are the duration of Israel's subjection. These seventy weeks however, take on the larger time period of **seven times seventy** or **four hundred and ninety years!** This period of 490 years has its time divisions and events lying between, which lengthen into history, but the original decree covers 490 years—a 49 with a naught added thereto making 490. The 490 years are the end of Israel's subjection and subjugation. After the 49th comes the **fiftieth** and the fiftieth year is the Year of Jubilee, when both land and people shall have their liberty and the restoration of their possessions which have been in subjection to others for the 490 years of the prophetic calendar. Therefore this is about the time for the proclamation of the year of Jubilee in Israel for with Israel and those that have ruled over her, these days have to do. We cannot expect to see the Church, the Body of Christ, here, and many an attempted interpretation to identify the Church with these scenes, brings but **confusion** and not right division and distinction.

It is a **Year of Jubilee scene.** The end of the 49 years has been reached. The assize is established, the throne set up, the throne sitter on the throne, the sealed parchment containing the title deed to the lost inheritance in the right hand of the throne sitter, the seven seals upon the parchment or book and a proclaimer asking for a kinsman to step forward, establish his claim to take the book and begin the process of seal breaking which will issue in the routing of the usurper and the return of the property to its proper and legal heirs! This is the event for which the 5th chapter of Revelation is making ready.

It is the time of jubilee—it is the "year of His redeemed." It is emancipation hour. The 490 years of servitude and subjection are near the end. The times of the Gentiles are about "finished." The city, the land, and the people are soon to be delivered. The heel of the oppreessor is soon to be lifted and the people shall rejoice.

The image seen by Nebuchadnezzar has about reached its extremity and the Stone is soon to strike! The rule of Gentiles is nearing its end and the supremacy of Israel is about to begin. The desolations of Jerusalem will soon be overpast and her glory restored. Surely, this is a crisis hour and a crucial time in the unfolding of the purpose of God for His people!

The time has come, the throne is established, there is him that "sat on the throne," the sealed book in the open palm and the trumpeter or proclaimer but where is the kinsman? Who will find him and bring him forward for this crisis hour? Who knows? There are many that could come forward but the challenge would prove their claim invalid. They must establish kinsman's rights beyond cavil, contest and controversy. Where will such be found? This is a legal transaction of such character that none may trifle.

That book of title deed is **sealed.** Let none assume to touch such a document without authority and legal right. "Who will take the book and break the seal thereof?" No such a question was ever asked in this universe of such vital importance as this. Where is the kinsman?

Lesson Twenty-four

## A KINSMAN IN HEAVEN (Rev. 5) Part 2

A search is now on for the Kinsman Redeemer. The throne has been set. The title deed to the last inheritance has been presented, and an angel has been chosen to issue the proclamation. This angel is known in the Book of Revelation as the "angel with a loud voice." He is an interesting person and should be considered. He appears here as a court crier, or an announcer, or proclaimer. With trumpet voice he proclaims the year of jubilee, a year which is by Isaiah, the Prophet, called, "the year of His redeemed." It will be noticed that the angel proclaimer cries and calls in three spheres—**heaven, earth,** and the **underworld.** In these three spheres he sounds the challenge and issues the call for some one to appear to take the Book of title deed, break off the seals and institute the judgments. Only a Kinsman would dare to do this without defeat. Others will be challenged and contested. He must be a Kinsman-Redeemer who attempts the work of redemption, recovery, reparation and restitution.

The angel cries, "Who is worthy to open the Book and to loose the seals thereof?" (Chap. 5:2). He called in heaven. Angels were there, how many we do not know. Daniel gives us a little idea, when he says "thousands, thousands ministered unto Him, and ten thousand times ten thousand stood before Him; the judgment was set, and the books were opened." Here we have a little glimpse upon the multitudinous number of angels in His presence. To these the call was made to find a Kinsman to recover the children's lost inheritance.

Michael was there, and he is the guardian angel of national Israel. This we learn at Daniel 12:1, where he is called "the great prince who standeth for the children of Thy People." Michael's delegated dignity is one of important responsibility.

Gabriel is among the angels and the hosts of heaven. He is the Evangelist of the Angels, and also the chronologer of heaven. The time of both advents of Christ were proclaimed by Him. See (Daniel 9:21-27). Indeed the entire history of Israel is found proclaimed before the time, in this remarkable passage which covers in its exent the time beginning with Nebuchadnezzar and the subjection of Jerusalem to Gentile nations until the time of Israel's national deliverance, salvation and glory.

There were myriads of angels besides of various ranks and ministry. Angels are "ministers" and "flames of fire" unto them that are the heirs of salvation.

Among these hosts of high heaven and of high honor the proclaimer calls, but there is no Kinsman Redeemer among the angels. Angels are not akin with those from whom the inheritance was wrested. Angels are the result of a direct act of creation. They are not the offspring of pro-creation. They are the fruit of no one's womb. They are not a race to propagate themselves, or reproduce themselves. We remember early in our Christian life what G. Campbell Morgan, the prince of expositors, said while lecturing on the Epistle to the Ephesians. "I used to sing,

> 'I want to be an angel,
> And with an angel stand,
> A crown upon my forehead,
> And a harp within my hand.'

But," said he, "I no longer sing this song. I do not want to be an angel. I am a child of God by the new creation, and in Christ I am far above all angels."

Dr. Morgan learned a great truth when this exalted position of the believer entered his understanding.

A study of the Scriptures will perhaps reveal that instead of an angel ministering unto the members of the Body of Christ, it is just the opposite. Angels are the object of a ministry from the members of the Body of Christ (Eph. 3:10).

Let it be remembered that Christ has two times passed the angels by, once when He went down in humiliation at the incarnation, and took on David's seed for the suffering of death. Again He passed the angels by, when He went up in exaltation at the resurrection to a seat at the right hand of God, "far above all principality and power and might and dominion and every name that is named not only in this world, but also in that which is to come." There is no use to call among the angels for a Kinsman Redeemer. There is no one of their kind, however exalted in rank and authority, that could stand before the call of the proclaimer and meet the demands of a Kinsman. The student must now pay close attention while reading Hebrews 1:1-18, and note each time the word, "angel," occurs.

This argument in the Epistle to Hebrews precludes any possibility of a Kinsman Redeemer to arise from among the angels. There must be One who can say, "Behold I and the children whom God hath given Me." There must be One who can say, "I will declare Thy Name unto My Brethren." There must be One of whom it is said, "He that sanctifieth and they who are sanctified are all of one." It must be one who is not "ashamed to call them brethren." That Christ is not an angel of exalted rank, but the Son of God, is among the contentions of this remarkable passage in the Hebrew Epistle. Says the writers of the Hebrews, "Verily He took not on Him the nature of angels, but He took on Him the seed of Abraham." Angel nature would disqualify any as a Kinsman and a Redeemer. **It must**

**be the seed of Abraham.** Only He can successfully pass every challenge and contest of the court of heaven. One must be found who was "made like unto His brethren." One must be found who became partaker of flesh and blood, as also the children were partakers of flesh and blood. The cry of the proclaiming angel finds no answer among the angels. Angels have great honor, but not a Kinsman's honor. Angels may minister to the redeemed, but they cannot appear as the executive and redeemer of the inheritance.

Somebody greater than angels must be found. Some one to whom angels bow in authority, and move to do His will. If there were ten thousand times ten thousand angels more than Daniel beheld, not one of them is good enough, or of a proper nature to "open the book and loose the seal thereof," and start the prosecution of the usurper, the Devil, the Old Serpent, that deceived them. The four hundred and ninety years have been fulfilled upon national Israel. The time of their captivity is near its end. The hour for their national deliverance is due, but where is the Kinsman Redeemer? He is not among the angels, where is He?

Lesson Twenty-five

## A KINSMAN IN HEAVEN (Rev. 5) Part 3

In our former lecture we beheld the "angel with the loud voice," crying in heaven among its inhabitants for a Kinsman who could take the Book and break the seals thereof. There was no one found in heaven to fill the office of a Kinsman Redeemer. He next calls to the earth in endeavor to find among the peoples of the earth one who could break the seals from the Seven Sealed Book. They search on the earth for one who could break the seals from the Book of Title Deed, but He was no longer upon the earth. There was no man among men who could act as Redeemer for man. Man cannot **procure** his salvation; there is no human market; man cannot **provide** his salvation; his genius is not sufficient; man cannot **purchase** salvation, he is bankrupt and without funds and is hopelessly overdrawn. Man cannot **produce** his salvation for every one born of man is but a fallen being, as was the man from whose loins he came. "Adam begat sons in his own likeness" and being a fallen man he has produced no other kind. "That which is born of the flesh is flesh." Nothing spiritual ever comes out of the flesh. There are no processes for the spiritualizing of the flesh. The flesh cannot be renovated, flesh cannot be recreated, the flesh cannot be regenerated. There is only one way in which God deals with the flesh,—He nails it to the cross and makes an open show of its rebellious character to the universe and executes upon it the full penalty, which is death.

The only man that ever came into the world that had no need of a Saviour was Jesus Christ. He is the Saviour because He had no need of a Saviour. If His need had been salvation He could never have been the Saviour to supply the need for others. He never came from Adam's loins, He was not of the first man of the earth, He was the Lord from heaven. He was not born as others were born. He never lived as others lived; He did not die as others died. His birth, His life, His death were unique and unlike anything in all the universe. It is said of Him that He never spoke as other men spoke. The reason why He spake as no man spake was because He lived as no other man ever lived, and the reason He lived as no other man ever lived was because He was born as no other man was ever born, and the reason He died as no other man ever died was because He was born as no other man was born. He lived as no other man ever lived, spake as no other man ever spake and therefore could die as no one ever died.

Jesus Christ cannot be classed with Adam's race; He took on in the incarnation, the likeness of sin's flesh, but He never **took on sinful flesh.** He was born of the Holy Ghost, and the Holy Ghost imparts no corruption, mortality, sin or death. In the crisis hour, which this fifth chapter of the Book of Revelation reveals, man will be in a high state of human exaltation. It will be a time after the Church, the Body of Christ has gone. The judgments of God will be upon the earth, upon the basis of Judgment and Retribution laid down in the second chapter of Romans:

"But unto them that are contentious and do not obey the truth but obey unrighteousness, indignation and wrath, tribulation and anguish upon every soul of man that doeth evil, of the Jew first and also of the Gentile."

In these dark days of tribulation there will be the cry for a superman. The superman will be produced. The thirteenth chapter of Revelation reveals him; he is known as the Beast King. He comes up out of the sea, but before his career is finished he is cast into the Lake of Fire. Revelation 20:10. The deification of man and the humiliation of God is the spectacle which shall yet receive the applause and approval of this world. There is no use for the angel with the trumpet voice to call upon the earth for one who can take the Book and open the seals thereof.

The angel crier having searched heaven and earth for one who could break the seals from the scroll of the Book, now cries unto the under world,—not the under world of submerged and defeated human beings but the under world of the dead, Hades and Sheol. Unto this world he cries: "Can any one take the Book and loose the seals thereof?" as if to say, "It is time for the heir of Jubilee when the inheritance is recovered, returned and restored." We have found no one in heaven, no one on earth, neither can there be found one in the underworld of the dead."

But it is as useless to search in Hades and Sheol for a Kinsman Redeemer as it was to search the heavens and the earth for there was One in Sheol and Hades but He is not there now. He had one time spoken of the impossibility of Sheol and Hades prevailing (Matt. 16: 18).

Peter on the Day of Pentecost had told of the visit this one had made to Sheol and Hades and declared their inability to hold Him prisoner. He Himself had said to John that He was now "alive forevermore" and had the "keys of Sheol and Hades." Indeed—

"Up from the grave He arose,
With a mighty triumph o'er His foes."

There cannot be found in the underworld any one to take the Book and loose the seals thereof. The cry had gone out, the challenge issued, but no one had been found. There was a time in the world when Jesus wept, it is now time for John to weep. Says he—

"And I wept much because there was no man found worthy to open and to read the Book, neither to look thereon."

John wept because the crisis hour had come in human history, the time decreed upon His people and the duration of their servitude was now finished. The four hundred and ninety years as prophesied by Daniel, have at last come to the point of final fulfillment and there is no one to appear who has the Kinsman's rights to take the Title and start the judgments which will issue in the return and the restoration of it to the people to whom it belongs.

John wept and so would we weep. The universe would be in darkness and total eclipse if Jesus Christ were not at the right hand of God. It is Jesus Christ who literally holds things together; it is Jesus Christ who upholds all things by the Word of His power; Jesus Christ is Providence. Throughout the entire universe there would be weeping and wailing and gnashing of teeth if Jesus Christ were not at the right hand of God. There would be universal suicide, there would be perhaps the immediate incineration of the material universe, fire, lava and smoke would rise in clouds, leaving the earth and all that is therein a clinker and a cinder. Rocks, hills and mountains would be a haven to a horror-stricken society. Order would once again become chaos and confusion and confounding would be the universal state of things if Jesus Christ were not at the right hand of God. There are no words in the vocabulary of all the languages of all the tongues of all the universe, to describe the catastrophe and the calamity.

Therefore John wept his lamentations over this seeming defeat as did Jeremiah over the fallen city of Jerusalem. But John's weeping endured but for a season; joy came, for lo, one of the Elders saith unto John "Weep not." Could it be that the Elder said indeed,

"Weep not"? Why should not weeping continue if there be none found in heaven, in earth or under the earth who could take this Book and break the seals thereof? Was there none who could act as the avenger for the children and bring execution upon this usurper of their possessions? It is true one of the Elders said "Weep not: behold the Lion of the Tribe of Juda, the root of David had prevailed to open the Book and to loose the seven seals thereof." John, wipe away tears, it is the hour of triumph; John, cease thy sobbings, it is the hour for shoutings, cease the dirge and the melancholy and join with the universe in one harmonious and heavenly anthem unto the Lion of Juda's Tribe and of the Root of David. Let Miserere give way to the Hallelujah Chorus, let the song of Jubilation and Emancipation begin. Surely the crisis is overpast, the cloud is gone and the darkness will flee with the breaking of the day.

Lesson Twenty-six

## A KINSMAN IN HEAVEN (Rev. 5) Part 4

John ceased sobbing, that he might see the One of whom it was declared, that He could loose the seals of the mysteriously bound scroll. He looked and in the midst of the throne, the four creatures, and in the midst of the elders, and lo, instead of a **Lion,** he beheld a **Lamb.** One must be strangely impressed, if when expecting to behold a lion, king of beasts, they confront a lamb, the kindliest of creatures. Not only did he behold a Lamb, but it was a Lamb that had been slain; it was a Lamb with the marks of sacrifice upon him.

It was indeed a Lamb of the Holy Scriptures (there on the first pages of Genesis to the last page of Revelation), it was the Lamb slain from before the foundation of the world. It was God's Lamb; it was the one John proclaimed, when he cried, "Behold the Lamb of God which taketh away the sin of the world." It was the Passover Lamb, and every Lamb in the types of Holy Scripture forecasting the vicarious death of Christ at the cross. It was the Lamb who had been for "sinners slain." John beheld, not only One who was Sovereign, but One who had been to the place of sacrifice.

When he saw the slain Lamb, he understood that the power to redeem belonged to the Person who had purchased the right of redemption. There is no escape from the cross. Whatever may be the future Sovereignity of Christ, it is based on His past sacrifice, whatever **crowns He takes** it is the result of the **cross He bore.** It is the One who was **slain** that will **reign.** The death of Christ underlies the super-structure of salvation; the death of Christ is the foundation of all Divine manifestations; redemption from the hands of the enemy can be accomplished only by the payment of blood, but no blood of less value than the blood of Christ; "A lamb without spot and blemish."

The year of Jubilee was proclaimed on the **"tenth day of the seventh month** in the Day of Atonement," says Leviticus, "Shall ye make the trumpet sound throughout all your land." The proclamation of jubilation, liberation and emancipation, could not be proclaimed **apart from atonement,** so here, the sounding of the angel, with the loud noise, in preparation for the year of jubilee, is associated with atonement. The Lamb approached the throne, took the Book out of the right hand of Him who sat upon the throne and upon taking the Book, the four living creatures and the twenty-four Elders, fell down before the Lamb, each of them with a harp and golden vials full of odors, and they sang a song. It is called a "new song," and the words of the song are found in vss. 9, 10.

This was the signal for the angels to join the anthem and the total number that sang with a loud voice was ten thousand times ten thousand and thousands of thousands, they sang:

"Worthy is the Lamb that was slain, to receive power, and riches, and wisdom, and strength, and honour, and glory, and blessing."

This song with its sevenfold note of triumph, so stirred the universe, that one universal anthem broke out from every creature, "which is in heaven, and on earth, and under the earth, and such as are in the sea, and all that are in them, heard I saying, Blessing, and honour, and glory, and power, be unto Him that sitteth upon the throne, and unto the Lamb for ever and ever."

There is no way to describe this song nor the singing. How many took part therein is beyond computation. The number of angels alone was "ten thousand times ten thousand, and thousands of thousands."

The subject of the song was "The Lamb" and His worthiness to take the title deed from the Throne-Sitter and break the seals thereof, and execute the judgments therein, which would issue in the restoration of all property, and the liberation of all slaves, and the inauguration of the Year of Jubilee. The cross which has been despised and the Christ of the cross who had been rejected, now receives the full praise, and glory, and honor, and adoration that is due. The Blood of the Lamb which has long been dishonored is now honored; the Redeemer is now acknowledged, the crisis hour of the universe is past, for the Christ of the Cross is now the Christ of the Crown; His redeeming results assures Him His regal reign. The Lamb that was slain is now Sovereign. The four creatures cried "Amen." The four and twenty elders fell down and worshipped, and homage to Christ was universally proclaimed.

The Book is now in the hands of the Lamb—all judgment in heaven and in earth is committed to Him **and the judgments must now begin.** The patience of God is exhausted, now the punishment of the inhabitants of the earth must begin, and the judgment which has long slumbered is now awakened.

Beginning with chapter 6 we shall see the Lamb breaking the seals from the Book, and the last week of Israel's servitude as outlined by Gabriel's chronology, will now be completed.

Lesson Twenty-seven

## PRE-MILLENIAL JUDGMENTS: SEALS, TRUMPETS, VIALS (Rev. 6-19) Part 1

At the 6th chapter of the Book of Revelation our attention is directed to the earth. From the beginning of the 4th chapter to the close of the 5th chapter, **everything is in heaven.** The throne, the One who sits upon the throne, the One who is in the midst of the throne and those who surround the throne, are all in heaven.

In chapters 4 and 5 the Bible student is privileged to glance within the secret of God's presence and behold preparation for the coming judgments. With the opening of the 6th chapter these judgments begin. The Lamb by right of the Purchase of Redemption now takes the Power of Redemption. He paid the price at the Cross, He now takes the power with the Crown. The One who has been sitting at the right hand of God in patient waiting for the cup of inquity to come to its full, is now ready to dash the bowls or vials of God's wrath upon the earth. He was found worthy to take the Book and open the seals thereof.

At the beginning of the 6th chapter begins the work for which He was found worthy. The judgment period includes chapter 6:1 to 19:4. The judgments are executed in three series:

I. **The Seals** (Chapters 6 to 8:5).

II. **The Trumpets** (Chapter 8:6 to 19:21).

III. **The Vials** (Chapter 16:1 to 19:21).

The Lamb breaks the seals. He only was found worthy to do this. The angels blow the trumpets; He holds them in His hand for this purpose (chap. 1:16). They are the seven spirits that are seen before the throne in chapter 1:4. The seven angels also pour out the seven vials of God's wrath upon the earth.

We are of the opinion that the seven seals include the entire judgment period and that out of them issue forth the seven trumpet judgments and the seven vials of judgment. The seven seals commence and conclude this judgment time.

It may be illustrated by a telescope comprising three sections, the original stock into which is enfolded two more sections. The second division of the telescope is drawn out of the first, and out of the second is drawn the third, for both were included within the first. The seals, in our judgment, may be likened to the original section with the trumpets and vials drawn out because they were included in.

Or, again, simple illustration may help us to make clear our understanding of these judgments. Who has not watched the great sky rocket which is sent plowing and scraping across a black sky on the night following a day of celebration or commemoration. Out of the great ball of fire one ball separates itself, shooting forth seven stars; soon another ball with seven more stars, but the original ball within which were included the two balls with seven stars each, **goes on to the end.** The seals are the original ball extending over the entire period of the judgment. Out of the seals come forth the seven trumpets and the seven vials. **The trumpets and the vials display in detail the judgments which were included in the seals in general.**

It will be well for the student to become familiar with these chapters; fix in the mind where each of the seven seals are mentioned and the principal thing connected with each; also the sounding of the trumpets and the pouring of each of the vials with the associated events thereof. A little hair line of ink marking under first seal, second seal, etc.; under first trumpet, second trumpet, etc.; under first vial, second vial, etc., will do much to aid the student in location of these great judgment events and the association of them with this most terrible judgment season. Be not afraid to mark your Bible. It is made for use.

Now we desire that it be understood that the author of these studies believes these judgments to be **future.** They have not yet been fulfilled. They are yet to be fulfilled. The Book of Revelation is a Book awaiting future fulfillment. We will not contend, nor shall we censor. We shall respect the viewpoint of others as we desire others to respect our viewpoint. Multitudinous interpretations and attempts at application of the prophecies of this Book to the events that have transpired in times past, in our sincere judgment, have created much confusion. There are most excellent men who seem to find the major portions of seals, trumpets and vials fulfilled in history, beginning the opening of the Christian era down to the present hour.

Frankly, we do not so interpret this Book. Though we have profound respect for many that do, we must confess we have received no help whatever from this method in the interpretation of the Book of Revelation. These judgments are future and are not contemporaneous with the dispensation now present. The Church, the Body of Christ, is not an object of these judgments. These judgments are upon the Jew as a **nation** and upon the Gentiles as **nations.** The Church, the Body of Christ, is neither Jew nor Gentile; it is one body of believers with the middle wall of partition which made separation and discrimination between the Jew and the Gentile removed, and thus creating of the twain, **one new man.** This wonderful peace which brought the Jew and the Gentile into one body, is the result of the Blood of His

Cross by which He made peace (Eph. 2). There are a number who differ with us. We thank God we have come to a place in our Christian life where we can continue our love where we cannot always harmonize the viewpoint of our Holy Faith. We rejoice that we can be tolerant without becoming indifferent. We cannot yield our convictions but we can respect the convictions of others.

During the present age God's judgments have not been in the earth. Instead of a **throne of judgment** it has been a **throne of grace.** Christ has been sitting at the right hand of God and He will sit there until the hour arrives for Him to make His "enemies His footstool." This hour has not yet arrived. Grace is still offered to the sinner; justice and judgment is held back. With this 6th chapter those judgments begin which will never cease until the enemies of the Messiah will be obliged to sit at His feet and the 2nd Psalm is fulfilled. In our judgment it does great violence to the present priesthood of the Christ in the heavens, to attempt to picture Him as fulfilling Apocalyptic judgments in the dispensation now present. He is not now breaking the seals, nor has He in any past period since the revelation of the Divine purpose in the Church. The trumpets have not been sounded in any of the events of the past 2,000 years nor have the vials been poured out anywhere between the Pentecost and the present. He has not been executing judgment upon the earth, He has been extending grace to the inhabitants of the earth with longsuffering and tender and compassionate waiting. These judgments are future. They occur after the Church, the Body of Christ, has been removed from the judgments which must fall upon the inhabitants of the earth. A clear distinction and discrimination between the Jew the circumcision and the Gentile the uncircumcision and the Church of God, which is neither of the circumcision or the uncircumcision, but is a new body, would clear the clouds of confusion and yield a better understanding of all the Scriptures from Genesis to Revelation.

This is not a careless utterance but one that deeply concerns the Church of God everywhere.

No, Christ has not been sitting at the right hand of His Father on the throne of grace and at the self same time executing the seal, trumpet and vial judgments upon the earth. When His season of succor at the right hand of God ends, then and not till then, will the execution of these judgments begin. This gives us courage to proclaim to lost men that the grace of God is extended for any who will receive it, and boldness to proclaim that judgment is impending from which there is no escape but to those who are in Christ Jesus.

Lesson Twenty-eight

## PRE-MILLENIAL JUDGMENTS: SEALS, TRUMPETS, VIALS, (Rev. 6-19) Part 2

At the opening of Revelation 6, we have reached chronologically, the last week of Daniel's **"Seventy Weeks"** (Dan. 9:26, 27). In chapters 4 and 5 we see the "throne set" and of this Daniel also spoke, when he said:

"I beheld till the thrones were cast down, or (set) and the Ancient of days did sit, whose garment was white as snow, the hair of His head like pure wool; His throne was like a fiery flame, and His wheels as burning fire" (7:9).

None can deny that these words practically summarize the first five chapters of the Book of Revelation.

Now the judgments of that **throne** and the **throne-sitter,** commence.

The sixty-ninth week came to an end at the time of the formal rejection of Christ as King of Israel. David's royal Son was rejected by David's seed. The throne was left vacant and the King rejected. The dynasty of David is without a King to sit upon its throne. The King is on His Father's throne "waiting," "until."

There are "seventy weeks" "determined" upon Israel. Between the 69th and the 70th is the **present purpose of God.** It is the time of the building and the perfecting of His Body the Church, which is not a racial or national institution—neither "Jew nor Gentile."

At the completion of this purpose, God shall again turn to His earthly program and to Israel and the nations. During this period occurs the "tribulation" and the "great tribulation." It is the day of "Jacob's trouble" and the "Day of the Lord." See Mathew 24; Isaiah 2:12-24; Joel 2:1-11.

It is that time in the program of God which Jesus,

when preaching at Nazareth, where He was brought up, called the **"day of vengeance of our God,"** He quoted from Isaiah the prophet. See Isaiah 61:1-3; Luke 4: 17-19.

These seals have not been broken as yet. No event in past history has fulfilled them. They are prophetic and **future.** The breaking of the Six Seals are found as follows:

First Seal—6:1.
Second Seal—6:3.
Third Seal—6:5.
Fourth Seal—6:7.
Fifth Seal—6:9.
Sixth Seal—6:12.

**THE SEALING OF ONE HUNDRED AND FORTY AND FOUR THOUSAND—Chapter 7.**

**Seventh Seal**—8:1-5.

It will be noticed that the Seventh Seal is separated from the other six seals by a sort of parenthesis, during which time occurs the **Sealing of the Remnant of Israel** and the **Salvation of a Great Number from the Nations.**

The 6th Chapter of Revelation may be divided somewhat as follows:

I. **THE FOUR STEEDS IN SUCCESSION,** 6:2-8.

1. **The White Steed** (vs. 2).
2. **The Red Steed** (vs. 4).
3. **The Black Steed** (vs. 5).
4. **The Pale Steed** (vs. 8).

II. **THE SLAIN SAINTS AND THEIR CRY,** 6: 9-11.

1. **Their Situation** "under the altar" (vs. 9).
2. **Their Condemnation**—"Slain for the Word of God" (vs. 9).

3. **Their Interrogation**—"How long, O Lord?" (vs. 10).
4. **Their Compensation**—"White Robes given them" (vs. 11).
5. **Their Consolation**—"rest until" (vs. 11).

III. **THE SEISMIC; SOLAR AND STELLAR DISTURBANCES.** 6:12-14.

1. **Seismic Disturbances**—"Earthquake" (vs. 12, 15).
2. **Solar Disturbances**—"Sun became black" (vs. 12).
3. **Lunar Disturbance**—"Moon became as Blood" (v. 12).
4. **Stellar Disturbance**—"Stars fell" (vs. 13).

IV. **THE SOCIAL STATE; ITS CONSTERNATION AND DESPERATION,** 6:15-17.

1. **Social Distinctions in Equation** (vs. 15). "Kings," "great," "rich," "chief," "captains," "mighty men," "bondmen," "freemen."
2. **The Common Refuge and Request and the Reason** (vss. 16, 17).
   "Hid themselves," "Hide Us," "From the Face of the Lamb."

We have outlined, in more or less detail this chapter, because of the fact that in it is contained six of the **Seven Seals.** We shall consider the Seals as the Lamb opens them.

## THE FOUR STEEDS IN SUCCESSION

1. **The White Steed** (vs. 2, 4).

"And I saw, and behold a white horse; and He that sat on him had a bow; and a crown was given unto him; and there was given unto him a great sword."

A white horse, a rider thereon, a crown, a bow and a sword!

Is the **white horse** the same steed as seen in 19:11? We think not, we are confident such is not the case.

Is the rider of this white horse the same One who rides on the white horse of chapter 19:11?

We think not. The rider in 6:2 does not come out of heaven; the rider of chapter 19 comes forth from an "open heaven." See 19:11. The rider on the white steed in Revelation 6, is an earth rider, not an heavenly. Besides, the armies of heaven follow Him on **white horses** (Rev. 19:14) but this white horse is followed by a black, red, and pale horse. **This rider is not Christ.**

Nor is this crown bestowed upon the Lord Jesus, for when He comes on the white horse, no gift of crown is in order, for "on his head were **many** crowns" (Rev. 19:12).

The sword is not in the hands of the Lord Jesus. When He comes forth on the white horse, "out of His mouth goeth a sharp two-edged sword" (19:15). When He comes He has no "bow" in His hand, but a "rod of iron" 19:15).

This rider of the white steed who rides at the head of the procession and after whom follow three other steeds in succession, is a great political leader and military strategist. He is a war lord crowned with the authority of government, riding as did the Oriental commander of old, upon a white and spirited steed in distinction from all other steeds in cavalry. He was distinguished upon a white horse. Napoleon had his little white mare. He was a striking figure on the only white horse among the horses. George Washington rode a white horse in Revolutionary days.

This rider may be the first manifestation of the man of sin, the first beast of Revelation 13. He is the accepted head of a confederation of ten nations and has come to this position by his great conquests for he is mighty in his conquests—"he went forth conquering" and "to conquer." Foch was made Generalissimo of all the armies of the allies—an unprecedented spectacle of military submission on the part of the nations. The rider of the white horse rises to this power and place. What a striking figure is he in the world's history! Riding on a horse which is white and the symbol of victory, this royal person moves into history. He has a genius for conquests which appears "diplomatic rather than sanguinary," for he is only armed with a bow. His triumphant march is unchecked—he marches with an iron heel and a nailed fist, commanded onward by one of the Living Creatures who are under the authority of the Lamb. "Come"—or "Go" is the command and he obeys. The Lamb reigns in the heavens regardless of who rides on the earth. They may arrogantly boast of their political authority, but all authority has been given unto the Son in heaven and on earth. The rise of the man of sin will be at first, perhaps unnoticed. Such a man may be necessary—a dictator and universal genius who will be able to quell and quiet national and international lawlessness. It will doubtless be found necessary to lift up a **"head over many countries"** (Psa. 110:6).

Appearing as a sovereign, he will be but a servant of God to carry out His purpose as was Pharaoh or Cyrus. Cyrus became great. It is reported that an ancient cylinder says of Cyrus, "He marched like a cloud, and his army like the waters of a river, opposition came to nothing before him." Yet he was but an instrument. This political genius may go forth "conquering and to conquer" but his power is but passing. We shall further consider this rider of the Klu Klux Klan of tribulation days in our next lesson. It will be well, for one of these days the whole world of earth dwellers will say:

> "Is this the Man that made the earth to tremble, that did shake kingdoms; that made the world as a wilderness, and destroyed the cities thereof" (Is. 14:16, 17).

Lesson Twenty-nine

## FOUR HORSES IN SUCCESSION (Rev.6:2-4) Part 1

"And when he had opened the **second seal,** I heard the second beast say, Come and see.

"And there went out **another horse** that was **red;** and **power** was **given to** him that sat thereon to take peace from the earth, and that should kill one another: and there was given unto him a great sword" (6:3, 4).

This is the second steed and its rider. The color of the steed is **red.** This **blood-like** color speaks of strife, violence and war.

Zechariah saw some such vision as this and among the four horses was one that was **red.**

"And I turned and lifted up my eyes and looked and behold, there came four chariots out from between two mountains; and the mountains were mountains of brass. In the first chariot were **red horses;** and in the second chariot **black horses;** and in the third chariot **white horses,** and in the fourth chariot **grisled** and **bay** horses" (Zech. 6:1-3).

Doubtless this vision of Zechariah is in full harmony with the vision of Ezekiel where the prophet says:

"Thus saith that Lord Jehovah, How much more when I send My four sore judgments upon Jerusalem, sword, famine, and noisome beast and pestilences?" (Ezek. 14:21).

These are His **"four sore judgments"** though the white horse did not at the first seem to indicate it, the second horse and its rider fully reveal the character of the time. The second seal, with **"The Red Steed and "Its Rider"** is in prophetic harmony with the words of Jesus in His great prophetic pronouncement on Olivet, or the **Second Sermon on the Mount.** Mathew 24. Said Jesus:

1. The appearance of false Christs (Matt. 24:5), the white steed.
2. "Wars"—"rumours of war"—"nations rising up" (Matt. 24:6, 7), the red steed.

3. "Famine" (Matt. 24:7), the black steed.
4. "Pestilence" (Matt. 24:7), the pale steed.

Matthew 24:5, 6 and 7 is an epitome of Revelation 6 and a remarkable illustration of the "harmony of the prophetic Word."

A glance at the following display will explain:

| JESUS<br>MATTHEW TWENTY-FOUR | JOHN<br>REVELATION SIX |
|---|---|
| **False Christ**<br>"For many shall come in My name, saying, I am Christ, deceiving many." vs. 5. | **The White Steed**<br>The First Seal—vss. 1, 2. |
| **Wars and National Uprising**<br>"Wars and rumours of wars, nations rise against nations, kingdoms vs. kingdoms." vs. 6. | **The Red Steed**<br>The Second Seal—vss. 3, 4. |
| **Famine**<br>"And there shall be famines." vs. 7. | **The Black Steed**<br>The Third Seal—vss. 5, 6. |
| **Pestilence**<br>"And pestilences." vs. 7. | **The Pale Steed**<br>The Fourth Seal—vss. 7, 8. |
| **Earthquakes**<br>"And earthquakes in divers places." vs. 7. | **Earthquakes**<br>The Sixth Seal—vss. 12-17. |

The **red horse** is war—national, international in other words, **world war.** With this steed and its rider, comes carnage and bloodshed. The red steed is an emblem of this. The wars stirred up by this rider have not yet occurred. This is future and occurs in the time after the Church has gone and the judgments of God are in the earth, which judgments can not and will not fall until the church, the Body of Christ has gone. These wars are not historical but prophetic—they are among the "things to come." Whatever wars of the past have had in general features, they are not the fulfilling of this prophecy. There are those who differ from us and we respect them, but we are convinced that these judgments **are all future.**

The rider of the red steed has "power to take peace from the earth" and taking peace from the earth is to turn the earth into a theatre of war. There will in these days predicted by the Revelator, be no national pacification in the earth. A Hague Tribunal will then be of no political value. Peace covenants and Treaties will be as but "a scrap of paper." Peace will be taken from the earth. There will be no peace. In his desolating dash across the earth on his bloody steed he will take away all peace. There will be no one in those days crying "Peace, Peace," for there will be no peace. Human life will have but little value for men will slay one another. The earth will be filled with internal fueds, civil wars and fomenting internecine strife. "Nation against nation and kingdom against kingdom" is a brief for an unspeakable situation!

Ezekiel, the prophet, doubtless spoke of the same period when he said—**"Every man's sword shall be against his brother"** (Ezek. 38:21).

Into the hands of this red-steed rider will be placed a sword. **"And there was given unto him a great sword,"** says the Record. Here the "sword is mightier than the pen." It takes all precedence. There will be no one to say, "Put up thy sword." It will be unsheathed for vengeance rather than victory. Blood will be spilled like water. Men will glut their vengeance on each other as in the days of a Robespierre and the Paris commune! Anything known to history will pale before this international blood-letting! As in the days of Asa, so in these days of the red horse rider.

"In those times there was **no peace** to him that went out, nor to him that came in, but great vexations were upon all the inhabitants of the countries, and nation was destroyed of nation, and city of city; for God did vex them with all adversity" (II Chron. 15:5, 6).

The **"sword"** is one of God's four sore judgments and it will be let out like a javelin on the earth!

By the mouth of the Prophet Jeremiah, God has declared He will call for a sword upon the earth.

"The Lord hath a controversy with the nations, He will plead with all flesh: He will give them that are wicked to the sword, saith the Lord.

"And the slain of the Lord shall be at that day **from one end of the earth even unto the other end of the earth;** they shall not be lamented, neither gathered nor buried; they shall be dung upon the ground" (Jer. 25:31-33).

Here is described terrible and universal bloodshed! Daniel also spoke of this when he said, "They shall fall by the sword, and by flame, by captivity and by spoil many days" (Dan. 11:33).

The sword will certainly be drawn to a universal extent and men's hearts will be so hard that there will be **no lamenting** and their hands will so cleave to the sword that none will bend a body to **bury a corpse.** Men will be but dung and manure on the earth and looked upon as fit only for fertilization.

The red steed and its rider is red war! But let it be remembered that Jesus has said, They that take the sword will perish by the sword, and there is yet to be another rider, coming from the opened heavens. His horse will not be red but **white.** His name is **"Faithful and True."** He makes war but His war is in "righteousness." See Revelation 19:11. He has a sword but it "proceeds out of His mouth." See Revelation 19:15 and 21. They who take the sword perish by the sword!

The fiery red steed and its rider will be followed by another—a **black steed.** One demands the other as one succeeds the other. They succeed in logical succession. A war lord will create war and war will produce famine.

Lesson Thirty

## FOUR HORSES IN SUCCESSION (Rev.6:5,6) Part 2

Following the **White Steed** was the **Red Steed,** and following the Red Steed, now comes the **Black Steed,** which will be followed by a **Pale Steed.**

First we saw the war lord on the white horse, who was followed by the red horse rider, who destroyed national pacification and took **"peace from the earth."** He was the destroyer of every national covenant and treaty, and to him they were but a "scrap of paper." The world had been saying "peace," but when he comes, there will be "no peace." He takes it from the earth, and within man's realm there is no way to restore it. Those days will be peaceless days and politics will be able to produce no better days. In those days man will take the sword to **perish by the sword.** Then comes

### 3. The Third Steed and Its Rider—

"And when he had opened the **third seal,** I heard the third living creature, saying, Come! And I saw, and behold, a black horse, and he that sat upon him had a pair of balances in his hand. And I heard as it were a voice in the midst of the four living creatures saying: A measure of wheat for a penny and three measures of barley for a penny; and see thou hurt not the oil and wine" (vss. 5, 6).

The next in the order of the judgments as outlined by our Lord, is **Famine** (Matt. 24:7). Here also as in Matthew 24, the third steed and its rider, introduce **famine.** This is according to the Word of the Lord as spoken by the mouth of His prophets. Said Haggai, the prophet:

"And I have called for a **drought** upon the land, and upon the mountains and upon the corn and upon the new wine, and upon the oil, and upon that which the ground bringeth forth, and upon men, and upon cattle and upon all the labor of the hands" (Hag. 1:11).

The steed is **black.** Black is the **color** of famine in the Bible. This is significant and interesting. In the midst of the desolation and devastation wrought by Nebuchadnezzar's third and final invasion, the Prophet Jeremiah in his Lamentation said,

"Our skin was black like an oven because of the terrible **"famine"** (Lam. 5:10). Thus **black** and **famine** are together associated.

Again he, Jeremiah, describes famine in a most realistic manner—

"Their visage is **blacker than coal;** they are not known in the streets; their skin cleaveth to their bones; it is withered, it is become like a stick. They that be slain with the sword are better than they that be slain with hunger; for these pine away, stricken through for want of the fruits of the field" (Lam. 4:8, 9).

In an earlier prophecy Jeremiah used also **"black"** as the famine color, if black be a color.

"The word of the Lord came to Jeremiah concerning the **dearth**—Judah mourneth, they are **black** unto the ground" (Jer. 14:1, 2).

Without a doubt, black denotes famine in the Word of God and **black** is a satisfactory word as famine comes to the mind of man. The former seal sent forth a rider who had a great **sword to kill** but Jeremiah says the judgment by famine is worse than that by sword. (Lam. 4:9) so it may be seen that with each steed and its rider, there is the intensifying of judgment. First, the **sword,** and then **hunger.** This is a tribulation description. In the glad millennial days, which follow the days described here, there will be a wonderful difference. Saith God by the mouth of His Prophet Ezekiel:

"I will call for the corn, and increase it, and **lay no famine upon you.** And I wil multiply the fruit of the tree, and the increase of the field and you shall receive no more reproach of famine among the heathen" (Ezek. 36:29, 30).

So here is the black steed—the black horse of **famine.** The future days will be days of food storage. Food stuffs are in these coming days to be apportioned by **measure** and by **weight.** The rider has a pair of balances in his hand. This denotes great scarcity of the very foundations of food supply. Many now living, will not soon forget what **weights** and **measures** mean when applied to food. Only so many pounds of sugar or flour, was the word we often heard from the lips of the produce dealer. Here they will be by **weight** and **measure** once again. Says the Prophet Ezekiel:

"Thy meat which thou shalt eat be by **weight.**"

"Thou shalt drink also water by **measure.**" See (Ezekiel 4:10, 11). This is all in harmony with the black horse and its rider. The use of weights or scales denotes great need of the conservatism of the food supply. In Joseph's days there was no such precaution. He used no weights or measures. Says the Book:

"And Joseph gathered corn as the sand of the sea, **very much,** until he left numbering for it was without numbering" (Gen. 41:49).

But it must be remembered that in these days of the breaking of the seven seals and the blowing of the seven trumpets and the pouring of the seven vials, there is no Joseph Jesus in Egypt providing against the famine days. Moses, telling Israel beforehand the distress which would come upon them in the latter days if they forsook the way and the word of their God, said:

"And when I have broken the staff of your bread, ten women shall bake your bread in one oven; and hey shall deliver your bread again by weight; and ye shall eat and not be satisfied" (Lev. 26:20).

While the famine may seem to come from a secondary and national cause, the fact of the thing is, that it comes **from the hand of God.** It is one of His "four sore judgments." "A voice from the midst of the throne," is heard. Man may **rule,** but God **overrules.**

Then follows the amount apportioned and the price fixed for the purchase of the same. There has been much written on this and doubtless much that is true interpretation and also much that is speculation. There is much here for those who are specialists in antiquarian research into weights and measures. **"A choenix of wheat for a denarius."**

From Matthew 20:2, 9 we learn that the value of a **denarius** was a day's wage and we know that a choenix of corn, about three pints, was the daily ration for a slave. History and contemporaneous literature throws considerable light on this money and this measure.

We are informed that a denarius would buy about sixteen choenixes of wheat in the time of Cicero, and twenty in the days of Trojan. Therefore it will be readily seen that there is a great advance in food and price and great reduction in the purchasing power of money. Money will be **below par** and food almost beyond **purchase.** The usual price of a choenix was one-eighth of a denarius, but here it is **eight times the usual price.**

But, if one considers the former steeds and their riders, they will find no difficulty in understanding the scale of prices fixed on food stuffs. The Red Steed Rider had a sword in his hand, and men are slaying one another and if the plough and the seed baskets have been neglected for more violent pursuits, it is easily seen from the human side how famine prevails. No sowing time means **no harvest**—so famine will prevail and food become scarcer day by day.

Other famines have been prophesied and have been literally fulfilled in history, so also will this predicted famine one day pass into history and the sooner it is history the better it will be for the world.

See II Kings 6:25. Here is the record of a famine most drastic and terrible, but there was a Prophet Famine breaker who appeared and according to his word, at the appointed time, food was at the bottom price. There will be no such an one to appear here, but rather **another steed and a rider.** Judgment will continue. Yet other woes are yet to come.

These judgments will not be executed upon the Church of God, the Body of Christ. In our judgment, the Scriptures teach the exemption of the Church from these judgments. There are others who differ and we respect their convictions and believe they do ours also.

"Who shall separate us from the love of Christ? Shall **tribulation** or distress or **persecution** or **FAMINE** or peril or sword? **Nay, in all these things we are more than conquerors though Him that loved us."**

There is no judgment for them that are in Jesus Christ, and this is the place of the believer "in Christ" in this age. "In Christ," means no judgments. We are already in the sight of God in heaven with Christ positionally. God has never seen us any other place, nor do the Scriptures, in our judgment, view us in the tribulation or any portion of the same.

If this be true let us live as men who are no longer of this world but hid in Christ, who is at the right hand of God.

Lesson Thirty-one

# FOUR HORSES IN SUCCESSION (Rev.6:7,8) Part 3

"And when he had opened the fourth seal, I heard the voice of the fourth beast say, Come and see.

And I looked, and behold a pale horse: and his name that sat on him was Death, and Hell followed with him. And power was given unto them over the fourth part of the earth, to kill with sword, and with hunger, and with death, and with the beasts of the earth" (Rev. 6:7, 8).

This pale horse follows the **white, red** and **black steeds** which we have considered in former lessons. This is the **fourth** of the **seven** seals. It is the **fourth creature** also that makes the call. They know the mind of the throne and still call for judgment, which, as in the days of Israel's deliverance from Egypt, is laid yet heavier with each succeeding judgment. This steed is said to be **"pale."** It was doubtless **pale green.** Pale, is strictly speaking, no color, it is the modification of color. We speak of the human face as pale. The rosy complexion is gone by the receding of blood. As used in other places in the New Testament, "green" is the meaning of the word. See Mark 6:39; Revelation 8:7; 9:4. In the Scriptures green is associated with the plague-stricken. (See leprosy and the laws governing the same [Lev. 13:49; 14:37]).

Behold, this pale or greenish steed! Who is he and what is his rider? The rider's name, in the A. V. is **Death.** The word used here for Death, the Septuagint Version uses about 30 times for "pestilence." See I Kings 8:37; Jeremiah 21:7.

The "pale steed" brings "pestilence." This is the order outlined by Christ in His second "sermon on the mount" known to us as the "Olivet discourse." Said He: "War, famine" and "pestilence" (Matt. 24:7).

Pestilence is followed by a strange and significant companion. Hell or Hades follows this rider, personifying Hell as the rider personifies pestilence. These two words, "pestilence" and "Hades" are found together, for one depends on the other. See Revelation 1:18; 6:8; 20:13; I Corinthians 15:55; Isaiah 28:15, 18.

So deadly is this plague that Hades follows as the reaper to gather up the awful harvest! Isaiah may have seen this judgment at the opening of the fourth seal, when he said:

> "Therefore Hades hath enlarged itself and opened her mouth without measure; and their glory and their multitude and their pomp, and he that rejoiceth, shall descend unto it" (Is. 5:14).

Here "death, and hell" are at an "agreement." They are allies. The men of Judah and Jerusalem are here under the scourge of the "man of sin." There is a "covenant." It must be "broken" and will be. The Prophet Isaiah also foretold these days when he said:

> "We have made a covenant with **death** and with **hell** we are at agreement.
> And your covenant with **death** shall be disannulled and your agreement with **hell** shall not stand; when the overflowing scourge shall pass through, then ye shall be trodden down by it" (Is. 28:15, 18).

The power or authority given unto this pale steed rider and his footman is limited. It extends over the "fourth part of the earth."

This may mean, political earth, inasmuch as we are in these apocalyptic judgments yet under the "times of the Gentiles," which "times" were politically and governmentally set forth by the "image" seen by Nebuchadnezzar and the "four beasts" seen by Daniel. The fourth world empire was the Roman Empire. This "fourth part" of earth rule may be indicated here, if so, then the power and authority of the rider of the pale or greenish horse, may extend over and include, the dominion of the original Roman Empire. This will be a large area of the earth and the student will readily see its extent and significance. The fourth part of the prophetic earth will fall under this scourge.

But the power given unto this rider and the one who follows him, exceeds pestilence. It is indeed a fourfold terror and horror! The authority given was to

First—"kill with the sword"
Second—"and with hunger"
Third—"and with death"
Fourth—"and with the beast of the earth"

All the judgments occurring under the two preceding steeds are repeated here, with addition and the added feature is **"beasts."**

Under this seal and with this rider, we have all the four sore judgments of God as predicted by Ezekiel. See Ezekiel 14:21.

"The **sword,** the **famine,** the **pestilence** and the noisome **beast."** They are all seen here with the pale steed.

Moses foretold these days and the wild beasts related to them.

"I will also send wild beasts among you" (Lev. 26:22). "I will send the teeth of beasts upon them, with the poison of the serpents of the dust" (Deut. 32:24).

The days of Israel's greatest sorrow has come. The tribulation days long foretold, are now upon the earth and among the other judgments are the "wild beasts."

Doubtless these "wild beasts" include the two beasts of Revelation 13, as well as the beasts of Daniel 7, which under the revived Roman Empire are all represented in the fourth beast, who has characteristics of the beasts which have come and gone before him. See Revelation 13:2.

God has often used creatures for His judgments. They fight on His side whether birds or beasts. He has sent locusts, flies, frogs and fiery serpents at His command

(Exod. 10; Num. 21:6). He sent hornets upon the Canaanites (Exod. 23:28; Josh. 24:12). Lions slew Samaritans and she bears, the mockers of a prophet (II Kings 17:25; II Kings 2:24).

These days will be the days of war, famine, death and wild beasts and pestilence! What days! Surely the Lord will punish the inhabitants of the earth! He comes forth for that purpose! These judgments will make man yet more defiant against God, as witnessed in the case of Pharaoh when the judgment hand was on the Egyptians. They will not inquire of the Lord nor petition Him for exemption or for mercy as did David.

David sinned against the Lord in the numbering of Israel. Three of these judgments were offered him.

"Thus saith the Lord; Choose ye either three years **famine**, or three months to be destroyed before thy foes while that the **sword** of Thine enemies overtake thee; or three days * * of **pestilence** in the land—" (I Chron. 21:12).

David cried: "Let me now fall into the hand of the Lord." The **pestilence** came and there fell in Israel **seventy thousand men.** The judgments of God are wonderful.

The day is coming when the brutal and beastly state of things as are here foretold, will maintain no more.

The Prophet Isaiah has declared the glory of these coming days!

The wolf shall dwell with the lamb! A leopard shall lie down with a kid! A calf and a young lion will lie down in domestication and pacification! The cow and the bear and their young will feed together! The lion will eat straw like the ox! A young weaned child will thrust its hand in the den of a cockatrice and a sucking child will be safe to play at the hole of an asp.

There will be nothing to "hurt or destroy in all My holy mountain; for the earth shall be full of the knowledge of the Lord as the waters cover the sea." Read Isaiah 11:7 to 9.

In those days men may dwell safely in the wilderness and **sleep in the woods.** See Ezekiel 34:25. It is not a safe practice in this present time and they who wander the wilderness know better than to assume such risks. May God hasten these times which are "His times." Other "times" maintain now, but soon "His times."

Lesson Thirty-two

## THE FIFTH SEAL (Rev.6:9-11)

The **Fifth Seal** is now opened and this is what is uncovered, or rather discovered:

"I saw under the altar the souls of them that were slain for the Word of God, and for the testimony which they held: and they cried with a loud voice, saying, How long, O Lord, holy and true, dost Thou not judge and avenge our blood on them that dwell on the earth? And white robes were given unto every one of them; and it was said unto them, that they should rest yet for a little season, until their fellowservants also, and their brethren that should be killed as they were, should be fulfilled" (Rev. 6:9-11).

The price paid for holding the Word of God in the days of the tribulation is revealed at the breaking of the fifth seal. This seal seems singularly marked off from the rest. We turn from steeds to saints. This is the order, however, that Jesus outlined in the second sermon on the mount, known generally as the Olivet discourse. Said He, False christs (1st seal), war (2d seal), famine (3d seal), pestilence (4th seal), and **"then** shall they deliver you up to be afflicted and shall kill you." These words are a key to the **5th seal.** (Matt. 24:9.)

These are the martyrs of the tribulation days. There need be no mystery here or confusion, nor time spent on the word **"souls."** It is used here as a figure for persons. The word "soul" in this passage does not mean the "part" of a man. The word "soul" is frequently put for a person. Said Stephen in his memorable address which cost him his life:

"Then sent Joseph and called his father Jacob to him, and all his kindred, three score and fifteen souls" (Acts 7:14).

"Soul" is used for person, and this statement here is simple and means that he saw the martyrs, their suffering and their slaying with their blood crying out as did the blood of Abel (Gen. 4:10). (See also concerning "souls" put for "persons"—Gen. 12:5; Gen. 14:21; Gen. 46:15, 26, 27. In Joshua 20:3, the word is translated "person"—Ezek. 18:4, 20; Rom. 13:1.)

John was exiled to the Isle of Patmos "for the Word of God and the testimony of Jesus Christ" (Rev. 1:9).

The tribulation martyrs are slain for the Word of God and their testimony. They will not believe the lie nor turn from the Truth. To hold the Word of God in those days, will bring the penalty of death. Those who hold it today must suffer, they will be slain. It is difficult, indeed, to stand for the Word of God and the Person of Christ today. What will it be in the days when the Church, the Body of Christ, is gone, and the "Man of Sin" is the autocrat of the hour? This seal shows us the persecution and affliction of those who thus stand. We can well understand the words, "Be thou faithful unto death" in the light of the fifth seal.

John saw them "under the altar." By this is always meant the altar of "burnt offering." The fire was continuous and the blood and limbs of animals slain in sacrifice could be seen. The blood was poured out at the bottom of the altar (Exod. 29:12; Lev. 4:7; 5:9). These slain saints are regarded as a sacrifice, not to make atonement, but a poured-out drink-offering.

Paul's words in Philippians 2:7 may be read, "But if I am even poured out as a drink-offering upon the sacrifice and service of your faith, I joy and rejoice with you all." Again when near the end, Paul said, "I am ready to be poured out as a drink-offering" (II Tim. 4:6).

These words indicate their sacrifice at the foot of the altar.

Their cry for vengeance is a sufficient evidence that the dispensation of the grace of God has concluded and that they are a faithful remnant in the days of tribulation.

"How long, O Lord, they cry, holy and true, dost Thou not judge and avenge our blood?"

This cry for vengeance is not on the ground of **the Gospels and the Epistles,** but on the ground of the **Law and the Prophets.** It is not **grace** but **law.**

They who are God's, in the time present, seek no vengeance and ask none. They "forgive one another," as God for Christ's sake has forgiven. They give no place to wrath or judgment. They have learned that **"vengeance belongeth unto God."**

But here their cry to the throne of God was judgment. They seek redress and sent their petition to the throne. This throne is set for that purpose. See II Kings 8:5; also 6:26.

"Help, my Lord, O King" the woman cried and so also this slain company cry!

According to His Word, He will avenge His servants, for Moses in his song foretold it:

**"He will avenge the blood of His servants and will render vengeance to his adversaries and will be merciful unto His land and to His people."**

They plead this promise. They cry to Him as **"Despot"** or **Sovereign Lord.** They call Him holy and true, and this is used in Revelation 3:7, and indicates God's relation to His covenant people as seen in Psalm 89:28, 35; Isaiah 55:3. He is **holy** and **true.**

This cry of the martyrs explains many of the Psalms, which represent the remnant of Israel as they cry to God in the midst of the days of tribulation.

Notice Psalm 13 and count the fourfold interrogation **"How Long,"** Psa. 79:5, which is Rev. 11 in summary has also the cry of these slain saints—"How long, Lord?" (vs. 5).

This cry for vengeance, which is not consistent with this dispensation, will be proper with those who utter it, and at the time they utter it. It will be uttered in the "day of the Lord," when His judgments are in the earth.

Psalm 54:5 said of the Lord, "He will reward evil unto mine enemies; cut them off in truth."

Psalm 143:12 is in full harmony with the cry of these slain saints.

But they had reward and recompense. Each one received a **"white robe."** Robes in the Old Testament were given for honor and reward.

Read Genesis 41:42; 45:22; Esther 6:8, 9; Isaiah 3:7; Zechariah 3:5. This was a definite promise to the overcomers in Revelation 3:4. Rewards will have a deep meaning in these days of suffering. Thus did God pacify them and instructed them that they were to do two things, viz., **"wait"** and **"rest."**

The persecution of the tribulation was not yet over. The trumpets were to follow the seals, in turn to be succeeded by the seven vials or bowls of God's wrath.

Their brethren were yet to be killed for the people are as Psalm 44:22 described them: **"Yea, for Thy sake we are killed all the day long, we are counted as sheep for the slaughter."** See also Romans 8:36.

This future killing mentioned here, may be seen in 13:7, 15 and 17:6. The extent of these massacres may be seen by a careful contemplation of these verses. The early martyrs of the **tribulation** period must **rest** and **wait** till the devilish work and murder of the **great tribulation** is finished. Blessed **resting** and blessed **waiting!**

If it were not for the sealing of the "one hundred and forty-four thousand" of Revelation 7, there would be none of the race of Israel left to tell the story of this awful period of time. The Lord will shorten it, thanks to His holy name! **No flesh** would be saved but for this. The furnace of the fury of these days none will know except those destined to go through it.

Lesson Thirty-three

## THE SIXTH SEAL (Rev.6:12-17) Part 1

"Thus saith the Lord of Hosts: Yet once more, it is a little while, and I will shake the heavens, and the earth, and the sea, and the dry land" (Hag. 2:6).

The "little while" of the Prophet Haggai is now past. The "yet once more" is at hand. The sixth seal opens and this time of shaking begins.

Not only the material universe comes into this shaking, but says the prophet,

"And I will shake all nations, and the desire of all nations shall come: and I will fill the house with all glory, saith the Lord of Hosts" (Hag. 2:7).

The prophet outlines the apocalyptic events beginning with this seal and reaching to the days of the millennial reign.

1. The shaking of heavens, earth and sea.
2. The shaking of the nations.
3. The coming of the "desire of all nations."
4. The return of the glory to the House of the Lord.

The sixth seal is one of great commotion and disturbance.

There is seismic disturbance—earthquakes.

There is stellar disturbance—the falling of stars.

There is solar disturbance—sun became as black as sack cloth.

There is lunar disturbance—the moon became as blood.

There is great social disturbance—see vs. 15.

Seven effects follow the opening of this seal and

above events. The seven effects are divided into four and three and four are comparisons and introduced by the word "as". The order is as follows:

1. A great shaking.
2. The sun black.
3. The moon blood red.
4. Stars cast down.
5. The heavens rolled up.
6. Isles torn from their bases.
7. Terror and fright among men.

These are to be taken literally and no other way unless indicated. We shall consider first the earthquake or

## SEISMIC DISTURBANCE

The shaking of mountains is not a new thing or a strange thing with God in his judgments.

Sinai **quaked greatly** when the Lord descended upon it in the fire. See Exod. 19:18. It greatly terrified the people who stood afar off and feared death (Exod. 20: 18, 19). In the days of Elijah when the Lord passed by in the mount, there was strong wind breaking rocks, and also earthquake (I Kings 19:11).

When Christ died there was an **earthquake**—indeed there was a little miniature of the scenes of this sixth seal judgment. There was **darkness** over all the earth till the ninth hour. The **sun was darkened.** The veil in the Temple was rent, and when He who died upon that cross, cried with a loud voice, the **"earth did quake and the rocks rent."** (Matt. 27:50, 51).

None doubt that the earthquake on Sinai or in the days of Elijah was literal and actual, nor can this earthquake be so interpreted otherwise, as some would do.

When Jesus died, the earth did actually quake; there was actual rending of rocks; there was darkness over the earth for the time mentioned; the sun was darkened.

These events took place at the death of Christ, and they will be as actually and literally fulfilled under this sixth seal judgment except the disturbance will greatly exceed that associated with the crucifixion. Nor can the sun, moon and stars here be taken figuratively. It means what it says and says what it means and this sixth seal judgment is a literal and actual judgment on the earth and upon the earth dwellers.

This earthquake is of tremendous energy and terrific rending power, for the islands of the sea were moved out of their place and mountains moved! It is the day of the Lamb's wrath, and He is shaking both the heavens, the earth and the sea.

## THE SOLAR DISTURBANCE

"The sun became black." It took on the appearance of sack cloth. It is said the tents of Arabs are often made of black hair cloth and the sun takes on this color. This is but one of several plagues that fall on the sun.

At the fourth trumpet a third of the sun is smitten. When the fifth trumpet sounds it is darkened and beclouded by a smoke from beneath.

When the fourth vial of God's wrath is poured out then the sun is called in to take agency in the judgments, and scorches men with a supernatural heat. This reference to the sun is literal and not symbolic or figurative and this principle of interpretation maintains throughout the Book of Revelation except when distinctly stated to be otherwise by such explanatory statements as, "As it were," or "a sign," etc., etc.

With the day in the shadow of a black sun, then comes the night with a

## LUNAR DISTURBANCE

and a blood-red moon. What terror and human fright this unnatural phenomenon will produce. In one of the plagues hereinafter mentioned, a third of the moon is stricken but here the whole is affected. God will shake the heavens and the earth. The great and terrible day of the Lord is the description through the lips of Joel and such it is. Then follows

## STELLAR DISTURBANCE

The stars of the heavens fall to the earth. There is a shower of stars. With a bloody moon and shooting stars what nocturnal terror this will display! God be thanked, the Church, the Body of Christ, will not pass through these judgments. There is no judgment for them that are in Jesus Christ.

A fig tree shaken by a mighty wind casts off her untimely figs and as such do the heavens cast away stars with a prodigality that is beyond description.

Following these things the heavens roll as a scroll, mountains moved and islands torn up and replaced!

Then the consternation of society, social and civil! Kings lead the crowd in their cry, then great men, and rich men join the agonizing hosts. This world has many kings, many great men and many rich men, but here they are a common crowd in the terror and horror of this season of judgment at the breaking of the sixth seal!

Lesson Thirty-four

## THE SIXTH SEAL (Rev.6:12-17) Part 2

In the former lecture we had the disturbances taking place in the realm of nature under the breaking of the sixth seal. We shall consider, in some detail the

### SOCIAL DISTURBANCE.

And the kings of the earth,
And the great men,
And the rich men,
And the chief captains,
And the mighty men,
And every bondman,
And every freeman
hid themselves in the dens and in the rocks of the mountains;
And said to the mountains and rocks,
Fall on us, and hide us from the face of Him that sitteth on the throne, and from the wrath of the Lamb;
For the great day of His wrath is come; and who shall be able to stand?

Society is divided into seven divisions by the word "and."

| | |
|---|---|
| **1. Kings and** | **CIVIL OFFICERS OF STATE.** |
| **2. Great Men** | **MILITARY OFFICERS.** |
| **3. Chief Captains** | **CAPITALISTS.** |
| **4. Rich Men** | **MEN OF SOCIAL AND** |
| **5. Mighty Men** | **POLITICAL INFLUENCE.** |
| **6. Bondmen** | **"EVERY MAN"—THE RANK** |
| **7. Freemen** | **AND FILE.** |

The Spirit of God has discerned the social situation of the end time. This is as it is today. That God is no respecter of persons, is again proclaimed. "Here beggars who walk and kings who ride" in the tribulation days are side by side. They are possessed by one common terror and are a commonwealth in fear and fright.

There is a twofold cause for their petition to the "mountains and the rocks"

First—"From the face of the Throne-sitter."

Second—"From the wrath of the Lamb."

What a visitation of God is this! Imagine the insecurity of houses, whether it be the palaces of kings, **who head the list,** or the hovels of bond men at the bottom of the list, when stars are falling, sun darkened, moon bloody, earth shaking until islands are removed from their places—what insecurity in ordinary habitats!

See kings and courtiers, chief military captains who led armies over the bloodiest battle-fields the world ever knew, see these military men who have faced all modern implements of warfare, in a state of complete consternation! The judgments of the Lord are in the earth. It is the time of **"the wrath of the Lamb!"** A disturbed Heaven and earth have brought this distraction and complete overthrow of all civil and social order.

Men are accustomed to social upheaval but not to physical upheaval.

Men have gone through the changing order of society and state with revolutions and anarchy on every hand. Men are accustomed to the melting pot of universal human struggle but without natural phenomena and change. Men are accustomed to the soil under their feet to remain solid, firm and unmovable. They are familiar with fixed stars and golden sun by day and silver moon by night. But when all these have failed in regularity and are changed, fear comes which knows no solace or quiet. This is the condition in which society finds itself. It produces a strange and unheard-of social situation. All society joins in petition for a hiding place.

History records the flight of men before volcanoes in action, of the fright of men when earthquakes were shaking the earth for but a few seconds, but here the heavens and the earth are at one time in an unnatural disorder. Surely the Lord cometh forth from His place to punish the inhabitants of the earth. Society from kings to bondmen know well how to interpret this phenomenon. They are conscious it is the judgment of God. They fear His face and acknowledged the wrath of the Lamb.

The judgments long held back are now let loose. "Then shall He speak to them in His wrath," said the psalmist—and the **"then,"** there foretold is here fulfilled (Ps. 2:5).

Isaiah saw this judgment of the sixth seal and described it in advance.

"Behold the day of the Lord cometh,
Cruel both with **wrath** and **fierce anger,**
to lay the land (or earth) **desolate;**
And He shall destroy the **sinners thereof** out of it.

For the **stars of heaven** and the **constellations** thereof shall not give **their light;** the **sun** shall be **darkened** in his going forth and the **moon** shall not cause her **light to shine.**

I will **punish the world** for their **evil,**
And the wicked for their iniquity;
And I will cause the **arrogancy** of the proud to cease and lay low the haughtiness of the terrible. (Kings, great men and rich men.)

Therefore I will **shake the heavens** and the earth shall remove out of her place in the wrath of the Lord of Hosts in the day of His fierce anger."

Isaiah in fullness of detail described the events connected with the **sixth seal.** The harmony of the Prophetic Word is impressed upon the student. Joel likewise foretold the conditions prevailing under the **sixth seal.**

"The sun and the moon shall be darkened and the stars shall withdraw their shining.

The Lord shall roar out of Zion and utter His voice from Jerusalem and **the heavens and the earth shall shake,** but the Lord will be the hope of His people and the strength of the children "of Israel" (Joel 2:9-17).

And I will show wonders in the **heavens and in the earth, blood, fire** and **pillars of smoke.** The **sun** shall be turned into **darkness** and the **moon** into **blood** before the terrible day of the Lord come" (Joel 2:30, 31).

Their cry goes up to the mountains and rocks. They are afraid of the face of the Throne-sitter and the wrath of the Lamb, and well they may be, for He "took the

Book" to break the seals thereof and execute judgment upon His enemies. At His first coming He proclaimed the acceptable year of the Lord; at this His second coming it is the "day of vengeance of our God" (Luke 4:18).

Isaiah spoke of this "day" and its terrors. The first mention of this day is found in his prophecy at chapter 2:10, 11, 19-21.

"Enter into the rock," said he, "and hide thee in the dust for fear of the Lord and the glory of His majesty.

The lofty looks of man shall be humbled, and the haughtiness of men shall be bowed down."

Here is a man "humbled," and "bowed down." All classes and conditions. Put them in fear, O Lord, cried the psalmist, that the nations may know themselves to be but men—and the prayer is answered here—they are but men and know their inability and equipment against such judgments and commotion. Jesus spoke of this scene in advance of John. "The days are coming," said Jesus, "when they shall begin to say to the mountains, Fall on us, and to the hills, Cover us" (Luke 23:30).

There is no hiding place from the wrath of the Lamb. There is no shelter from the coming judgment. Nature's hiding places are inadequate. There is but One Rock for a hiding and that is

"Rock of Ages, cleft for me
Let me hide myself in Thee."

O, that men would "Kiss the Son" before His anger is kindled. O, that men would seek exemption from wrath through the Blood of redemption! "Being justified by His blood we are saved from wrath through Him" (Rom. 5:9).

The interrogation which closes the chapter **"Who shall be able to stand?"** is answered in the next chapter 7.

Lesson Thirty-five

## SIXTH AND SEVENTH SEALS (Rev.7:1-3) Part 1

The judgments which we saw moving in rapid succession in chapter 6, wherein six seals are broken, suddenly cease. There is a Divine arrest. Judgment cannot continue further until permitted by the Lamb, for unto Him is all authority given in both Heaven and earth.

This chapter is a pause in the purpose of God. It is an interlude which is a prelude to judgments of greater Divine severity.

The chapter may be analyzed for the student after the following:

**I. THE ANGEL AGENTS AND THEIR INSTRUCTIONS—vss. 1-3.**

**II. THE SEALING OF A NUMBERED COMPANY OF ISRAELITES—vss. 4-8.**

**(Sealed to Pass through Tribulation)**

**III. THE SAVING OF AN UNNUMBERED COMPANY OF GENTILES—vss. 9-12.**

**(Saved to Come Out of Tribulation)**

**IV. THE ELDER'S INTERROGATION AND THE GENTILES' DESTINATION—vss. 13-17.**

We shall look upon the chapter in the light of these divisions.

### I. THE ANGEL AGENTS AND THEIR INSTRUCTIONS—vss. 1-3.

Angels and their ministrations come to view again. There are

(1) "Four angels.

(2) Four corners or quarters of the earth.

(3) Four winds of the earth" (vs. 1).

They are ministers to force exemption from judgment for a short season upon

The earth.

The sea.

Or any tree (vs. 1).

Land, water and forest come under the protection of the edict of the Lamb and executed by the four angels commanded by fifth. **Four winds** and **angels** were associated in our Lord's words in Matthew 24:31.

In the prophecy of Daniel they are seen holding the four winds of the earth. See Daniel 7:2; 8:8; 11:4.

The wind is in their control for a season. Wind is a very destructive force. It destroys on land by great tornadoes, it destroys the ships at sea and is disastrous to the trees.

In the Book of Jonah the great wind is seen in its destructive and retributive power. "The Lord sent out a great wind into the sea and there was a mighty tempest in the sea so that the ship was like to be broken" (Jon. 1:4). See also Jonah 1:10, 11, 12.

In the Book of Job there is also a display of the power of the wind.

"Behold there came a **great wind** from the wilderness and smote the **four corners** of the house and it fell upon the young men and they are dead; and I only am escaped alone to tell thee" (Job 1:19).

There are **four** angels here and "another angel" (vs. 2). The four angels who are executors of the will of "another angel," stand at the four corners of the earth.

The fifth angel "ascends" from the east or the sunrising. He "ascends" not "descends."

The **east** is the direction from which God manifests

Himself. His star at the first advent was seen in the **east.** See Matthew 2:2.

The coming of the Lord will be manifested from the **east** unto the **west.** See also Isaiah 41:2.

Ezekiel saw the glory of God come back to the forsaken Temple by the way of the **east** (Ezek. 43:1, 2).

"The Sun of Righteousness will arise," in the **east** (Mal. 4:1, 2).

Some think this "another angel" is Jesus Christ. There is some ground for the viewpoint. This is not evident to us.

This angel has the "seal of the Living God," and as a seal signifies among other things authority and authenticity, this angel is an authentic and authoritative agent of God.

**His Coming**—"from the east."

**His Commission**—"the seal of the Living God."

**His Command**—"cried with a great voice to the four."

How wonderful are all these things! There is not a breath of air to stir a rustle among the leaves of trees or a ripple on the bosom of the sea. It is almost a **breathless silence.**

"Hurt not," is the command, for these are the days of "hurting."

### The Cause

This arrest of the wind was for a cause and purpose. The earth, sea or trees could not come under the designed judgments of God **"till"**;

"Till we have sealed the servants of our God in their foreheads" (vs. 3). This brings to consider.

## II. THE SEALING OF A NUMBERED COMPANY OF ISRAELITES—(vss. 4-8)

### (Sealed to Pass Through Tribulation)

Tribes of the children of Israel! Who are the children of Israel? We have no time to deal with the foolish and unscriptural attempts at the interpretation of this passage. It means just what it says and says just what it means.

There is positively no way **theologically, logically,** or **etymologically** to make **ISRAEL,** in the Bible to mean any other but the **natural descendants** of Jacob, who are nationally known as Israel.

The tribulation days develop a great anti-Semitic persecution. There is attempt to blot Israel out "forever as a nation." The hatred of Satan and the Beast and the False Prophet is for Israel. They are the covenant people with whom God's oath has been made for the blessing of all the families of the earth and establishment of the earth's rightful King on the throne of David. The wrath of these tribulation days will be so great that unless shortened, there would be universal death and "no flesh," saved, either Jew or Gentile.

God seals a remnant of the chosen races and secures them through the tribulation.

A seal is for the preservation of an object, Israel through this remnant is to be preserved through the tribulation.

They will come through as certainly as Noah and his sons passed through the judgment of water when shut or sealed in the Ark, for the Lord shut them in.

A seal is set to **prevent molestation.** A seal is official and any tampering with or fumbling at, are the subjects of law and government.

God will seal a remnant of Israel beyond the molestation of the Devil, the Beast or the False Prophet who appear in chapters 12 and 13.

God has a sealed people now whom He will take out before tribulation. Believers of this age are sealed with the Holy Spirit of promise unto the day of redemption.

God will have a people in the tribulation days, who will be sealed to pass safely through them.

Satan will imitate God and will set a seal or mark of distinction on the worshipers of the Beast. See chapter 13.

God set a mark on Cain. It was a visible mark. The mark was to prevent any one from hurting him. This seal is to preserve **His true** servants.

The number of the sealed was one hundred and forty-four thousand. This number was divided into twelve equal parts or **twelve thousand** from each tribe.

This is the **new Book of Numbers.** In the Book of Numbers under Moses the nation failed but in this new numbering the remnant will not fail to enter the land and possess it.

They may be driven into the wilderness as chapter 12 indicates, but they will not **perish in the wilderness.** Of this remnant of the nation it will never be said as of the nation:

"I was grieved with that generation and said: they do always err in their heart; and they have not known My ways" (Heb. 3:10).

They will not "harden their hearts" nor will there be a "day of provocation." This remnant sealed from among the nation of Israel is mentioned by Joel and harmonizes with this 7th chapter both in the order of events preceding and succeeding.

Joel speaks of

"The wonders in Heaven and earth" (2:30) and of blood, fire and pillars of smoke.

He then sees in detail the events recorded under the sixth seal in Revelation 6.

The sun turned to darkness

The moon to blood

And the "great and terrible day of the Lord."

This is the order of the **sixth seal.** See Joel 2:30, 31

and Revelation 6. Then Joel sees the future glory of Israel and the salvation which follows Israel's restoration to Jerusalem and Mt. Zion and also the remnant by whom it is accomplished. Says the prophet:

"And it shall come to pass that whosoever shall call on the name of the Lord shall be delivered; for on Mt. Zion and in Jerusalem shall be deliverance **and in the remnant whom the Lord shall call"** (Joel 2:32).

Lesson Thirty-six

## SIXTH AND SEVENTH SEALS (Rev.7:4-8) Part 2

### (Sealed to Pass through Tribulation)

These are Israelites and no one else. A company is sealed out of each of the "twelve tribes" and this is no reference to the Church, for there are no "tribes' in the Church of God but **one body** the unity of which must not be broken nor indeed can be. These of Israel, are sealed to **pass through** the tribulation—the Church takes no such passage. As in the days of Ahab, so in the days of a greater persecutor than Ahab, God will preserve a remnant of the nation. As in those days God cared for His overwrought and much sought Prophet, so will He in these days care for His overwrought people. Elijah, in a most trying and terrible **three years and a half,** was the object of the wrath of Ahab.

Israel in a **more terrible three years and a half** will be the object of the wrath and the persecution and the power of the Beast out of the sea and the second Beast out of the earth, both of them energized by Satan.

In the days of wicked Ahab, God said:

"Yet I have left me **seven thousand** in Israel, all the knees of which have not bowed unto Baal, and every mouth which hath not **kissed him**" (I Kings 19:18). See also Romans 11:4.

In Elijah's days **seven thousand** who had not bowed to or kissed Baal, and in the tribulation days **twelve thousand** who do not bow to or acknowledge the Beast.

The tribes as mentioned here in chapter 7 are the following order:

| | |
|---|---|
| Judah | Simeon |
| Reuben | Levi |
| Gad | Issachar |
| Asher | Zabulon |
| Nepthalim | Joseph |
| Manasses | Benjamin |

The order of the tribes here differs considerably from that in Genesis 49, where Jacob delivers his dying benediction and prediction. They were born in a different order, blessed in a different order and now sealed in a new order. There is a significant omission of Dan and Ephraim and in their stead we find Levi and Joseph. There has been a great deal of speculation concerning this omission and to explain it some have read into the Bible what is not there.

The Scriptures we think are plain as to this omission. In the law of Moses we read:

"Lest there should be among you any man, or woman, or family, or tribe, whose heart turneth away this day from the Lord our God, to go and serve the gods of these nations,

The Lord will not spare him, but then the anger of the Lord and His jealousy shall smoke against that man, and all the curses that are written in this Book shall be upon him, and the Lord shall **blot out his name** under Heaven.

And the Lord shall separate him unto evil **out of all the tribes** of Israel, according to the curses of the covenant that are written in the Book of the Law."

The tribe of **Dan** came first under this curse. The record of his idolatry is recorded in Leviticus 24:10-16. ("The tribe of Dan" vs. 11).

**Dan** and **Ephraim,** the two missing ones in Revelation 7, introduced idolatry among the people in the times of the judges. Read carefully Judges 18:2 also verses 30, 31. Golden calves were later set up in the tribe of Dan (I Kings 11:26; 12:28-30). Is it any wonder that

God has said, Ephraim is joined to his idols, **let him alone.**

In this sealed company Dan and Ephraim are **"let alone."** They **are "blotted out."** They are **"separated out of the tribes."**

The day this the remnant of Israel is sealed is no day for idolators. The beast has set up the image and decree has gone out to worship the same and no Danites or Ephraimites are wanted now. None who ever set up a golden calf are safe in a day. There must be in these days a company that will not "worship the beast nor receive his mark in their foreheads."

The whole earth is filed with idolatry. Any who will not worship the image of the beast will be killed (Rev. 13:15). It is not the day for a Dan or an Ephraim. There must not be idolators in this company and Dan and Ephraim are missing.

None of these sealed ones will fail God in this crucial and crisis hour of history; nor will they fail their nation in this, the greatest of all Anti-Semetic persecution.

This is God's wonderful tribulation company! They stand for the whole nation. They are protected through all the judgments. They are seen a little later in the Book on Mt. Zion in great victory (chap. 14:1-5). There is no way to blot out Israel "forever from being a nation." "He that keepeth Israel shall neither slumber nor sleep." There is no slumber nor sleep with God in these days. God knows how to hedge about His people and keep them in the hour of trial.

There was a time in Old Testament history where God would send judgment upon the Midianites. There must be a mobilization for warfare. God conscripted without respect of persons or tribes. "Out of every tribe," said Moses "a thousand for war." **Twelve thousand** were chosen. It was indeed a remarkable military achievement. The record of this campaign is found in Numbers 31. Time fails us to narrate the details as set forth in this chapter. The remarkable fact however, is that the **twelve thousand** went safely through the season of strife. When the conflict was over it was said, **"And there lacketh not one man of us"** (vs. 48). In this day when the "Beast" makes war on the saints the **twelve times twelve thousand** all pass safely through. Not one is missing will be the result.

Lesson Thirty-seven

## SIXTH AND SEVENTH SEALS (Rev.7:9-17) Part 3

Having seen **The Sealing of a Numbered Company of Israelites,** who were sealed to pass through the tribulation we are now ready to consider the remaining portion of chapter 7 and the **third** and **fourth** divisions of the chapter.

### III. THE SAVING OF AN UNNUMBERED COMPANY OF THE GENTILES (vss. 9-12).

**(Saved to Come Out of Tribulation)**

### IV. THE ELDERS' INTERROGATION AND THE GENTILES' DESTINATION (vss. 13-17).

**"After this,"** says John, (after sealing of the twelve tribes of Israel vss. 9-12).

"I beheld, and lo, a **great multitude,** which no man could number, of **all nations,** and **kindreds** and **peoples,** and **tongues,** stood before the throne, and before the Lamb, clothed with white robes, and palms in their hands, and they cried with a loud voice, saying, Salvation to our God which sitteth upon the throne, and unto the Lamb" (vss. 9, 10).

In the act of sealing there was but **one nation,** the nation Israel, but here **"all nations."** The Jew is **first** here again, then the nations or Gentiles. Israel is never "reckoned among" the nations. See Numbers 23:9. They "dwell alone." The order with God has been "Jew first" then the nations.

| **ISRAEL** (Jew) | **THE NATIONS** (Gentiles) |
|---|---|
| "I will bless thee" (Gen. 12:2). | In thee, all the **families of the earth** (Gen. 12:3). |
| "He will be merciful unto His land, and to His people" (Deut. 32:43). | "Rejoice, O ye nations, with His people" (Deut. 32:43). |
| "God be merciful to **us** and bless **us** and cause His face to shine upon **us**" (Ps. 67:1). "God shall bless **us**" (Ps. 67:7). | "That Thy way may be made known upon the **earth**, Thy saving health **among the nations**" (Ps. 67:2). |
| In that day there shall be **root of Jesse**, which shall stand for an ensign of the **people** (Is. 11:10). | "To it shall **the Gentiles** seek" (Is. 11:10). |
| Throughout the Gospels and Acts it is to the "**Jew** first." "To every one that believeth; to the Jew first" (Rom. 1:16). | and **then** to the **Gentiles.** "And also to the Greek" (Nations). |
| "Now I say that Jesus Christ was a **minister of the circumcision** for the Truth of God, to confirm the promises made to the fathers" (Rom. 15:8). | "And that the **Gentiles** might glorify God for His mercy, as it is written, For this cause I will confess to Thee among the Gentiles, and sing unto Thy name" Rom. 15:9, 10, 11, 12). |

It will be seen by the above that in the counsels and plan of God blessing for the Gentile or nations is dependent upon **the blessing of Israel** and that Israel is placed **first.** This is not only true of Israel in blessing, but also in judgment, for says Paul in Romans:

"Tribulation, wrath and anguish, upon the soul of every man * * **to the Jew first**——————————**and also to the Gentiles**" (Rom. 2:9).

As in the tribulation days the Jew is first then Gentile, so also in the millennial days the blessings are also on the same basis:

"But honor and glory and peace, to every man that worketh good, **to the Jew first**——————————**and also to the Gentile.**" (Rom. 3:10).

After John saw the one hundred and forty-four thousand sealed from the twelve tribes of Israel to pass through the tribulation, he then beheld this great company from the nations.

Israel was **numbered,** but this company **unnumbered.** The **twelve tribes** are distinct from **all nations.** Let us consider this great company.

## 1. THE PERSONS

This great company in its personnel, is cosmopolitan. The division is described as fourtold.

(1) All nations
(2) and kindreds
(3) and peoples
(4) and tongues.

2. THEIR POSITION

**They stand before the throne.** The Elders **sit,** but this company **stand.** They have a position of great honor. When Saul sent for David it is written,

"Let David stand before me for he has found favour in my sight" (I Sam. 16:21, 22).

This great company have a place of honor and favor. **They stand before the Lamb.** Their position before the throne and the Lamb, partially answers the question as who can stand before the Lamb and the throne. See 6:16, 17.

3. THEIR PRAISE

They praise God and the Lamb and ascribe unto Him, "Salvation." Their praise is the cause of general praise. It includes "angels about the throne," the eiders and the living creatures who in prostration worship God and the Lamb. As in the song of praise in chapter 5, so here there is sevenfold note in their praise:

Blessing
and glory
and wisdom
and thanksgiving
and honour
and power
and might (vs. 12).

4. THEIR PERSONAL APPEARANCE

They are clothed with white robes and palms in their hands. The psalm branches may speak victory, but these claim nothing for themselves. That their garments are white is a testimony to the Blood of the Lamb in which they were washed. See vs. 14.

The palms may be in celebration of the Feast of Tabernacles which is about to be kept in the land and when blessing comes both upon the Jew and the Gentile. Read Leviticus 23:39, 43; Ezra 3:11, 12; II Chronicles 20:19.

## IV. THE ELDER'S INTERROGATION AND THE GENTILES' DESTINATION—vss. 13-17.

It is with difficulty one refrains from both weeping and shouting aloud upon reading these words. How wonderful and surpassing and marvelous they are! What a recompense and what a reward! What a great salvation was theirs! This company of tribulation saints experience a wonderful deliverance in the midst of earth's darkest hour, the hour of tribulation. See their happy lot:

1. **They Stand**—"before the throne of God."
2. **They Serve**—"Him day and night in the temple."
3. **They Are Satisfied**—"No hunger, no thirst."
4. **They Are Sheltered**—"neither shall the sun light on them, nor any heat."
5. **They Are Sustained**—"the Lamb shall feed them and lead them to fountains of living waters."
6. **They Are Solaced**—"God shall wipe away all tears from their eyes."

Instead of standing in the presence of the wicked one, the beast and his seat of authority, they stand before God.

Instead of the suffering of the days of tribulation, when food stuff is all under the control of the Man of Sin and none can either buy or sell without the mark of the beast, this company have food and will **never again** know hunger.

When the rivers and the fountains have become blood as they will under the pouring of the third vial (Rev.

16:4) these are led to living fountains of water and will never again know thirst.

In the days, which follow under the pouring of the **fourth vial,** when the sun becomes scorching, it shall not light on them, and when men are scorched with a great heat none of it comes upon them. See Revelation 16:8, 9.

When the fifth angel has poured out the fifth vial of God's wrath and the kingdom of the beast is filled with darkness and men are gnawing their tongues for pain, God is wiping away all tears from their eyes.

O what a destination is theirs! They have come out of **tribulation** into a great **triumph!** This day of tribulation is an awful day. See Daniel 12:1; Matthew 24:21.

They are now Blood-washed and beautiful! They had once been of the earth and of Adam. They were as the cleansed leper now washed (Lev. 14:8, 9. They had been "world-infected," but now washed (Lev. 14:47). They had once touched the unclean thing but now washed (Num. 19:19).

This vision seems to take us out even beyond millennial days. Time evidently does not change their destiny, and their condition is as is described when the new heaven and the new earth have come into view at the close and succeeding the millennium. The new peoples are common in blessing with this great multitude except in the days of the new heaven and earth, it is a general and universal condition and blessing while with this great company, it is a special deliverance and destiny.

Lesson Thirty-eight

## SEVENTH SEAL, SILENCE, SEVEN ANGELS AND SEVEN TRUMPETS (Rev.8:1-14:20)

Between the opening of the Sixth Seal and the Seventh Seal, we have considered the arrest of judgment and the events of the 7th chapter, which we found to be concerned with Sealing of Israel and the Saving of a Company of Gentiles. At the opening of the 8th chapter the Seventh Seal is opened. The opening of this seal is followed by the **Seven Trumpets**. These Seven Trumpets continue through to chapter 15, when the Seventh Trumpet sounds and following the sounding of the Seventh Trumpet, the events of chapters 12, 13 and 14 are recorded, bringing us in the judgment period to the preparation of the pouring out of the **Seven Last Plagues or the Vials of God's Wrath** (see Rev. 15:1).

The period covered by the **Seven Trumpet Judgments** begins at chapter 8:6, where the **seven angels** prepare to sound, unto chapter 15: where the seven angels prepare to pour out the vials of wrath. Chapter 15 is preparatory to the pouring of the vials, which are actually poured out in chapter 16.

These pre-millennial judgments of **Seals, Trumpets** and **Vials,** constitute this judgment period, therefore we adhere closely to the divisions of this portion of the Book with reference to them.

And when he had opened the seventh seal, there was silence in Heaven for about the space of half an hour.

And I saw the seven angels which stood before God; and to them were given **seven trumpets.**

And another angel came and stood at the altar, having a golden censer;

and there was given unto him much incense, that he should offer it with the prayers of all saints upon the golden altar which was before the throne.

And the smoke of the incense, which came with the prayers of the saints, ascended up before God out of the angel's hand.

And the angel took the censer, and filled it with fire of the altar, and cast it into the earth: and there were voices, and thunderings, and lightnings, and an earthquake.

And the seven angels which had the seven trumpets prepared themselves to sound (chap. 8:1 to 6).

We shall consider the opening of this Seventh Seal and the chapter also by means of the following divisions:

1. **The Seal**—"the seventh seal" (8:1).
2. **The Silence**—"there was silence in Heaven" (8:1).
3. **The Space**—"about the space of half an hour" (8:1).
4. **The Seven Servants**—"seven angels which stood before God" (8:2).
5. **The Special Servant**—"and **another** angel came and stood at the altar" (8:3).
6. **The Saints**—"the prayers of the saints ascended up before God" (8:4).
7. **The Sounding**—"the seven angels prepared themselves to sound" (8:6 to 13).

1. **THE SEAL**—"the seventh seal" (8:1).

The Seventh Seal is quite unlike the others. The six seals at their opening produced rapid and revolutionary results. There were the four **Steeds,** the Seismic, Solar, Stellar and Social disturbance, but here, at the opening of the Seventh Seal, it is **Silence.**

The sixth seal brought us up to the great day of wrath and appears co-terminous with the seventh trumpet (see chap. 11:17, 18).

The seven trumpets expand or merge into the seven vials, but between the seals and trumpets, the continuity is broken by this silence.

The events connected with six seals occurred on the earth and while the scene of this seventh seal is laid in

Heaven, the results are seen upon the earth and in effect, much after the results of the sixth seal.

"And the angel took the censer and filled it with fire of the altar and cast it into the earth and there were voices, thunderings, lightnings and an earthquake."

The seventh seal as the six preceding it, affects **the earth** and is a disturber of the elements.

This fourfold manifestation is a sort of a preface to the coming judgments of the seven trumpets. Indeed the Seventh Seal as a preface and preparatory event to the trumpets.

This Seventh Seal indeed may be called the seal of the **Pause, the Praise, the Prayer and the Preparation.** The above all are seen in it.

**2. THE SILENCE**—"there was silence in Heaven" (8:1).

There is but little silence in the Book of Revelation. So far as we know the word does not occur again in the Book. It is not the Book of silence; it is the Book of speech. This is the day of the silence of God. The day of the Lord in this Book is not a day of silence. Says the Psalmist when speaking of this judgment period, "Then shall He **speak** to them in His wrath." This silence was in Heaven, there was **none on the earth.** Praise has ceased, service is suspended, all is still. **Silence** and **waiting** are expressed by the same word in Hebrew. This is a waiting time as well. There is an illustration of this in the 65th Psalm—"Praise waiteth (is silent) for Thee, O God in Zion."

There will be days when the Lord is in His holy temple, that the earth will keep silence before Him (see Hab. 2:20), but here it is **Heaven silent.** This is a voiceless silence. The word voice occurs **many, many times** in the Book of Revelation, but this is the one speechless season of the Book. This is a stillness before the storm. The Lord is about to come out from His holy place and punish the inhabitants of the earth. It is a momentous time, a thrilling period! Silence, suspense, hush and stillness in a Divinely dramatic degree! Expectation is a great silence!

3. **THE SPACE**—"about the space of half an hour" (8:1).

The duration of this strange and significant silence is about half an hour—about 30 minutes—no longer. God's patience has been long-suffering, but preceding the clang and blast of the trumpets there will be but brief delay. If the time of this judgment period be limited to seven years, as many believe the Scriptures to teach, then "half an hour" is long silence in the midst of such voices. The work of this judgment period is to be a **"short work."** It must be or no flesh could be saved so severe is it all! One-half hour for pause, praise and preparation—then the seven angels.

4. **THE SEVEN SERVANTS**—"seven angels which stood before God" (8:2).

These seven angels have been seen before and will be seen hereafter. They are the Divine executors of God's will. They are first seen in 1:4 and introduced as "the seven Spirits which are before His throne" for His angels are "ministering spirits" (see Heb. 1:7, 14). The distinguishment of these seven angels is denoted by the articles, "the seven angels." They are servants for they **stand** before the throne. Gabriel had such a place (see Luke 1:19). He may have been included among the seven—we do not urge it. In earthly courts men "stood before the king" as in the case of Daniel and his companions (see Dan. 1:19). There are angels in Heaven that always behold the face of the Father. This we know by the words of Jesus (see Matt. 18:10). In the days of Ahasuerus the king—**"seven** chamberlains served in his presence" (see Esth. 1:10). We are here privileged to see the favored ones which stand before God. To them are delivered **seven trumpets.** There is a change of agency here for in the case of the seven seals, the Lamb opened them for among angels none were found worthy "to take the Book and open the seals thereof," but here the trumpets, are committed to the **seven angels.** These seven trumpeters are heralds of the King of all the kings. Royalty is about to be displayed!

**Trumpets were used in war to assemble the host** (see Judg. 6:34; 7:16, 18; I Sam. 13:3; Jer. 4:5). Job connected trumpets and battles in a suggestive way—

"He saith among the **trumpets,** Ha, ha; and he smelleth the battle afar off, the thunder of the captains, and the shoutings" (Job 39:25).

This is a description of Calvary, for the horse is the subject of Job's discussion (see Job 39:19-26). **Trumpets, battles, thunders** and **shoutings** are associated in Job and they are all here at the breaking of the Seventh Seal, also, see verse 5. God gave instruction to His people Israel:

"And if you go to war in **your land** against the **enemy** that **oppresseth** you, then ye shall **blow the alarm** with the **trumpets**; and ye shall be **remembered before the Lord your God,** and shall be **saved from your enemies**" (Num. 10:9).

Here are the Trumpets and the Seven Trumpeters at the opening of the seventh seal for the "enemy that oppresseth," the great oppressor, the Beast, the Man of Sin is soon to come up against Israel and the **land.** Blow the alarm! Blow the alarm with trumpets! It is the "great and a terrible day of the Lord" at the hand. Zephaniah the Prophet foresaw and foretold this event:

The great day of the Lord is near, it is near, and **hasteth greatly,** even the voice of the day of the Lord; the **mighty men shall cry** there bitterly. That day is—

(1) **A day of wrath,**
(2) **A day of trouble and distress,**
(3) **A day of wasteness and desolation,**
(4) **A day of darkness and gloominess,**

(5) **A day of clouds and thick darkness,**

(6) **A day of the TRUMPETS** and alarm against the fenced cities and high towers.

"And I will bring distress upon men, that they shall walk like blind men, because they have sinned against the Lord: and their blood shall be poured out as dust, and their flesh as the dung.

Neither their silver nor their gold shall be able to deliver them in the day of the Lord's wrath; but the whole land shall be devoured by the fire of His jeolousy; for He shall make even a speedy riddance of all them that dwell in the land" (Zeph. 1:14-18).

At this place in the Book of Revelation the "day of the Lord" "is near—very near." It "hasteth greatly" only thirty minutes of silence and suspension in the midst of judgment. The "mighty men who cry bitterly" are seen under the sixth seal (see 6:15, 16). They cry because it is "a day of wrath" (6:17). In a sixfold detailed description of the day of the Lord, the Prophet summarizes these apocalyptic judgments and among other things it declares it a day of **"trumpets and alarms."** These seven trumpets will bring "distress upon men." This will be herein after discussed. Men shall walk as blind men. Blood will be flung away like dust, flesh will be treated as dung. "Speedy riddance" will be the work of that day.

No wonder there are thirty minutes for pause and preparation! The bombardment of the earth is about to begin, but **"ye shall be remembered before the Lord your God,"** says Numbers 10:9 and this brings us to the work of

**5. THE SPECIAL SERVANT**—"and another angel came and stood at the altar" (8:3).

Who this angel is we know not. We can not agree with some that it is the Lord Jesus Christ. He comes to do a priestly service. He takes his stand at the altar (the golden altar in the Holy Place, not the brazen altar at the door of the court), and bears in his hands a golden censer at the golden altar of inense. He is a nameless angel with a priestly ministry for this time.

The scene speaks of the realities of the "Temple not made with hands" after which the Tabernacle and Temple of olden days, was patterned. Moses made things after the "pattern of things in the Heavens." Here we see things in the Heavens. Once an angel was seen over Heaven with a **sword** in his hand, but here it is a **censer.** His fellows are about to sound their trumpets of judgment and like Aaron and Hur of old, he goes to prepare the way for the avenging of God's people upon the Amaleks of the last days.

His service must be performed in half an hour—this is the time allotted for the transaction, so there he stands at the golden altar that was before the throne, thus placed as was the golden altar in the Tabernacle before the veil wherein God dwelt. What an august and wonderful person and what a wonderful performance!

**"There was given him much incense."** There was no Judas here to complain at the misuse of ointment or precious offerings—, "much incense."

His work was first "upon the altar"—the incense and the prayers of saints; then the "censer and fire." The fire **ascended** up to God, the second **descended** into the earth"—it was "cast into the earth."

It is here that according to Numbers 10:9 God **remembers** His people and will deliver them and we see

6. **THE SAINTS—**"the prayers of the saints ascended up before God" (8:4).

God is hearing the prayers of the tribulation saints which are going up to Him. They are as sweet incense. The prayers of martyred saints went up at 6:10. These are living saints who are passing through these days. They are the saints of the faithful remnant, and we believe, the sealed ones of chapter 7. They are crying unto Him day and night, and He is remembering them. These prayers are as sweet-smelling incense as they ascend. Many of these prayers are in the Psalms. Canon Barnes, a rationalist of the Church of England, called these Psalms the "cursing Psalms" and says they are **"obviously un-Christian."** They are "un-Christian" in the present time but they will be in full harmony with the days when they are uttered. In the lips of the remnant of Israel in the tribulation days, they will come up before God as incense. Read Psalm 83:9; Psalm 78:4.

In one of these prayers the Psalmist cries:

"Lord, I cry unto Thee; make haste unto me; give ear unto my voice, when I cry unto Thee. Let my prayer be **set forth before Thee as incense**; and the lifting up of my hands as the evening sacrifice" (Ps. 141:1, 2).

These prayers are now coming up as incense before God. He hears their prayers. They are sacred and sweet to Him, and He will speedily answer.

**The fire was cast into the earth,** resulting in the voices, the thunderings, the lightnings and the earthquake. This fire is a token of destruction. In Ezekiel 10 fire was taken from between the cherubim under the throne and scattered as a token of judgment. It would be well to take time to consider "fire" in the light of such Scriptures as Ezekiel 39:6; 38:22; Hosea 8:14; Deuteronomy 32:22; Amos 1:4, 7, 10, 12. Surely, "a **fire is kindled in Mine anger,"** and it shall burn to the lowest Hades and shall consume the increase of the earth and set on fire the foundation of the mountains.

It is now time for the baptism of fire. Baptized with the Holy Ghost was Israel's privilege in the Acts, but **"with fire"** here. So the seven angels with their seven trumpets, are ready. They will sound in succession. This will bring us to

**7. THE SOUNDING—**"the seven angels prepared themselves to sound" (8:6).

Lesson Thirty-nine

## SEVEN TRUMPETS (Rev.8:7-11:19)

At the close of our last lesson we beheld the **Seven Angel Trumpeters** ready to sound. With this sounding begins the **second** of the **three** divisions of Apocalyptic judgments. The trumpet blasts of Angel trumpeters will now be heard, each introducing an imminent judgment.

"And the seven angels which had the seven trumpets prepared themselves to sound" (vs. 6).

These seven trumpets are divided into four and three, and the **first four** are separated from the **last three** by the **"flying eagle."**

The Sounding of the First Trumpet (vs. 7).

The Sounding of the Second Trumpet (vs. 8).

The Sounding of the Third Trumpet (vss. 10, 11).

The Sounding of the Fourth Trumpet (vs. 12).

### THE FLYING EAGLE
(vs. 13).

The Sounding of the Fifth Trumpet (chap. 9:1).

The Sounding of the Sixth Trumpet (chap. 9:13).

The Sounding of the Seventh Trumpet (chap. 11:15).

Thus we see that the **last three of the trumpets** are distinguished from the **first four.**

The **first four** appear in rapid succession with but little description, while the **last three** are described with considerable detail.

The **first four** trumpet judgments are described **in**

**seven verses,** while more than fifty verses are necessary to the details of the **last three.**

The **last three trumpets** are further distinguished from the first **four** by the word **"woe."** The last three are the **"Woe" Trumpets** (see 8:13; 9:12).

The voice of the **"eagle"** in verse 13, introducing the remaining three, is also a matter of their distinguishment.

The **first four,** are connected and are interdependent with intrinsic features, while the **last three,** on account of the character of the plagues, seem to stand apart for fuller consideration. (See Dean Alford.)

The first four, are visited upon **places.**

The last three upon **persons.**

The first four upon things **material** and the last three upon **men.** The **first four** affect the accessories of life and the **last three, life itself.**

And as in the case of the **seals,** so with the trumpets. Six of the seals were associated with the **earth** and the **seventh** with **Heaven.** The six trumpets are related to the **earth,** but the **seventh,** with **Heaven** (see 11:15).

We shall study the trumpet judgments in the order of the **first four**; then the **remaining three.**

## THE FIRST FOUR OF THE SEVEN TRUMPETS 8:7-13.

1. **The First Trumpet Judgment Fell Upon the Earth.** (The instrument was "fire, hail and blood" [see vs. 7]).
2. **The Second Trumpet Judgment Fell Upon the Sea.** (The instrument was a burning fire ball [see vs. 8]).
3. **The Third Trumpet Judgment Fell Upon the Rivers.** (The instrument was "a great star" [see vs. 10]).
4. **The Fourth Trumpet Judgment Fell Upon Sun, Moon and Stars.** (The instrument was partial eclipse or obscuration [see vs. 12]).

**Three spheres** are brought under the judgment of the first four trumpets—the earth, the sea, and rivers—the solar, lunar, and stellar bodies of the heavens. We thus display:

| | | |
|---|---|---|
| 1. **The First Trumpet** | Agricultural | green grass, trees. |
| 2. **The Second Trumpet** | Aquatic | sea. |
| 3. **The Third Trumpet** | | rivers. |
| 4. **The Fourth Trumpet** | Astronomic | sun, moon, stars. |

The above is not to be lightly considered. These words are not used for alliteration, but for analysis and better interpretation. One can see at once what it will mean in these tribulation days to suffer an interference of the products of agriculture—green grass and herbs, and doubtless the trees, include **many fruit bearing trees.** Consider this.

With the seas filled with blood and ships destroyed and the water corrupting with dead marine life, one must see the problems of **export** and **import** to relieve the famine produced by blight of trees and grass.

With the rivers, the source of water for domestic purposes, and human existence, poisoned, what a personal problem is here suggested.

And if upon things follows eclipse of the lightbearers in the heavens, what will be the condition under which earth dwellers will exist or attempt to exist? These things will be more fully taken up in detail after a little further analysis of the four trumpet judgments.

1. The First Trumpet Affects **Vegetation.**
2. The Second Trumpet Affects **Transportation and Importation.**
3. The Third Trumpet Affects **Sanitation.**
4. The Fourth Trumpet Affects **Illumination.**

And these considered together with the first four

seals, which present four steeds in succession, will be found to further develop the features of **famine, pestilence, disease,** and **death,** predicted under these first four seals. We shall now develop what we have sought to introduce in the above.

THE FIRST TRUMPET—Its Effects upon **Vegetation** (vs. 7).

"The first angel sounded, and there followed hail and fire mingled with blood, and they were cast upon the earth; and the third part of the trees was burnt up, and all green grass was burnt up" (vs. 7).

Hail and fire mingled with blood! God is once again saying, "Let My people Israel go," as in the days of Egyptian bondage. Indeed, in these trumpet judgments, we are reminded of the judgments upon Pharaoh and the Egyptians. The seventh plague sent on Pharaoh, greatly resembles this first trumpet judgment. The Prophet Micah assures us there is good ground to expect the judgments in Egypt repeated in the end time judgments (see Mic. 7:5; also Is. 11:15, 16; and Jer. 23:7, 8).

In Egypt there was "hail and fire," but **no blood. "The Lord sent thunder and hail, and the fire ran along the ground"** (Exod. 9:23). "The hail smote every **herb of the field,** and brake **every tree of the field"** (Exod. 9:25).

With the fire and the hail, in this first trumpet judgment was **blood.** This judgment of blood and fire had been foretold and is now being **fulfilled.** Joel in speaking of the terrors of the "great and terrible day of the Lord," said, "I will shew wonders in the heavens above and signs in the earth beneath, **blood and fire"** (Joel 2:30). "This is that," may again be Scripturally proclaimed (see Acts 2:16).

It will be noticed that under this first trumpet, the prohibition placed between the sixth and seventh seal is **removed.** In that instance there was command that the **earth** should not be hurt, "neither the sea nor the trees"

(7:3). This exemption no longer maintains. The angels to whom "it was given to hurt the earth and the sea" (7:2), are no longer under the Divine restraint. The trees and the grass are the first to receive a judgment blow under the trumpet judgments.

The judgment, as we have seen above, was directed against the realm of **agriculture** and **horticulture**, the grass or herbs and the trees. Without doubt these are herbs for food and fruit-bearing trees. This was the case in Egypt.

"And the flax and the barley was smitten; for the barley was in the ear, and the flax was bolled. But the wheat and the rye were not smitten; for they were not grown up" (Exod. 9:31, 32).

So also here, this judgment falls upon the **food stuff** —both green edibles and fruit. A **third** part of it was burned by the fire. There was a reduction of **one-third** the regular supply. This was a serious matter. This was a harbinger of famine, and God used the hail and the fire tc produce it. It was to Jcb God addressed this question:

"Hast thou entered into the treasures of the snow? hast thou seen the treasures of the hail, which I have reserved against the time of trouble, against the day of battle?" (Job 38:22, 23).

Here are some new agencies brought into battle, and the sounding of the first trumpet reveals them.

Fire has been an instrument of judgment at other times. Fire fell on Job's sheep—they were burnt up (see Job 1:16). Here it falls on pasture, and not only is the green herb destroyed, affecting the food of man, but food of beast also, and therefore—there is not only **a famine for foodstuffs,** both flesh and fruit, but the **wool and flax for clothing** are also imperiled. It is difficult to **fully** understand to **what extent** this first trumpet judgment may affect the earth.

With the destruction of the green grass, the beasts would suffer with man. Joel the Prophet must have spoken of these trumpet judgments when he said:

"How do the beasts groan! the herds of cattle are perplexed, because they have no pasture; yea, the flocks of sheep are made desolate.
O Lord, to Thee will I cry: for the fire hath devoured the pastures of the wilderness, and the flame hath burned all the trees of the field.
The beasts of the field cry also unto Thee; for the rivers of waters are dried up, and the fire hath devoured the pastures of the wilderness" (Joel 1:18, 19, 20).

It is an hour of judicial retribution upon the earth-dwellers. It is the time foretold by Moses and the Prophets. The very accessories of life are ravished. Hail and fire and blood—a strange chemical situation with destruction to vegetation. Grass for the cattle was a promise of the Law. "I will send grass in thy fields for thy cattle, that thou mayest eat and be full" (Deut. 11:15). But here the favor is no more. The beasts are groaning—cattle and sheep are in a famine. The fields are black as fields of burnt stubble.

The Psalmist in recalling the judgment in Egypt gives graphic account and says:

"He destroyed their vine with hail, and their sycomore trees with frost. He gave up their cattle also to hail and their flocks to hot thunderbolts" (Ps. 78:47, 48).

This first trumpet judgment may also include the **vines** and add yet further to the food shortage for both man and beast. Again we say, it is well nigh **impossible** to forecast the results of this one trumpet, without even taking into consideration those yet to come. One can not withhold from turning a moment from these terrible judgments to look ahead a little space and spy out Millennial Glory and blessedness, for such glory is depicted in glorious words by the Prophet Joel, and are indeed in strong contrast with Revelation 8 and 9. Says the Prophet:

"Be not afraid, ye beasts of the field: for the pastures of the wilderness do spring, for the tree beareth her fruit, the fig tree and the vine do yield their strength" (Joel 2:22; Read also Zech. 10:1).

How blessed and beatific! How great and gracious is the Lord but how terrible His judgment!

Nor can we refrain from looking back to chapter 7, to

the "Great Multitude" that had been saved out of the great tribulation, to see there is **no hunger** for them—no **burning heat** and no **poisoned waters** and **no weeping.** Says the Revelator;

"They shall hunger no more, neither thirst any more; neither shall the sun light on them, nor any heat. For the Lamb which is in the midst of the throne shall feed them, and shall lead them unto living fountains of waters: and God shall wipe away all tears from their eyes" (Rev. 7:16, 17).

Lesson Forty

## SECOND AND THIRD TRUMPETS (Rev.8:8-11)

In our previous lesson we considered the results of the sounding of the first of the seven trumpets. We found this judgment fell upon things agricultural and horticultural—the "trees" and "green grass." The sounding of the second and third trumpets will engage our attention for a time. See 8:8-11.

The **first** trumpet judgment, as we have seen, fell upon things in the realm of **agriculture.** The products of forest, fruit and pasture, were affected.

Under the **second** and **third** trumpets things **aquatic** are brought under judgment.

First—The waters of commerce and transportation (vs. 8).

Second—The waters used for domestic purposes (vss. 10, 11).

The **sea,** the **rivers** and the **fountains** were all included in this visitation of judgment. Both **salt** and **fresh** waters are polluted. The extent is to the third part upon all waters. This judgment covers an extent equal to that upon the trees and the grass—the "third part." The location is within the prophetic zone or area upon which these judgments fall.

The great burning or blazing object which was cast into the sea is not called a mountain. The record reads, "As it were a mountain" (vs. 8), or like a mountain. The Holy Spirit with Divine care guards all **the words of Holy Scriptures.**

It is by such expressions as, "as it were," "like unto,"

"a sign," and similar figures, we may discern between the literal and the figurative. This great burning mass had the appearance of a great mountain. It was a literal object that actually fell into the sea. It is not to be spiritually interpreted. There is no event in history for which it stands. This event is not history fulfilled in any time in the past, but a prophecy **yet to be fulfilled.** This is our conviction, though we respect the opinions of those who differ. The events of this portion of Revelation are future.

Water has been turned to blood at other times in the history of God's dealings with the earth and His people Israel, why not again?

During the plagues in the days of Pharaoh, Moses lifted his rod and the river turned to blood (see Exod. 7:20). The Psalmist in recalling the early history of Israel in the 105th Psalm, says plainly, "He turned their waters into blood" (Ps. 105:29).

What chemical qualities this burning ball contained, we know not, but they were of character and kind to turn salt sea water into bloody water. Pharaoh did not deny the bloody waters of his beloved Nile in the days of Moses; it is only "modernists" who do such things. Let it be said for us, we believe God and to us His Word is authority.

The effect upon the sea life was severe. A third part of the creatures in the sea died. "Which had life," may refer to fishes and sea creatures used for food.

That sea life should die in bloody water or water turned to blood, is not a new thing and is recorded in the past annals of Israel's history. The fish in the Nile in the days of Pharaoh and Moses died when a plague fell on that so-called sacred river. "The fish that was in the river died." This is a plain statement. See Exodus 7:21. Fish are most sensitive to water and the elements introduced into the same. Dead fish are often seen washed ashore as the result of even slight disturbances. Even the gold fish in the bowl in the home die easily from change of water or lack of change. Those who have attempted to maintain a miniature aquarium understand well.

The Psalmist in commenting on the plagues in the days of Pharaoh says: "He turned their waters into blood, **and slew their "fish"** (Ps. 105:29).

This great ball of fire, with its heat to boil the water, and the gases which escape from it, thrown suddenly into the sea, produces a bloody water within which fish cannot live. What a basin of stinking fish and disease! This destruction of fish life in the sea, adds to the famine of the first trumpet. Their **fruit** and **field** was cut off and now **fish.** With the products of the fields and the fisheries cut off, one can see somewhat of the food shortage and the famine that will follow.

But to add to this, the ships are plowing their prows **through seas of blood.** The result of this flaming burning ball issues in the third of the ships being destroyed. This greatly affects transportation upon the seas and creates a serious problem in famine days—the problem of **imports** and **exports.** England well knows the difficulties the shortage of tonnage creates. When the submarine warfare was sending her ships to the bottom of the sea, there was a serious national problem of food. The nation was facing a famine. For not only was there the loss of the ship, but also the cargo, for it was a submarine warfare **against the merchant marine.** It was food stuff sent to the depths of the sea. Such was the main object of attack and cause for the same. When imports and exports are impossible because of marine conveyance, famine is greatly accentuated.

Think of a bloody sea filled with sunken ships and

dead, putrefying, stinking fish with white bellies upturned on the bosom of a scarlet sea! Think of the stench and pestilence arising therefrom to be carried by the winds to the land and inland!

These are the days of tribulation. In their foretelling there has been forewarning. They shall be "shortened"; if they were not, there would be no flesh saved. Doubtless the Prophet had these days in mind when he said:

"Therefore shall the land mourn, and every one that dwelleth therein shall languish, with the beasts of the field, and with the fowls of heaven; yea the fishes of the sea also shall be taken away." (Hos. 4:3).

In the millennial days, which immediately follow this tribulation these waters will be healed and fish life restored. Says the Prophet Ezekiel:

"And it shall come to pass, that everything that liveth, which moveth whither soever the rivers shall come, and shall live; and there shall be a very great multitude of fish, because these waters shall come thither; for they shall be healed; and everything shall live, whither the river cometh" (Ezek. 47:9; see 8-10).

He who filled the waters of the seas at the **Creation** (see Gen. 1:22) will destroy them in the **tribulation** but will restore them in the days of the **regeneration.**

The third trumpet adds to the severity of the situation. The sea, **under the second trumpet,** becomes bloody and the basin for dead fish and sunken ships, but the third trumpet makes the rivers and fountains, the object of retribution.

The **second** trumpet had the appearance of a **mountain.**

The **third** trumpet has the action of a **meteor.**

There fell a great star from Heaven. It was not a nameless "wandering star;" it had a **name.**

Said the Psalmist: "He telleth the number of the stars; He calleth them all by their **names."** He made these stars in the beginning and gave them their Heavenly locality (see Gen. 1:14-16). A star appeared over the birthplace of the Lord Who made the stars (see

Matt. 2:2, 7). That was a literal star and so also is this one.

The name of this star is "Wormwood." Its name and nature agree. It is "bitter" and creates bitterness in whatever it touches.

Why should it be considered but a figure of speech rather than a fact, that such a star should appear? Why will men believe anything science may predict and reject the predictions of Scripture?

"Wormwood" may not now be catalogued among the stars, but depend upon the veracity of God's Word this star **will visit the earth and just as this Book of Revelation describes it!**

Who called attention first to the constellation of Orion? Was it a modern scientist or an ancient Scripture? Who spoke of Orion before there was a calculating telescope in all the world? Job, the most ancient Book in the world, gives to God this praise. Says he:

"Which maketh **Arcturus, Orion,** and Pleiades, and the chambers of the south. Which doeth great things past finding out; yea, and wonders without number" (Job 9:9, 10).

It was God who asked Job, "Canst thou * * loose the bands of **Orion?"** (Job 38:31).

If a noted scientist has found in the constellation of Orion, a giant star, it is because God has "loosed" it and permitted it to come into human vision. "He doeth wonders without number" says Job, and this great star "Wormwood" is among the coming wonders.

It would be well for man to follow the instruction of Amos when he exhorts:

"Seek Him that maketh the **seven stars and Orion,** and, turneth the shadow f death into the morning, and maketh the day dark with night; that calleth for the waters of the sea, and poureth them out upon the face of the earth; The **LORD** is His name" (Amos 5:8).

This star makes bitter and undrinkable the water of both rivers and fountains, or the fresh water supply. Why consider this a strange thing?

It is reported that the German army in retreating from France poisoned the wells.

Isaac digged out the wells the Philistines had filled (see Gen. 26:15).

Hezekiah sought to stop Sennacherib by stopping the waters at the fountains (see II Chron. 32:3, 4).

When man, in the full display of his hate for holiness and God, showed his contempt for the Son of God Whom the Father sent unto the world, they gave Him the bitter cup of gall to drink, and now the cup is at the lips of the world dwellers in the dark hour of the world's tribulation.

Israel must drink the cup they gave Him. Said Jeremiah:

"Thus saith the Lord of Hosts, the God of Israel; I will feed even this people with **wormwood**, and give them water of gall to drink" (Jer. 9:13-15).

"Behold, I will feed them with **wormwood**, and make them drink the water of gall" (Jer. 23:15).

The rivers in the days of Pharaoh were actually bitter, so will they be in these days also—"The Egyptians could not drink the water" (Exod. 7:20). See also verses 18 and 24.

It was a tree cast into the bitter waters in the wilderness that made them **sweet,** here it is a star cast into sweet waters that makes them **bitter** (see Exod. 15:23-25).

In Egypt the rivers, ponds and pools were polluted, here also fountains.

In the days of Elisha in the city of Jericho, the waters were found bitter. He ordered salt put in them and the bitter was made sweet (see II Kings 2:19-22). There is no Elisha the Prophet with healing salts in these days recorded in the Revelation. There are false prophets and **the false prophet,** but no Prophet of God with the power of miracle working to heal these rivers and fountains. Thirst has followed hunger and there are yet many other woes to come.

These are the days when many of the curses spoken under the Law are fulfilled. Perhaps this bitter water which causes death may fulfill one of the types of the Law.

The suspicious man under the Law of Moses would test the fidelity of infidelity of his wife. She, if suspected, was brought to the priest and put through the crucible of the **bitter water test.** Read Numbers 5:12-31.

In the Book of Revelation, the one who stood at the golden altar, poured not dust from the floor of the tabernacle, but commanded a star to embitter the waters and **many died.**

Is there anything in the Scriptures to indicate the prevalence of adultery and social evils in the earth at the end of this age? Is there secret adultery in the earth? Is there any evidence today? See chapter 9 and verse 21 and with this ponder Matthew 12:39; 16:4; II Peter 2:14, and in this reference found in Peter, notice the words, **"cursed children."** Does not Ezekiel say: "I will judge thee, as women that break wedlock and shed blood, are judged?" Could Ezekiel have this judgment under the third trumpet in mind?

Lesson Forty-one

## THE FOURTH TRUMPET (Rev.8:12,13)

"And the fourth angel sounded, and the third part of the sun was smitten, and the third part of the moon, and the third part of the stars; so as the third part of them was darkened, and the day shone not for a third part of it, and the night likewise.

And I beheld, and heard an angel (eagle, R. V.) flying through the midst of Heaven, saying with a loud voice, Woe, woe, woe, to the inhabiters of the earth by reason of the other voices of the trumpet of the three angels, which are yet to sound" (8:12, 13).

Under the former trumpets, we have seen the judgment of God laid on things. **Agricultural** and **aquatic.** With the sounding of the fourth trumpet, the judgment on things **astronomical.** The sun, moon and stars, as under the sixth seal, are now the object of God's visitation. Both day and night are to be darkened and thus add to the reign of terrors already commenced with the sounding of the three former trumpets. From the earth and the sea we now turn to the heavens and see the Divine draping of solar, stellar and lunar bodies.

This astronomical disturbance is the fulfillment of prophetic forecast. Jesus spoke of this eclipse and spoke of it as "signs."

"And there shall be **signs** in the sun, and in the moon, and in the stars" (Luke 21:25).

In fact the sun, moon, and stars were originally placed in the heavens not only to be light-bearers and to divide the day from the night and for seasons and days and years, but they were also placed there for **"signs"** (see Gen. 1:14-16). The order in Revelation is as that in Genesis:

## "GOD MADE TWO GREAT LIGHTS"

1. **Sun**—"The greater light to rule the day."
2. **Moon**—"The lesser light to rule the night."
3. **Stars**—"He made the stars also" (Gen. 1:16-19).

He Who made them for the light now uses them to make darkness. Read also Matthew 24:29; Mark 13:24.

It is interesting in passing to notice the **fourth** day of the creative or rather the recreation week, and it is the **fourth** trumpet that smites and shades them.

The Prophets foretold this natural and supernatural phenomenon following the judgment of the fourth trumpet.

Said Isaiah: "Behold darkness and sorrow, and the light is darkened in the heavens thereof" (Is. 5:30).

Here the prophet sees the human sorrow and nocturnal darkness of these days.

So also did Amos the Prophet catch foregleams of these times of distress and darkness, and declared that, God would **"cause the sun to go down at noon, and I will darken the earth in the clear day"** (Amos 8:9).

Here is midnight at midday and a clear day turned into a lightless night!

Said Jeremiah: "And the heavens, and they had no light" (Jer. 4:23).

Ezekiel summarized these tribulation days in a graphic and dramatic manner. Said he:

"I will cover the heaven, and make the stars thereof dark; I will cover the sun with a cloud (see also Rev. 6:12), and the moon shall not give her light. All the bright lights of heaven will I make dark over thee, and set darkness upon thy land, saith the Lord God" (Ezek. 32:7, 8).

Joel the prophet of the "day of the Lord" foretold this day and the judgment thereof. John fills in with detail what Joel saw in general. Said Joel:

"The sun and the moon shall be dark, and the stars shall withdraw their shining" (Joel 2:10).

"The sun shall be turned into darkness, and the moon into blood" (2:31).

"The sun and the moon shall be darkened and the stars shall withdraw their shining" (3:15).

Let us conceive, if we can, sunless, moonless, and starless days and nights when the judgments of the Lord are in the earth. The partial eclipse under the fourth trumpet is quite serious enough, what will the total eclipse be, "before the great and terrible day of the Lord?"

But what will be the result of this diminishing of light both in the day and at the night, and especially, in the light of the results of the former trumpet judgments?

The first trumpet fell upon the products of agriculture and horticulture. There was a reduction of field and fruit to **one-third.**

The second trumpet fell upon things aquatic and **one-third** of fish as food destroyed with transportation reduced **one-third,** thus greatly interfering with import and export.

The third trumpet fell upon rivers and fountains used for domestic purpose with their reduction to the amount of **one-third,** and of course this greatly affected both beasts for food, and fruit and field production as well as water for irrigation and distillation.

This fourth trumpet reduces the light of sun by day and moon by night and the stars, and of course this also retards vegetation for the influence of both sun, moon, and stars upon vegetable growth is established beyond controversy. The reduction of one-third of these luminaries will affect the earth greatly. How often have we heard agriculturists and horticulturists say—"Too much cloudy weather," "Not enough sun," "The crops are rotting in the ground—too many clouds, not enough sunshine."

The sun by day and the moon by night have a mission to the growing things of the earth. There are wise agriculturists, who speak of planting "in the light of the moon." Think of these things and consider the effect of these trumpet judgments upon all food stuff and products of provision for man's sustenance. Surely the famine of these can be but a natural and forthcoming result as well as terrible pestilence.

If time would permit us to go to length, we would show the scientific accuracy of the Book of Revelation. There is yet to be written a valuable book on this subject. The **astronomy of the Apocalypse** alone would be a subject worthy of deepest consideration. It can be readily seen that this diminution of light and heat would have a chilling effect upon vegetation, and fruit would not ripen or field come to maturity. Who can now imagine the result of one-third of the reduction of the sun's light upon the earth? Deprive the earth of one-third of the light of sun, moon and stars and you have indeed turned the laws of vegetation away back and retarded maturity beyond understanding. But such will be the condition in these days!

And this Book means what it says and says what it means and we understand, the sun, moon, and the stars to be **the actual, literal sun, moon, and stars.** They do not stand for generalities or uncertainties. The "sun" is not some Emperor, the moon, the church, or the stars some bishops or ecclesiastical potentates. These are not political symbols, but just what God says—**the sun, the moon, and the stars.** We believe God.

In the Book of Revelation a sign, a symbol, or a figure of speech is clearly designated and only such may be used figuratively. To treat this Book otherwise will end in hopeless confusion and never come through symbolic and figurative chaos and, confusion to sound interpretation.

### The Flying Eagle

That this should read **"eagle"** instead of "angel" is

established by the best manuscripts and is adopted by the critical editions. The Revised Version uses the word **"eagle"** (Alford, Bengel, Tischendorf, Tregelles and many others upon the use of the word "eagle" here, instead of "angel." The Greek word is "aeton," "eagle.")

This eagle separates the four trumpets from the three. The former four have fallen upon things in the earth, the next three fall upon the inhabitants of the earth.

The appearance of an eagle here is not strange. The eagle is connected with judgment in the Scriptures. Jesus spoke of them in Matthew 24:28 in His great prophetic discourse. They are called to prey on men in Revelation 19:17. This is a single eagle. He flies in mid-heaven where eagles are wont to fly in the face of the sun. God made in the beginning fowl to fly in the "open firmament of heaven" (Gen. 1:20). So here is one of the flying fowl.

It was the **fifth day** of the creative week that brought forth the fowl. It is at the sounding of the **fifth trumpet** this eagle flies in midheaven. This eagle not only flies but he **speaks.** The burden of his scream is the coming judgments. Things are not better but rather worse.

**"Woe, woe, woe, to the inhabitants of the earth by reason of the other voices of the trumpet of the three angels, which are yet to sound" (Rev. 8:13).**

Does this eagle speak? It does. Birds have been known to speak words and do. There are birds that use human language this day. God opened the mouth of an ass to speak and He can and will open the mouth of an eagle to speak. Men use birds and beasts for communication, why may not God? Man has developed both birds and beast up to an intelligence near the point of almost human expression, can not God break the natural barriers and make an eagle scream, "Woe, woe, woe"? He can and will.

The story of the dogs trained for war is most engaging, their instincts were developed up to an intelligence that was remarkable. In many cases they received special recognition for valiant duty on the battle fields. Not only were beasts used in the world war but also birds.

Canaries were used to detect the presence of gas in the trenches and the pigeons played prominent part. They carried the messages through "mid-heaven." Messages, sketches, and maps were sent through the air by these wonderful birds. One pigeon was known to fly eleven hundred miles, from Rome, Italy to Durham, England. In the Mense-Argonne sector alone, birds delivered 403 messages, many of them very important.

Man will receive the exploits of men however marvelous, without the least doubt or incredulity. Science may claim anything and there is never a sneer on the face of man. He is willing tc believe in the power and possibility of nature, but when asked to believe the Scriptures and the power of God, it is then he shows his contempt and unbelief.

If God will use an eagle in the world's worst hour, when natural phenomenon is surpassing anything ever known and every sphere of nature over which the first man lost dominion, is invaded by the miraculous power and movements of God, shall it be counted a thing incredible?

This "flying eagle" screaming out his triple "woes" of coming catastrophe and world cataclysm is a messenger of God heralding the coming events of a day dark with God's wrath.

Lesson Forty-two

## THE LOCUST SCOURGE (Rev.9:1-12)

The eagle's scream announced the coming "woes" (see 8:13) under the sounding of the trumpets succeeding the **first four.** At the sounding of the **fifth** trumpet these "woes" begin. Read 9:1-12.

We have here introduced a new sphere, the underworld or the **bottomless pit.** The three spheres mentioned here are—(1) Heaven, (2) earth, (3) bottomless pit.

From this time forward the bottomless pit will come under consideration. At chapter 11:7 the beast that ascends out of the "bottomless pit" is mentioned, and at 17:8 again. At 20:1 we have an angel with the key to the "bottomless pit" and at 20:3 the incarceration of Satan into the "bottomless pit." Under this trumpet the underworld begins an invasion of the earth. Demons begin to play their part in the drama of the "day of the Lord." The prison pit and abode of demons opens its mouth to belch out upon the earth a vomit of demons. It is but little wonder the eagle cried, "Woe, Woe, Woe!!" It is always woe, whether the devil comes down or up. In Revelation 12, it is "Woe unto the inhabitants of the earth for the devil is come down unto you" (12:12). Here it is woe because of that which comes up out of the earth.

Many think with this first woe at the fifth trumpet, the **"great tribulation"** of which Jesus spoke in Matthew 24:21, 22, commences and is in point of time, the same as the casting of Satan out of Heaven in chapter 12. There is no objection to this viewpoint and one thing is certain, except such days be "shortened" no flesh could survive. The things that have come to pass under seals and trumpets, have been severe enough, but under these woes, with the demon hosts from the prison pit of the underworld, we may expect the worst. In these judgments, the worst is yet to come. It is the order. This bottomless pit is God's prison house or dungeon. In Old Testament times prison houses were underground (see Jer. 38:6), and the experience of the Prophet also.

This pit was sometimes in the court of the prison. See Jeremiah 38:13. It does not only say, "the key to the bottomless pit" but some of the translators agree that it is the "key of the well of the bottomless pit." This may throw some light upon the interrogation put to Job by the Almighty (see Job 38:17). It seems to be the dungeon of demons. They manifest fear lest they be imprisoned there.

Demons acknowledged Christ when He was on earth and confessed what the wise of the world knew not. They knew He was the Lord and Despot of demons. They saw in Him both His manhood and Godhead and confessed His millennial authority in the use of three of His titles. They said: "Jesus, **Thou Son of God Most High."** They acknowledged their guilt and knew well the place of imprisonment and asked present exemption on the ground of future penalty and punishment (see Matt. 8:29; Luke 8:28-30). They besought Him that He would not command them to go away into the "bottomless pit."

Here the bottomless pit is **opened**; at Revelation 20:3 it is **closed** for a thousand years with its inmates awaiting further disposition.

We will look at this locust scourge and its results.

**1. The Place from Which They Came.**

They came out of the smoke out of the bottomless pit. The smoke which shrouded them was as the smoke of a great furnace. It came from the seething boiling lava of the pit. Smoke is associated with the place of torment. When Sodom was destroyed it was as the smoke of a great furnace. But here is a judgment in which it would be "more tolerable for Sodom," on that day (see Gen. 19:24-28). Look again at Revelation 14:10, 11 and see the "smoke of torment."

The excess of smoke resulted in the obscuration of the sun. Upon the horrors of this judgment there comes partial, if not almost complete eclipse. Under the former judgments the sun has been included, but here the darkness is the result of the smoke. The entire scene is like a great eruption of volcanic character with an awful brood of locusts as the product. Moses perhaps was foretelling this day and time in Deuteronomy 29:23.

**2. The Power Committed to Men.**

They have power. The word "power" is three times used in the record (see vss. 3 and 10). Their power is "as the scorpions of the earth." We have but to turn back to the Book of Exodus to behold the power of ordinary locusts but these from the bottomless pit are of greater power. History tells of locust invasions with terror and waste as the result.

**3. The Prohibitions under Which They Scourge.**

These locusts from the bottomless pit are under certain prohibitions. Twice we have the statement—**"They should not."**

"They should not hurt the grass of the earth," or any green thing or trees" (vs. ). "They should not kill them" (vs. 5).

The destroying of one-third of the green grass, the food for stock and domestic animals, was inflicted under the first trumpet. The trees bearing fruit were also destroyed to the amount of one-third. There is to be no further reduction of the food supply of the earth under these locusts, though green stuff, though trees and grass are the objects of locust invasions. They are prohibited from touching all such. It is a command (see vs. 4). Behold the desolation that came to the vegetation in Egypt when the plague from the hand of Jehovah came upon that land:

"Eat every herb of the land that the hail left"
"The fruit of the trees"
"Any green thing in the trees"
"Or in the herbs of the field."

Read the record in Exodus 10:5, 12, 15. But here a strict command and prohibition. There is also instruction that they "should not kill." Their scorpion character permits them to strike and sting, but not to kill. If they could kill it would be pleasant to men compared with the sting of their tails. In these days which we call "the deathless days of the locust scourge," men will do what men have never done in the world—"seek death!" Men have sought by all means to extend, further and protect life and escape death—but not at this time—"Death shall flee from them," says the record (see vs. 6). "The Society for the Extension of Life" of which Ex-President Taft was the President (if we remember correctly) would be indeed an unpopular one in these days. Just think of the character of these dreadful days; men desiring death, seeking death and death fleeing from them. The razor refusing to cut the throat, the gun shot to penetrate the heart and the poison to burn out the vitals. See to it, O man, that you are in Christ, for to such no judgment will come!!

In the present day man takes the life of man and the world is filled with murder, but in these days men would gladly murder each other but it can not be accomplished. Surely the judgments of the Lord are in the earth. As a rule, men dread death with its sting, but here the sting of death would be desirable. It is said that "all a man hath he will give for his life" but here he would give as much for his death.

**4. The Period of Time Covered by the Locust Scourge.**

The period of time covered by this scourge is **"five months."** This is twice mentioned as the duration of time (see vss. 5 and 10). This will be a period of great length for such a judgment. Five months of it will be quite enough. These are actual months and are to be taken literally.

In the Book of Numbers is recorded the judgment of God upon His wilderness people who provoked and despised the Lord. It was for **one month** (see Num. 11:20). This is for five months and the only plague we recall that the time or period of it is made known.

**5. The Particulars of the Appearance of the Locusts.**

The particulars in the description of the appearance of these locusts is interesting in the details. They are not common locusts or such as the world has before seen. They are of strange creation. "They are shaped like horses prepared unto battle." "On their heads were crowns like gold with faces like men." "They had hair like women" and "teeth of lions." They were armored with "breastplates" and "wings" which create a sound like horses and cavalry running to battle. Their tails were "like scorpions" with a "sting in the tail." It would seem a demon imitation of the four living creatures in chapter 4. In the Epistle to the Romans, Paul perhaps had these and "other creatures" of the Book of Revelation in mind when he said, **"Nor any other creature"**

(Rom. 8:39). In Romans 8:35 he got a sort of summary of the judgments of the Book of Revelation:

| | |
|---|---|
| 1. "Tribulation | 5. Nakedness |
| 2. Distress | 6. Peril |
| 3. Persecution | 7. Sword" |
| 4. Famine | |

for these things maintain throughout Revelation from chapter 6 to 19.

The Apostle continues to speak of

| | |
|---|---|
| 1. Life | 6. Things present |
| 2. Death | 7. Things to come |
| 3. Angels | 8. Height |
| 4. Principalities | 9. Depth |
| 5. Powers | 10. **"Any other creature."** |

Along with the former list of seven, these things are also a summary or a resume of the judgment period of the Book of Revelation, for all these persons, things and conditions make the tribulation period. There are strange creatures due in the manifestations of the Book of Revelation and insomuch as they are beyond classification with ordinary creatures, they are included in the statement, "any other creature." Whatever other creatures may appear, and there are others, they also are covered by this one sentence "or any other creature."

### 6. The Punishment They Inflict.

They sting with their tails, for they have tails like scorpions. The weakness of the serpent is in its tail, but not so with these scorpion-like locusts. They **hurt** men for five months. It is bodily pain they inflict. There is exemption only for those who are the sealed of God.

This judgment comes upon those which have "not the seal of God in their forehead." The sealed ones of chapter 7 escape this judgment.

The Prophet Ezekiel doubtless foretold these days:

"And the Lord said unto him, Go through the midst of the city, through the midst of Jerusalem, and set a mark upon the foreheads of the men that sigh and cry for all the abominations that be done in the midst thereof. And to the others He said in mine hearing, Go ye after him through the city, and smite, let not your eye spare, neither have ye pity; slay utterly old and young, both maids and little children, and women; but come not near any man upon whom is the mark, and begin at My sanctuary."

These days are the days when the "Lord is wroth" and has "delivered men to their tormentors" (Matt. 18:34). They would not have eggs, they must take scorpions (see Luke 11:12). If chastisements with "whips" will not suffice, then men must be chastised with scorpions. To His own, God has promised power to tread on "serpents and scorpions" and also victory over "all the power of the enemy." He fulfills His promise. In chapter 9 we have the **scorpions** and in 10, the **serpents,** but they hurt not the sealed ones—they have power to tread on these scorpions.

God has His sealed ones **now** and His sealed ones **then.** We are sealed with that Holy Spirit of promise (see Eph. 1:13), they are sealed with the "seal of God in the forehead" (Rev. 7:3).

**7. The Political Head Over Them.**

"They have a king over them." They are therefore not ordinary locusts for they have no king (see Prov. 30:27). These have a political head and they are commanded by him. Their king is the "angel of the bottomless pit."

This may be the beast that cometh up out of the bottomless pit (see 11:7, 17:8), but, whoever he is, the king of these locusts and his name is made known to both the Jew and the Gentile. His **Hebrew** name is given and also the **Greek.** These judgments are upon both Jew and Gentile. Paul indicated this clearly—said he:

"Unrighteousness, indignation, and wrath, tribulation and anguish, upon the soul of every man that doeth evil, of the Jew first, and also to the Gentile" (Rom. 2:8, 9).

The name of this demon king is made known to both Jew and Gentile.

The two names given here mean "Destroyer" for such is he. Daniel predicts one who will "destroy wonderfully"—"destroy the mighty and holy people" (Dan. 8: 24, 25). Jeremiah refers to him perhaps when he says, "The destroyer of the Gentiles is on his way" (Jer. 4:7), and indeed he is "on his way," everything points to this. The king of the locusts will come, he will see, and succeed in a short-lived conquest.

But kings of any dominion will reign but a brief space, for the King of kings will be shortly and speedily on His way for yet "other woes are to come" (vs. 12).

There can not be anything but "woe," "woe," "woe," for a world that has

1. "Gone in the way of Cain
2. run greedily after the error of Balaam
3. and perished in the gainsaying of Core" (Jude 1: 11).

Lesson Forty-three

## HORSEMEN OF THE APOCALYPSE (Rev.9:13-21)

Under the **fifth trumpet** we saw the "first woe" as **The Deathless Days of the Locust Scourge.** "Two other woes" are "yet to come" (9:12). With the sounding of the **sixth trumpet** is the "second woe." The record of the sounding of this sixth trumpet and the judgment following is found in chapter 9, commencing with verse 13 and extending to chapter 11, verse 14. A total of thirty-four verses are required for description and detail of this period of Divine affliction upon rebellious man.

In the 6th chapter of the Book of Revelation, and under the judgments of the **seven seals**, we saw the four steeds in succession. Ibanez, the great Spanish writer and romanticist, has called the attention of the reading public to **"The Four Horsemen of the Apocalypse."** This book has had unprecedented reading and many who never knew anything about the Book of Revelation, know that in chapter 6, there are four horses and their horsemen which signify **militarism, war, famine** and **pestilence.** He has used fiction to indicate the stubborn facts of a world situation.

In this 9th chapter of Revelation it is not "four horsemen" but **"Two Hundred Thousand Thousand Horsemen of the Apocalypse."** Of these we concern ourselves at present. See 9:13-21.

We shall consider three aspects of this strange judgment.

I. THE UNLOOSED ANGELS—9:13, 14, 15.

II. THE UNRESTRAINED HORSEMEN—9:16-19.

III. THE UNREPENTANT MULTITUDE—9:20, 21.

**I. The Unloosed Angels.**

At the sounding of the sixth trumpet there was a "**voice.**" The word "voice" occurs many times in this Book. The voice came out from the four horns of the "golden altar which is before God." The voice was from the presence of God. It seems to be a cry for vengeance, for no longer are the four horns of the altar available for the sinner, for in these days there is no place of resource from judgment left for the sinner and the ungodly. There was a time when murderers were taken to these, but the murderers of these days of tribulation are not of the repentant sort (see vs. 21). Read II Kings 2:28; Exodus 21:14. These judgments are moving out from the presence of God to the earth. It is the day of His wrath. Remember the words of the 2nd Psalm, "Then shall He **speak** to them in His wrath, and vex them in His sore displeaure" (vs. 5). This is His vexation and His sore displeasure.

At the opening of chapter 7 there were four angels standing at the four corners of the earth. These angels were ministers of God, but the four introduced here are evil angels and have need to be loosed for they are bound or imprisoned.

Of these angels both Jude and Peter have written. There are a number of them "reserved unto judgment" (II Peter 2:4; Jude 1:6) and these are the days **when God is ordering out the reserves.** Four of them are ready and ordered out by the voice of command,

**"Loose the four angels which are bound at the river Euphrates!"**

The prison and demon spirits come at the command. God is permitting them to be unbound that soon their head and king may be bound, and the time of Satan's liberty is greatly limited, when this command goes forth (see Rev. 20:2-7).

Their prison house is at the "river Euphrates" and this is not a figure but a fact.

The river is often mentioned in Scripture. It is of name and fame.

It was one of the four first mentioned in the Bible. See Genesis 2:14. It was mentioned as the eastern boundary of the land as promised to both Abraham and Moses (see Gen. 15:18; Exod. 23:31; Deut. 1:7; 11:24; Josh. 1:4).

David gained a great victory at this river (see II Sam. 8:3). Solomon's reign and its dominion are associated with this river, and horses and horsemen are not foreign to this river, for Solomon had **forty thousand** stalls for his horses and chariots and twelve thousand horsemen (see I Kings 4:24-26).

Here in the Revelation at this river, the horses and horsemen are **millions.** God used a river in the judgments upon the Egyptians and here also.

Jeremiah along with John, saw in prophetic vision this judgment. Said he:

"Order ye the **buckler** and the **shield,** and draw near to **battle. Harness the horses;** and get up, ye **horsemen,** and stand forth with your **helmets;** furbish the **spears,** and put on the brigandines. * * Let not the swift flee away, nor the mighty man escape; they shall stumble and face toward the north by the **river Euphrates.** Who is this that cometh up as a flood, whose waters are moved as the rivers? Come up, ye horses! and rage, ye chariots * * for this **is the day of the Lord God of Hosts,** a day of vengeance, that He may avenge Him of His adversaries: and the sword shall devour, and it shall be satiate and made drunk with their blood; for the Lord God of Hosts hath a **sacrifice** in the north country **by the river Euphrates"** (Jer. 46:3 to 10).

This drive of demons is to cover a definite period of time as also did the scourge of locusts. That scourge covered five months; this appears to cover **thirteen months.**

They are to slay the "third part of men." As food

stuffs and water was reduced **one-third,** here also men are reduced **one-third.** It will be a most terrible scourge of God. We do not know how to compute the number killed as we do not know the extent of the territory included in this judgment, but the slain will doubtless reach millions.

**II. The Unrestrained Horsemen.**

What a cavalry is this! Two hundred thousand thousand horsemen and their horses! And such horses and such horsemen! These come doubtless under the "any other creature" of Romans 8:39. There is no classification for them otherwise, for they are not ordinary creatures. They are demon incarnations. In the days of the Lord, they entered into swine, here the horse.

Demons are "legion," they are many and these two hundred million horses are required for this Klu-Klux-Klan of the underworld of demons! They are the "night riders" of the world's darkest hour! There is no mention of a political head over them as in the case of the locusts, but are under command and conscripted for a definite period of warfare. John saw these horses and the ones sitting on them, and the vision is sure of fulfillment. We believe God and find no difficulty in accepting the Bible as the true and trustworthy Word of God from the beginning to the end.

The war which has just turned the world into a Saturnalia of blood, produced a barrage of fire, gas and brimstone, and if man by science can create instruments and implements of warfare most astounding and unusual, what may the Holy Omnipotent God do when His wrath is kindled?

Can one imagine the charge of this cavalry of horsemen—each horse—with a head in appearance to that of a lion and smoke, fire and brimstone issuing therefrom? It will be the moveable barrage of hell! It will be the demon drive of two hundred million! All other battles will sink into insignificance before this one! And again; imagine thirteen months of it!

The smoke and fire and brimstone is used to kill men. What a furnace this world will be! Stifling brimstone and strangling gas filling the air men breathe! They employ also their tails in this judgment. It is certainly **wonderful,** but God will make these judgments an object of wonder. He has said so (see Deut. 28:5, 9; Exod. 34:10). Read also Jeremiah 8:17 and ponder in the light of this description.

Horses and chariots of fire have been associated with Heaven (see II Kings 2 and 6); they will be also with earth in these days of God's retributive justice. These creatures are God's reserves for battle and war.

Isaiah has spoken of these days when he said, "The inhabitants of the earth are **burned,** and **few men left"** (Is. 24:6). This will indeed be torment before the time for fire and brimstone after this time will continue to be God's instruments of punishment. Men are promising peace for the earth but can not keep their promise as noble as are their hearts to perform it. There is no peace until these days are over. These things must **first** come to pass. The Prophet is right when he says:

"We looked for peace, but no good came; and for a time of health, and **behold trouble! The snorting of his horses** was heard from Dan; the **whole land** trembled at the sound of the neighing of his strong ones: for they are come and have devoured the land, and all that is in it; the city, and those that dwell therein" (Jer. 8:15, 16).

### III. The Unrepentant Multitude.

The goodness of God does not bring men to repentance nor does the wrath of God. The judgment upon Pharaoh did not soften his heart, indeed it "hardened his heart." He became defiant under the hand of God. So also in these days, men are not brought to repentance. When repentance is gone out of the earth, you may be sure the devil is in the earth! They who escaped this death inflicted by the horses, the other **two-thirds** repent not. They continue to worship devils and idols. We are permitted to get a look in upon the world at this time and behold its ungodliness. No wonder Jude says the Lord cometh with ten thousand of His saints to execute judgment upon all that are ungodly—in ungodly deeds and ungodly speeches against Him (see Jude 1:14, 15).

Men will worship the metals and materials, for this is the result of an age of materialism and mammonism. They prefer demons to Deity and stones to a Saviour!

Six, man's number and the number of sin, is here found;

| | |
|---|---|
| 1. Devil worshipers. | 4. Sorceries . |
| 2. Idol worshipers. | 5. Fornication. |
| 3. Murders. | 6. Thefts. |

It is into this sort of a world our Lord will make His advent and not into any other kind. Let us not be **of it,** though while in it bear faithful testimony.

God has forewarned men of His judgments upon such things, therefore let none complain if God be true in His judgments.

Men will not repent of sin, therefore must take the penalty for their sins. See the summary of the situation by the Apostle Paul: **"They which commit such things are worthy of death,"** and this after he has catalogued the very sins mentioned here in the Revelation. Compare Romans 1:24 to 31 with Revelation 9:20, 21. Ponder also Isaiah 8:9; Acts 16:16-18; I Chronicles 10:13; Deuteronomy 18:10 and many such verses in which may be found God's condemnation of all such as are mentioned with this remnant of **two-thirds** of men who have survived the horrors of the horses. May God help us to consider what these things mean to a Godless world. Amen.

Lesson Forty-four

## LION-VOICED ANGEL (Rev.10)

With the sounding of the **Sixth Trumpet,** we beheld **"The Two Hundred Thousand Thousand Horsemen of the Apocalypse"** (see chap. 9:13-21). We considered the unloosing of the angels, the unrestrained horsemen, and the unrepentant multitude. This fulfilled **two** of the **three** woes announced by the eagle (see chap. 8:13).

The events recorded in chapter 10:1 to 11:14 lie between the sounding of the **sixth** and **seventh** trumpet. The **sixth angel** sounds at 9:13 and the results are depicted down to verse 21. The **seventh angel** sounds at 11:15 and therefore the events between those two points are parenthetical and preparatory.

After the breaking of the sixth seal and between the seventh (see chap. 6:12), there was a period of time and a number of significant and important events (see chap. 7). So here also, between the **sixth** and **seventh** trumpets, there are details preceding the sounding of the seventh trumpet which are made known.

In chapter 5 we saw the "Throne Sitter" in whose hand was a book. Here again we have a book, but it is known as the "little book."

In chapter 5 the book was closed waiting for some one to open. Here in chapter 10, the book is **"open."** In chapter 5, the book was in the right hand of Him that sat on the throne. In chapter 10, it is said to be in the hand of an angel who is known as "another" and a "mighty" angel. This "another angel" is distinguished from the seven who sound the seven trumpets.

This chapter, which is introduced by "another" and "mighty" angel, may be divided for the sake of the student as follows:

**I. THE ANGELIC DEPUTATION—10:1 to 5.**

**II. AN OFFICIAL NOTIFICATION—10:6, 7.**

**III. A STRANGE MASTICATION—10:8 to 11.**

We shall look at this in their order and as a preface to **The Two Witnesses.**

## I. THE ANGELIC DEPUTATION—10:1-5.

This angel is cloud-clothed and rainbow-circled. His head, his face, his hands, and his feet came in for special mention. He is an angel minister of authority and majesty. This, his cloud-clothing indicates. The scene recalls Sinai and its clouds and fire. This is a judgment scene indeed. This angel has come with special deputized authority. The parchment, scroll, or little book is a legal document having to do with the earth and its claimants. The little book in chapter 5 was found to be the title deed to an inheritance which had been held by a usurper who must be officially and authoritatively ousted. There was found the **"Kinsman Redeemer"** who could "take the book and open the seals thereof" and begin the persecution proceedings which would ultimately issue in ejection of the squatter from his position and possessions. These proceedings have been in continuance since the Lamb broke the first seal (see Rev. 6:1). They are progressing and have about reached the end. This angel with a special deputation and with this end in view, appears. How striking his appearance! He "came down from Heaven"—from the seat of authority and Divine rule. We have seen the underworld opened, but now the upper-world again—"Heaven." He comes, doubtless straight from Christ, Who is still in Heaven at the "right hand of God." He is one of the "ministers that do His will." When Christ hung on the Cross He could have commanded this angel and legions of them besides, but He did not, for the **first time** He came it was to **put away sin by the sacrifice of Himself.** Now, He comes not as a **sacrifice,** but as a **Sovereign.** "Angels and principalities are subject unto Him," so this one comes at the command of Him Who has **"all** authority in **Heaven** and in **earth."** This authority will soon be on universal display. Clothed with a cloud, crowned with a rainbow, his feet in fire and his face as solar light, in his hand a book and in his mouth a loud cry—what a minister and executor of the Divine vengeance and judgment!

When the little book of chapter 5 was presented and a proper person found to open or break the seals thereof, it was found that the only person in the universe to do this was the **"Lion** of the tribe of Judah."

Here, with this little book, the angel has a voice so loud and of such terror as a **lion** when he **roareth.**

It is a time of vengeance. It is said the lion roars just before he springs upon his prey. From chapter 12 we find the devil come down to the earth. He is as Peter declares, "goeth about as a **roaring lion** seeking whom he may devour." Here is an angel with a voice with the thunderous roar of a lion's voice. The Prophet Joel evidently spoke of this time when he said,

> "The Lord also shall roar out of Zion, and utter His voice from Jerusalem; and the heavens and the earth shall shake: but the Lord will be the hope of His people, and the strength of the children of Israel" (Joel 3:16).

When the angel cried with the strength of a lion's roar, seven thunders answered back in agreement—in one continuous **Amen!** Angel voices and thunders are at other places associated (see John 12:29). John heard the seven thunders and was proceeding to write when he was prohibited. God referred secrecy, and not publicity concerning the events immediately at hand.

## II. THE OFFICIAL NOTIFICATION—10:6, 7.

Notice the action of this angel with the little book and the loud lion-like voice.

He set his **right** food on the **sea** and his **left** foot on the **earth.** He is officially taking possession. He is ready to make an official notification by the way of an official proclamation. He is, so to speak, **staking his claim.** Not as a **prospector,** but as a **prosecutor** who has authority beyond question and controversy to claim an inheritance which has already been judicially conceded with every legal transaction and the demands thereof, fully met and confirmed, so that the One Whose right it is, may take possession thereof and possess His possessions.

In oath and in unquestioned authority, he lifted his hands to Heaven and swore. He took oath in the name of

> "Him that liveth for ever and ever,"
> "Who created Heaven and the things that therein are,"
> "And the earth and the things which are therein."
> "And the sea and the things which therein are."

It is not difficult to understand in Whose name the mighty cloud-covered angel swore, for the Scriptures tell us Who He is "that liveth for ever and ever" (see Heb. 1:8; Rev. 4:9; 5:14; 10:6; 15:7). **It is Christ the coming Lord!**

The Scriptures tell us Who it is that made things in Heaven and earth and in the sea (see Col. 1:16; Eph. 3:9; Eph. 2:10; Rev. 4:11). **It is Christ the coming Lord!**

In His name he sware, for in Him, Christ, all the promises and purposes of God are **"yea"** and **"amen."**

This angel makes official notification, with his feet

on the sea and the land; he takes possession of both in the name of the Lord. This is a formal expression of a matter of which due notice had long since been given. The ruler of this world has long since been an outlaw, but now the official notification of immediate prosecution for the ejection of the false land and sea lord. The kingdoms of the world will soon be the Kingdoms of our Lord and His anointed Christ!

His feet are in possession of **sea** and **land!** The prince of this world has long before been condemned, but now for the **execution of the sentence!** (See John 12:31 and 16:11).

The events in this portion of the Revelation are of a startling significance. The end will soon be reached—justice is speeding forward. The usurper's time is short. He offered the kingdoms of the world to Christ in Matthew 4. Christ refused them. Now, they are His by the Divine right of His heirship and as the purchase of His Blood! Praise the Lord! "Time shall be no more." The sand in the glass of the ages has run out. The dispensation is coming to a close. The millennial age will soon be here. The calendar is about complete. **"Time shall be no more."** The "times of the Gentiles," about fulfilled. The age has finished its period, and probation. "The Lord cometh." This the angel proclaims in official notification. The seventh trumpet will finish and fulfill the words of promise made to the Prophets. They were His servants. He will vindicate each prophecy and the time is at hand.

### III. A STRANGE MASTICATION—10:8 to 11.

The Prophet asked for the book. It was given him with a command to **eat it.** It was a strange mastication! It was strange food. A book became Prophets' food!

It is **sweetness** to know that soon all the promises of

God made for ages unto His people in the Prophets will soon be fulfilled. It is **sweet** to know that soon the earth's rule will pass from the hands of the enemy to the hands of Christ. It is **sweet** to know that soon the evil age will be ended and the Sabbatic age will begin. O, how sweet and solacing!

It is **bitter** to know the final judgments that are to fall under the seven vials!

It is **bitter** to know the terrors of the Lord which will yet fall upon the earth-dwellers.

It is **bitter** to contemplate the fall of Babylon and the Battle of Armageddon which are yet to be!

As with the little book of chapter 5, the mention of kindreds, tongues, peoples and nations, so here with this little book is mentioned "peoples, nations, tongues, and kings" (see 10:11 and also 5:9). John must prophesy unto them. His is yet a wide ministry. Even kings must be the object of his message.

These words "peoples," "nations" and "kings" remind us much of that judgment Psalm, Psalm 2, where they are each and all mentioned.

"Why do the **heathen** (nations) rage, and the **people** imagine a vain thing? The **kings** of the earth set themselves, and the rulers take counsel together, against the Lord, and against His anointed" (Ps. 2:1, 2).

It is to this company of raging **"nations"** and vain imagining **"people"** and confederated **"kings"** that John must prophesy. But the result will be, that in the end;

"Thou shalt break them with a rod of iron; thou shalt dash them in pieces like a potter's vessel" (Ps. 2:9).

And this is fulfilled in Revelation 19, where we read:

"And out of his mouth goeth a sharp sword, that with it he should smite the nations; and **he shall rule them with a rod of iron**; and he treadeth the winepress of the fierceness and wrath of Almighty God" (Rev. 19:15).

Lesson Forty-five

## THE TWO WITNESSES (Rev.11) Part 1

We now come to the Two Witnesses. We approach this subject with prayer and care. Much has been said that perhaps should have been left unsaid. When men go beyond God's revelation, what they say is but speculation. This is not the Book of **speculation,** but the Book of **Revelation.** Again may be repeated that this Book, the Bible, is a book that **says what it means and means what it says.** These two witnesses are two persons who shall appear as the witnesses of God in the days of the tribulation. They have not yet fulfilled their ministry. There is no event in history which has fulfilled it. Though men who have not known that the Book of Revelation is a Book of which the events are future, have made attempt to find the two witnesses, all their findings have failed to fill up the details of this prophecy. These two witnesses have not yet appeared. They will appear in the days when the Church is gone and the "tribulation wrath and anguish" spoken of by Paul is upon the soul of every man, to the Jew first and also to the Gentile.

The Church of God, the Body of Christ, cannot be here, for the Church is "neither Jew nor Gentile" and there is no judgment or tribulation or wrath appointed for any but nations—viz.,—the Jew and the Gentiles.

The **persons** and **things** many have tried to make these two witnesses to be, would be ludicrous, if it were not so serious a matter.

We have tried always to respect the convictions of others, as we desire others to respect our convictions, but by our convictions we must stand. The Book of Revelation is not a Book that is being historically fulfilled. The events of history have not fulfilled the prophecy of this Book. Prophecy is the mold of history, not history the mold of prophecy.

We shall not take the time of our students in discussing the matter.

These two witnesses are two witnesses that will actually witness upon the earth in the coming tribulation days, after the Church, the Body of Christ is gone.

1. They are real persons, not principles or practices.
2. They actually stand upon the earth and prophesy.
3. They prophecy literally and actually a "thousand two hundred and three-score days."
4. They are clothed in sackcloth as they prophesy.
5. They are empowered of God to "shut heaven" and withhold "rain."
6. They have "power over water" to turn water to blood.
7. They have power to smite the earth with plagues —"all plagues, as often as they will."
8. They finish their testimony in the earth.
9. War is made against them by the beast that ascendeth out of the pit.
10. They are overcome by him.
11. They are actually killed.
12. Their dead bodies lie in the streets of Jerusalem, the city where the beast sitteth as God and where our Lord was crucified.
13. Representatives ("they of the" [Rev. 11:9]) of peoples, nations, and tongues shall see them there.

14. They shall remain there for "three days and a half"—**actual time.**

15. Attempt will be made to bury them which will be prevented.

16. It will be a time of merry making for the people of the earth.

17. They shall enjoy the exchange of gifts as the expression of their joy.

18. This is an open show of their contempt for the prophecies they uttered.

19. An actual miracle of resurrection will occur, for the two witnesses shall be raised up.

20. This will create great fear upon those who had been making merry over their death.

21. The miracle of ascension shall then take place and the two witnesses will ascend into Heaven.

22. This will be followed by a great earthquake causing the fall of one-tenth of the city.

23. As a result of the earthquake seven thousand men will be slain.

Now these are the facts as they will occur. These things have not yet occurred. Why turn from the plain and simple Word of God to spiritualize and symbolize these things? Why try to corrupt prophecy to make history? Why try to interpret these prophecies, **which will be literally and actually fulfilled,** into events of the past which they do not fulfill and cannot fulfill? Without doubt, the Lord's table and the believer's baptism has been neglected and even set aside in history, but they are not the two witnesses of this chapter.

The Word of God has been rejected in time past by an apostate church and the Holy Spirit of God has been grieved and sinned against, but these two are not the two witnesses of Revelation 11.

There have been times when God in Heaven has withheld spiritual blessing from the people of God, and there has been famine and thirst for the Word of God; but that period was not the time mentioned in the 11th chapter of Revelation, for it is a time after the Church has been taken from earthly testimony and service.

This will do all right for **application,** but in our judgment, utterly fails as **interpretation.** Why cannot men see that **"interpretation** is one and **application** is many"? There is a wide field for **application,** but interpretation is single and solitary in the Scriptures. If the Bible is a Book other than of this sort, it is no better than the **Book of Mormon** or Mrs. Eddy's so-called and misnamed **"Key to the Scriptures."**

Whatever testimony of witnesses in the past has been rejected, it does not set aside the fact that in the "tribulation" days, the time known as the "day of the Lord" and the "last week" of Daniel's prophecy, two special witnesses of God will appear and prophesy with all the events recorded in Revelation 11, coming to a **literal fulfillment.**

If this 11th chapter of Revelation is not future, but is by application to be fixed as fastened somewhere in the past, then one man has as much right as another to make application. Also one man's application has as much authority as another's, and we may choose to believe whom we will, but this is indeed a poor foundation for faith to rest upon. We are left to believe any man whose application we prefer. But if this is a chapter of prophecy and these things are among the "things to come" and will have their interpretation only in the **actual fulfillment** of them, then we are not left to believe in any man but in God alone Who "cannot lie" and Whose Word is dependable. We prefer this and turn away from the **speculations** and **applications** of man, to the **interpretation** of prophecy which will come to **complete, actual** and **literal fulfillment in all the verbal details of the text.**

We are glad for all of God's dear children who attempt to arrive at the truth of God's Word. We do not think we know it all, for how very ignorant we feel ourselves to be, nor do we consider ourselves the censor of Bible students, but we are confident we cannot arrive at sound and safe understanding of the Scriptures by spiritualizing the same. The Book of Revelation is to be taken literally except where the Spirit of God **expressly speaks,** and the Book of Revelation is thus safeguarded. At the opening of chapter 12 this is signally and simply illustrated and will be considered when that chapter is reached.

Lesson Forty-six

## THE TWO WITNESSES (Rev.11) Part 2

It has been said that "the Bible is the best commentary on the Bible." This is often demonstrated. In the light of the Bible we see light. To compare "spiritual things with spiritual things" is God's way. As we begin the study of the 11th chapter of Revelation, again we see the value of this principle of interpretation. Zechariah's prophecy of the two olive trees is here set out into the light. Let us consider the prophecy of Zechariah briefly:

> "Then answered I, and said unto him, What are these two olive trees upon the right side of the candlestick and upon the left side thereof? And I answered again, and said unto him, What be these two olive branches, which through the two golden pipes empty the golden oil out of themselves? And he answered me and said, Knowest thou not what these be? And I said, No, my Lord. Then said he, These are the two anointed ones, that stand by the Lord of the whole earth" (Zech. 4:11-14).

We now have the confirmation of this prophecy and its true interpretation and are able to identify the two witnesses. Says the Book of Revelation, in speaking of the two witnesses:

> "These are the two olive trees, and the two candlesticks standing before the God of the earth" (Rev. 11:4).

The two "olive trees" were **two persons** in Zechariah's prophecy. The two witnesses are **two persons** in this period of the tribulation. They are not symbols or figures of **anything,** they are **two of God's servants** who will **actually** live and prophesy in the days of the Beast. There were two witnesses in the days of which Zechariah prophesied.

There was **Zerubbabel** the Prince, Zerubbabel means **"dispersed, or begotten in Babylon."** In the first year of Cyrus he was living in Babylon and was there called the **"Prince of the Captivity"** or the **"Prince."** He was head of the tribe of Judah at the time of the return from the captivity. He was raised up to "go build the House of the Lord in Jerusalem." When the Chaldean Kingdom became subject to Cyrus and the second world empire of Daniel's prophecy subjected Jerusalem at the close of the seventy years in Babylon, a notable company marched and moved back to Jerusalem.

With the sacred vessels which Nebuchadnezzar carried away, and copious presents of silver and gold and goods and beasts, Zerubbabel, with Joshua the High Priest, the Prophets Haggai and Zechariah, and a notable company of Levites, the heads of the houses of Benjamin and Judah, marched to "Zion" to the city of God. With a grant from Cyrus he set about at once to rebuild the Temple.

**Joshua the High Priest** witnessed and worked with Zerubbabel. They were God's witnesses in the days of the return of the remnant. They were His two olive trees and lampstands. The two men returned together and worked for the restoration and rebuilding of Jerusalem. Read the following: Haggai 1:1, 12, 14; 2:4; Zechariah 3:1, 3, 6, 8, 9; 6:11.

Under the ministry of these two Old Testament witnesses, Jerusalem was rebuilt after the captivity of seventy years. Under these Old Testament witnesses there was a measuring of Jerusalem (see Zech. 3:1-3).

Under the two witnesses of Revelation, there is a measuring of Jerusalem.

We place the record of the two surveys beside each other for comparison.

**Zechariah**

"I lifted up mine eyes again, and looked, and behold a man with a measuring line in his hand.

Then said I, Whither goest thou? And he said unto me, To measure Jerusalem, to see what is the breadth thereof, and what is the length thereof.

And, behold, the angel that talked with me went forth and another angel went out to meet him" (Zech. 2:1-3).

**Revelation**

"And there was given me a reed like unto a rod: and the angel stood saying,

Rise, and measure the Temple of God, and the altar, and them that worship therein. But the court which is without the Temple leave out, and measure it not; for it is given unto the Gentiles; and the holy city shall they tread under foot forty and two months" (Rev. 11:1, 2).

In the Book of Zechariah, the captivity and servitude is over and Jerusalem is to be rebuilt and with the measuring of the city the two Old Testament witnesses are introduced. But the "seventy years" are to be lengthened intc the **490 years** of Daniel 9. Zerubbabel and Joshua, nor the rebuilt city of Jerusalem **fill the prophecy.** It takes on larger proportions and reaches to the end time for its final and complete fulfillment.

In the Book of Revelation the "times of the Gentiles" are coming to a close. The long servitude of Daniel's calendar is near its end. The long captivity is soon to come to its end. The temple is to be rebuilt for the home coming nation and therefore the measuring angels appear, and with them, the two witnesses. These two may be called the **Zerubbabel and Joshua of Great Coming Restoration.**

They are now ready for their ministry. We will consider them carefully, remembering this is the Book of **Revelation** and not the book of **speculation.** In order to help the student we shall outline the study as follows:

**I. The Period They Prophesy.**

**II. The Provision for Their Protection.**

**III. The Power They Possess.**

**IV. Their Persecutor.**

**V. Their Persecution.**

We shall discuss each of the five divisions briefly.

**I. THE PERIOD THEY PROPHESY. "They shall prophesy a thousand two hundred and three-score days"** (vs. 3).

In verse 2 we find a period mentioned in **months.** There it is 42 months but here the period is computed in **days**—1260 of them.

These **three years and a half** are the years of the great tribulation or the **last half** of **Daniel's seventieth week.**

The time computed into **months,** will be found **twice** in the Revelation—11:2 and 13:5.

1. Connected with the down treading of Jerusalem (see 11:2).

2. The time period of the power of the "beast" (see 13:5).

The time computed in **days,** occurs **twice.**

1. The time period for the ministry of the two witnesses (see 11:3).

2. The time period for the exile of the sun clothed woman unto the wilderness (see 12:6).

These synchronize and harmonize perfectly. These are all events occurring at the same time and covering the same period. They are the events occurring in the last half of the final or seventieth week of the "times of the Gentiles" as outlined in the chronology of Daniel. These three and a half years will be the most momentous and tragic perhaps human history has ever known. This is the "time, times and a half" (three and a half years) of which Daniel also foretold (see Rev. 12:14 and with this Dan. 7:25; 12:7).

Prophecy converges without the least confusion. There is a Divine dove-tailing and morticing in fulfillment that is evidence of the veracity of prophecy.

Elijah had power from God to shut up heaven for this period of time (see James 5:17; Luke 4:25). Thus we see that the "coming evangelists," as Mr. Panton has called them, will exercise their ministry for three and one-half years. Under the conditions that will exist, this will be a long period and only God can sustain and uphold them. This leads us to consider:

## II. THE PROVISION FOR THEIR PROTECTION.

"And if any man will hurt them, fire proceedeth out of their mouth, and devoureth their enemies; and if any man will hurt them, he must in this manner be killed" (vs. 5).

Elijah had power to command fire down from heaven by the command of his mouth and so also will these two witnesses (see II Kings 1:10).

God will make the very words in their mouth fire and will protect them till the time period be fulfilled. They are invulnerable to assault till the work is done. "When they finish their testimony" God permits their enemies to lay hold upon them but for a short time (see vs. 7). Said God unto Jeremiah:

"Wherefore thus saith the Lord God of Hosts, Because ye speak this word, behold, I will make My words in thy mouth fire, and this people wood, and it shall devour them" (Jer. 5:14).

God will make His Word good and He of the eyes of flaming fire will endow His servants with the miracles of combustion and ignition. The elements are all His and He will use them. Man seeks to use fire for destruction by the laws which govern chemistry but when God **of Whom** is all law, declares to make use of them in a time of judgment, man laughs, but this merry-making will not set aside the miracle and its manifestation. At the first coming of Christ when the disciples desired that "fire come down from Heaven and consume them" (Luke 9:54), Jesus rebuked them but in this dispensation of God's severe judgment the fire descends. There is no "grace" at this time nor are judgments tempered with mercy. **It shall be even as God has spoken.** We believe God and if He causes fire to come forth from the mouth of a prophet He can create the chemical elements.

Lesson Forty-seven

## THE TWO WITNESSES (Rev.11) Part 3

In the former lesson we considered these two witnesses as follows:

**I. The Period They Prophesy.**

**II. The Provision for Their Protection.**

We now continue the study to behold,

**III. The Power They Possess.**

**IV. Their Persecutor.**

**V. Their Persecution.**

These, we shall consider in the order above.

### III. THE POWER THEY POSSESS.

**"And I will give power unto My two witnesses"** (vs. 3).

These two are empowered of God. "Power belongeth unto God" and never has this been so strikingly confirmed and exemplified as at this time. It is the earth against **two** and an angry earth at that. We must remember that if men's hearts are not softened by the grace of God in Christ, they will not be by the judgments of God. Man was never so defiant as in these days of tribulation. Revelation 10:21 is still the **social state** and **rebellious condition** of the world of mankind—**they have not repented of murders,** nor will they at this time but prepare to perpetrate yet further murder and rid the world of the two witnesses, for they **will not tolerate a testimony against them.** This is the natural heart of man **at all times,** but especially at this time. But God has given His two witnesses power. Their power is threefold and as follows:

1. **They have power to shut up heaven that it rain not** (see vs. 6).

2. **They have power over waters to turn them to blood** (see vs. 6).

3. **They have power to smite the earth with plagues at will** (see vs. 6).

It will be seen their power reaches to the air, the clouds even unto the astronomical world. They shut up heaven and hold back rain. They bring drought into the earth. They leave a dry and parched world for angry and aroused men! This is a cause for a new outbreak for wrath! They are empowered to hold back rain the days of their prophecy which is **"three years and a half."**

This will add to the famine and pestilence already in the earth, by the reason of the trumpet judgments. The fields will be burned and non-productive, the fruit trees will yield no fruit and the rivers and foundations are dried up. The hand of death and famine and pestilence is laid on everything. This is charged to the two witnesses and it is only fear that holds back the wrath of the earth-dwellers against these two anointed ones of God. They would hurt them and doubtless some have attempted this, but to find that fire comes down from heaven and devours them. There have been perhaps many examples of this and fear is upon men, though hate is in their hearts (see vs. 5). These are dark and terrible days and it is cause to praise God that we, the members of Christ's Body the Church, will not come into these days. These days are the days of judgment and they can not be spiritualized away or vaporized by application into meaninglessness. They are the judgments upon the Jew and the Gentile, when the Church which is "neither Jew nor Gentile," is gone.

The power to shut heaven for three years and a half reminds us of Elijah and it may be that one of these is Elijah, though the Book of Revelation does not say so, nor does the prophecy of Zechariah when these two witnesses are mentioned there.

It would be speculation for us to affirm assuredly that Elijah and Enoch, or Elijah and Moses, or either of the two together, are the two witnesses, as there is "no sure word of prophecy."

Many think these two are Elijah and Moses, or Elijah and Enoch, and we have no quarrel, as there is much to indicate this, but we do not know. We know they are God's two witnesses and the names He has been pleased to withhold. Elijah is to "appear," perhaps this is that appearance, though we could not be over sure, though many far better taught teachers than we, think so and we are thus inclined, but will not be dogmatic. Elijah prayed and heaven was closed for three and a half years, and he also brought down fire from heaven. Moses also had power to turn water into blood and smite the earth with a plague and with plagues. These may be Moses and Elias. It is difficult to settle and we feel a little timid and speak sparingly.

**They have power over waters** to turn them to blood and this adds also to the famine, pestilence and distress of the earth. For the flocks may not drink nor the cattle. This further imperils the food supply and increases the pain of famine. And to this famine, brought about by the power of the two witnesses to withhold the water from above and turn to blood the water already beneath, power to bring plagues, adds yet another feature of these days.

It will be seen how with famine comes pestilence. But

this is the order of the former "four horsemen"—famine, pestilence and death (see Rev. 6:1-5). This is the order as outlined by Jesus in this second sermon on the mount, or the Olivet prophecy—"war, famine, and pestilence" (see Matt. 24:5, 6). This is the order of Ezekiel's prophecy (see Ezek. 5:17).

These two witnesses have power and none can prevail against them till their ministry is finished. They are invulnerable and unconquerable till their work is done.

We will next consider:

**IV. THEIR PERSECUTORS. "The Beast that ascendeth out of the bottomless pit shall make war against them"** (vs. 7).

The record of the appearance of the Beast is left till the 13th chapter, but he is on the earth in the 11th chapter and the two witnesses are upon the earth during the events of the 13th chapter. His revelation has taken place before or during the ministry of the two witnesses, for he is their persecutor. The Beast that cometh up out of the abyss is the one who leads this persecution. It will be well to take a general look at him now and later we shall go into general detail when chapter 13 is reached. This glimpse at him now will accentuate the record of the persecution and the persecutor. Rev. 13:1-8.

The two witnesses exercised their ministry for the forty and two months and so also was power given unto the Beast to continue **forty and two months.** Perhaps the ministry of both the witnesses and the Beast was exercised at the same period.

**V. THEIR PERSECUTION. The Beast * * shall make war against them, and shall overcome them, and kill them." "Their dead bodies shall lie in the street of the great city"** (vss. 7, 8).

This war against the two witnesses is commenced by the Beast, when their **ministry is finished,** he **"overcomes them."** The world rejoices—it is the hour of a great triumph! The word is sent from mouth to mouth and sent by rapid despatch to all the world! The papers will doubtless bear great headlines,

**"THE BEAST HAS OVERCOME THE TWO WITNESSES!!"**

**Their Power Gone They Become Easy Prey!!**

There will be a celebration and a jubilation! It will be a time of "merry-making." Another message by wire or cable or through the air may state:

**"THE BEAST HAS KILLED THE TWO WITNESSES!!"**

**These Two Troublers Are Triumphed Over at Last!!**

The two witnesses are dead. It is a tragic hour in the history of the world! Who knows all it may mean? What days will these be in the world of men and nations? God help us to think!

Three days and a half their dead bodies are on the streets of Jerusalem, the city where our Lord was crucified. Not since the death of Christ has such a tragedy ever been enacted, and now, in addition to the death of Christ, another judgment is due the nations. There is international joy and rejoicing. **All Nations** celebrate and send gifts, one to another. Commerce is thereby quickened and trade improved. The shops are astir. A time for exchange of gifts has come. There is celebration and jubilation everywhere. Every one is purchasing gifts and every means of transportation is taxed to the limit. Gifts are passing to and fro with each gift bearing a congratulation and satisfaction.

**The two witnesses are dead!** All methods of communication are put to full use. The **cable** and the **wire** and the **air** and whatever other method of communication may then maintain, are all put to full use. Message after message is sent to celebrate the victory over the two witnesses of God. **They are dead.** After three years and a half of power, they are now captured and their bodies are on the street of the city! This is the cause of all the merry-making.

One can imagine a message after this manner from one political leader to another. It might be somewhat after this order;

"Thanks to the Super-man the Beast, we are now rid of the two tormentors, known as the two witnesses. Now let joy be unrestrained and revelry begin. Let commerce be resumed and the world again follow its pleasures and pursuits."

Thus they make merry over murder. They rejoice that heaven can not be shut and rain withheld. They are merry because there is no more fire to come down from heaven and no more plagues, little knowing that **the vials of God's wrath,** are yet to be poured out upon the earth. They are glad because they hate God! This will be the world's most godless period. Jude 1:15 will have much meaning here.

But now turn your attention to the streets of Jerusalem, and behold the bodies of the two witnesses. The Psalmist had foreknowledge and prophetic foreview of these two witnesses. Long before John saw the visions on Patmos the Spirit of prophecy came upon David. He describes this scene. Let us go back to David to better understand John.

"O God, the heathen are come into Thine inheritance; Thy holy Temple have they defiled; * * The dead bodies of Thy servants have they given to be meat unto the fowls" (Ps. 79:1, 2).

"Wherefore should the heathen say, Where is their God? Let Him be known among the heathen in our sight by the revenging of the blood of Thy servants which is shed" (Ps. 79:10).

"Preserve Thou those that are appointed to die" (vs. 11).

And the prayer is answered—they are "preserved" for

behold, in the midst of the merry-making a great miracle occurs.

They are passing the bodies as they rest in the street. Most bitter and cruel are the utterances. They are cursed in death. We might hear such insults and denunciations as these:

"Now where is your power to shut up heaven?"

"You brought plague upon us, now we take pleasure in your death!"

"Honor and majesty and might and power be unto the Beast who brought thy death!"

"You trusted in your God let Him deliver thee!"

When suddenly, after three and a half days of such scorn and contempt and carnival had been in the earth, **life from God entered into them** (see vs. 11) and **"they stood upon their feet"** (vs. 11). The frolic was turned to fright and fear, and terror seized upon all, and revelry was turned to consternation. **"Great fear fell upon all of them"** (vs. 11).

O, what an hour, what a sight, what a vindication of God's servants.

A great voice like thunder said, **"Come up hither"** and they ascended up to Heaven in a cloud in **full sight of their enemies** (see vs. 12).

Was there ever anything like this in the world before?

The same hour there was a great earthquake. The tenth part of the city fell with a casualty list of **seven thousand!** (see vs. 13). Surely the judgments of God are in the earth. It is the day of His wrath.

Lesson Forty-eight

## PROCLAMATION, PRAISE AND PROGRAM (Rev.11:14-19)

In the preceding studies we have seen **"The Testimony, Tragedy and Triumph of the Two Witnesses."** They gave their testimony under the sounding of the **sixth trumpet.** It was also the time of the **"second woe."** See 8:13 and 11:14, 15. The events related beginning with 8:13 to 11:15 have all occurred under the sounding the **seventh trumpet** and the **"second woe"** of which the loud-voiced eagle gave notification at chapter 8:13. We are now ready for the sounding of the **seventh trumpet** and the beginning of the **third woe.** Read: Rev. 11:14-19.

Once again from the judgments upon the earth we turn our eyes to **Heaven.** The sounding of the **seventh angel** with the **seventh trumpet** is an introduction to the final series of judgments upon the earth known as the **seven vials,** indeed, it is our conviction that the **seventh trumpet** includes the **seven vials** as the **seventh seal** included the seven trumpets. The **seven vials** or seven last plagues of the **"third woe"** begin to be poured out in chapter 16:1, 2. Before the first vial is poured out, and under the seventh trumpet period, there is what seems to be a break while the details of the "great sign" of chapter 12 is explained in chapters 12, 13 and 14. The result of the sounding of the seventh trumpet is resumed at 16:1 when the vials are poured out, one succeeding the other.

This **seventh trumpet** is not, in our judgment, the

**"last trump"** of I Corinthians 15:52. It is called the **seventh trumpet** and is but the last of a series of seven. It does not convey that there are no more trumpets. The record here says the **"seventh angel sounded."** That does not infer it is the last angel and that there are no other angels. Personally, we are convinced that the "last trump" of I Corinthians 15:52 does not refer to any event occurring in the time of the tribulation which is recorded in Revelation 6 to 19. There are some who hold, and we respect them, that the church passes through the tribulation period up to the point of Revelation 11:7 and identify the seventh sounding angel with the "last trump" of I Corinthians 15. We can not accept this, for in our judgment the Church, the body of Christ, does not come into the tribulation or any part of it. That the Church will be raised and raptured prior to these days, is in our sincere conviction, the teaching of the Scriptures.

At the sounding of this seventh angel, there was much interest and activity in Heaven. The long ages of **foretelling** are now about to reach their **fulfilling.** The Kingdom long promised is about to be established. The rejected King is to be the returning and reigning King. The prayer in which is the petition, **"Thy Kingdom come, Thy will be done on earth as it is in Heaven,** is about to receive its answer. **"Great voices"** were heard in Heaven saying:

> "The kingdoms of this world are become the kingdoms of our Lord, and of His Christ; and He shall reign for ever and ever."

It is an official announcement—a sort of a proclamation. This is the long-looked for event. The "ruler of this world's darkness" will soon yield the kingdoms to Christ which he at another time offered to Christ, (see Matt. 4:8, 9), as a bribe for worship. The "times of the Gentiles" have run their course and the kingdoms of the world must pass under the rule and reign of Messiah, David's Son and Lord! The dynasty of David that is "fallen down" is now to be "raised up" and "a King shall reign in righteousness." The days of the "overturning" are about at an end and the days of the Sovereignty of Christ at hand! The time has come when He shall bruise Satan under His heel. It will indeed be "shortly" now. See Romans 16:20. Soon there will be a shout in the land. **"The Lord is king for ever and ever."** The song at the sea is about to be sung anew —"The Lord shall reign for ever and ever" (Ps. 10:16; Exod. 15:18). Daniel's prophecy is now to be performed in dramatic fulfillment. The days of "these kings" which Daniel mentioned are about complete. It is time for the "God of Heaven to set up a Kingdom." It is a Kingdom which shall never be destroyed. It is the Kingdom of Christ, God's Divine Despot—**"It shall break in pieces and consume all these kingdoms and it shall stand forever"** (Dan. 2:44). It is near the time of the advent of the Lord. It is the hour of His coming and coronation. It is time for the vindication of Daniel's prophecy and the manifestation of the King he promised in his holy prophecy. Says Daniel,

> "One like the Son of Man came with the clouds of Heaven, and came to the Ancient of days, * * and there was given Him dominion, and glory, * * which shall not pass away, and His Kingdom which shall not be destroyed" (Dan. 7:13, 14).

This announcement brought forth again expressions from the **four and twenty Elders.** When at the opening of the Book of Revelation there was a search to find some one who could take the book and open the seals thereof, and there was one found—then they broke into praise and worship and now that the work is about accomplished, they again adore the Lord and Lamb. In their first praise they voiced especially His purchase (see 5:9), but here they speak of His **power.** There was a time when Jesus stood before the tribunal of an earthly ruler and said:

"My Kingdom is not from this world, if My Kingdom were from this world, then would My servants have fought, that I should not be delivered to the Jews, but now My Kingdom is not from hence" (John 18:36).

But this time is now past, the dispensation of His exile from the earth is finished, His Heavenly work now gives place to the exercise of His earthly power and He takes the Kingdom and reigns and the trumpet proclaims and the elders praise, as the time of the event draws near. The testimony of the two witnesses and the tragedy which followed their testimony, has filled up the cup of the world's defiance against God. He now takes the power and authority that is His and with rapid succession the remaining judgments will be poured out upon the earth. As one day the trumpet sounded and the people said "Absalom reigneth in Hebron," so one of these days David's true Son and the Greater than Solomon will be proclaimed king of all the earth! Amen! and Amen !!

After the **proclamation** and the **praise,** there is outlined a **program** or a resume of events in anticipation (see vss. 17, 18).

**I. His Right**—"taken to Thee Thy great power."

**II. His Reign**—"and hast reigned."

**III. The Rebellion of the Nations**—"the nations were angry."

**IV. His Retribution**—"Thy wrath is come."

**V. His Recompense**—"time of the dead to be judged."

**VI. His Reward**—"give reward unto servants, prophets and saints."

**VII. His Righteous Judgments**—"and destroy them which destroy the earth."

These seven events will quickly follow. In the following chapters these things are each accomplished. Keep an open eye for the immediate fulfillment of this program. Following this outlined program of events which are looked upon as accomplished, once again is the opened Heaven and within the opened Heaven an **"open temple"** and a repetition of the events that preceded the sounding of the **seven trumpets** (see 8:5). There were "lightnings, and voices, and thunderings, and an earthquake and great hail" (vs. 19).

There are **seven** great **"openings"** in the Book of Revelation and this is the **fourth.**

1. **A Door** is opened in Heaven (see 4:1).
2. **The Seals** are opened (see 6:1-9).
3. **The Abyss** is opened (see 9:2).
4. **The Temple** of God is opened (see 11:19).
5. **The Tabernacle** of testimony is opened (see 15:5).
6. **The Heaven** is opened (see 19:11).
7. **The Books** are opened (see 20:12).

Lesson Forty-nine

## MAN-CHILD AND THE DRAGON (Rev.12) Part 1

At the close of chapter 11, where we beheld the tragedy and the triumph of the Two Witnesses, our gaze was directed to Heaven. Chapter 12 is a continuation of chapter 11 and begins with the word **"and."** Every verse of chapter 12, save one, begins with the word **"and."**

There are **two "wonders"** in this chapter and both of them will now come under our consideration. The first **wonder** is called a **"great wonder"** (see 12:1). The second **wonder** is called **"another wonder"** (see vs. 3). **Both** of these "wonders" appear in Heaven.

We shall read the inspired record of these two "wonders."

### THE FIRST "WONDER" ("Great").

"And there appeared a **great wonder** in Heaven; A woman clothed with the sun, and the moon under her feet, and upon her head a crown of twelve stars. And she being with child cried, travailing in birth, and pained to be delivered" (12:1, 2).

### THE SECOND "WONDER" ("Another").

"And there appeared **another wonder** in heaven, and behold a great red dragon, having seven heads and ten horns, and seven crowns upon his heads.

"And his tail drew the third part of the stars of Heaven and did cast them to the earth, and the dragon stood before the woman which was ready to be delivered for to devour her child as soon as it was born" (vss. 3, 4).

The word "wonder" here is **"sign."** The Greek word is **"semeion"** a sign, and not **"teras,"** "wonder." In this we see the unerring guidance of the Spirit of God Who makes plain throughout this Book what is figurative and what is symbolic, and distinguishes between them and the literal.

That a sign should appear at this important place in the Book of Revelation is not the unexpected. Special **"signs"** had been prophesied and are now to come to fulfillment. This is the sign of things yet to come, just as a cloud in the sky is a sign of rain at hand. See Matthew 16:3.

The Pharaisees asked for a "sign" and we must not think it strange in these days when the Church, the Body of Christ, is gone, that these signs be granted.

Doubtless this particular "sign" was spoken of by Jesus when He said, "There shall be signs in the **sun,** and in the **moon,** and in the **stars"** (Luke 21:24, 25).

The sun, moon and stars were given originally for "signs." "Signs" is first in the Divine Record, then "seasons." Said God:

> "Let there be lights in the firmament of the heaven to divide the day from the night, and let them be for signs, and for seasons, and for days, and years" (Gen. 1:14).

These are at Revelation 12 employed for an end-time-of-the-age sign. This is most significant, for in this "great sign" is mentioned each of these:

1. A woman clothed with the **sun.**
2. The **moon** under her feet.
3. Upon her head a crown of twelve **stars.**

These lights have not only through the centuries and millenniums of time served as lights for the world of mankind by day and by night, but now in a sign language they are to speak in the darkest night the world of human history has ever known. God will employ them as symbols as He has used them for seasons.

Nor is this the first time God has ever used the sun, the moon and the stars for signs to signify and communicate His Divine will and program.

By these, doubtless, early revelation was made prior to revelation in the **Written Word.** This may have been and doubtless was God's way of speaking before the call and choice of Abraham. This was God's **primitive** revelation and the written Word of God coming through the Jewish race given later, became **permanent** revelation. This revelation in the things God had created, was so plain, legible and sufficient, that a Holy and Righteous God could condemn the Gentile world and all the world, prior to Abraham, and from Adam to Abraham, as **"without excuse."** God's judgments are righteous and unless the revelation has been sufficient the judgment would never have been pronounced.

This is a passage of Scripture which confirms this position and in our judgment could be understood no other way.

We read in the Epistle to the Romans:

"For the wrath of God is revealed from Heaven against all ungodliness and unrighteousness of men, who hold the truth in unrighteousness;

Because that which may be known of God is manifest in them; for God hath shewed it unto them.

For the invisible things of Him from the creation of the world are clearly seen, being understood by the things that are made, even His eternal power and Godhead; so that they are without excuse."

There was a time when God made known His redemptive plan by another and earlier reading than the alphabet. God has never been shut up that He could not speak to man. It distinctly says, "That which may be known of God is manifest." And again: **"For God hath shewed it unto them."** This is sufficient. What did "He shew unto them"? **"Invisible things,"** that is, things that are of the spiritual world and having to do with things affecting faith and destiny, things that abide in the realm of faith and beyond the realm of reason.

How did He show these invisible things?

By the use of things visible—they were "understood by the things which were made."

By the visible things, things which were made, He made known His **"eternal power and Godhead,"** the **Father, Son and Holy Spirit!** These are staggering Scriptures but **truthful!** This revelation of the Godhead was ample, it was enough that the rejection of it would bring a "without excuse" judgment and indictment from God. God made the heavens intelligible to the mind of man and through the lights in the heavens, the "sun, moon and stars," He communicated His great purposes of Redemption by this means. He used the sun and the moon and the stars. There are those today who attempt to read the stars and the heavens but with little success, for this was God's primary way before the permanent revelation in the Written and Living Word of God. He has erased that communication from the blackboard of His revelation and calls men to read the full and final revelation in His Word, the Bible, and His Son, Christ! Men will not do this and still attempt to read the heavens, but with no deciphering or understanding.

There is no doubt in our mind that God preserved the great prophecy of Genesis 3:15 in the configuration and constellation of the stars. They had a language. They had a speech; it was heard. It had a universal publication. The heavens were used as a document, as a papyrus or a scroll. This may seem startling and such it is! The 19th Psalm is as a book with two chapters or two divisions. It has two pages—on one of them we see the revelation of God in His works. On the other we see the revelation of God in His Word. The **first** division of the 19th Psalm is the book of nature. The **second** division of Psalm 19 is the book of things spiritual. One division—verses 1 to 7—shows God's speech in nature or His works. The other division—verses 7 to 14—show God's speech through His

Word. We place these in comparison for the student's consideration.

**Revelation in the**
**WORKS OF GOD**
(Primeval)

"The heavens declare the glory of God; and the firmament sheweth His handiwork.

"Day unto day uttereth speech, and night unto night sheweth knowledge.

"There is no speech nor language, where their voice is not heard.

"Their line is gone out through all the earth, and their words to the end of the world. In them hath He set a tabernacle for the sun,

"Which is as a bridegroom coming out of his chamber, and rejoiceth as a strong man to run a race.

"His going forth is from the end of the heaven, and his circuit unto the ends of it: and there is nothing hid from the heat thereof."

**Revelation in the**
**WORD OF GOD**
(Permanent)

"The law of the Lord is perfect, converting the soul: the testimony of the Lord is sure, making wise the simple.

"The statutes of the Lord are right, rejoicing the heart: the commandment of the Lord is pure, enlightening the eyes.

"The fear of the Lord is clean, enduring for ever: the judgments of the Lord are true and righteous altogether.

"More to be desired are they than gold, yea, than much fine gold: sweeter also than honey and the honeycomb.

"Moreover by them is thy servant warned: and in keeping of them there is great reward.

"Who can understand his errors? cleanse Thou me from secret faults.

"Keep back thy servant also from presumptuous sins; let them not have dominion over me: then shall I be upright, and I shall be innocent from the great transgression.

"Let the words of my mouth, and the meditation of my heart, be acceptable in Thy sight, O Lord, my strength, and my redeemer."

In the first division we have the heavens with the **SUN** in them.

In the second division we have the Scriptures with the **SON** in them. Thos. Boys has given us a valuable skeleton of this Psalm. There is nothing better; we publish it here:

**PSALM NINETEEN—The Skeleton.**

A. **Verses 1 to 4—The HEAVENS.**

B. **Verses 4 to 6—The Sun in them.**

A. **Verses 7 to 10—The SCRIPTURES.**

B. **Verses 11 to 14—Thy Servant in them.**

We see by a glance at the above comparison that the "heavens declare the glory of God." The glory of God is a result of a manifestation of God resulting from redemption accomplished. It is not the power of God here in creation, but the glory of God. The heavens declare this redemption and such was the case in the early times. There was a speech, a logos, a word that went out to all the earth. Each speech and language heard this primitive voice and saw the recordings of redemption in the signs of the heavens. There was nothing hid.

Then at **verse 7** is the record of God's Word, and under the words "law," "testimony," "statutes" and "commandments" the written Word of God is declared and praised.

That the heavens did bear witness for God and was the recording of God is confirmed by Romans 10:18, where verse 4 of this Psalm is significantly quoted. Says Paul,

> "So then faith cometh by hearing, and hearing by the word of God.
>
> "But I say, Have they not heard? Yes verily, their sound went out into all the earth, and their words unto the end of the world."

Now again, in the Book of Revelation God turns to the heavens for a "sign," a "great sign" and another sign. This 12th chapter is of vast importance. Its symbolism takes on a great realism. It is a summary of the past and a sign for the immediate present in the tribulation days.

Lesson Fifty

## MAN-CHILD AND THE DRAGON (Rev.12) Part 2

We have, at this 12th chapter, which is the "Great Sign Chapter" come to the very heart of the Book of Revelation.

We cannot introduce the Church, the Body of Christ, here, for the Church is not, in our judgment, in the tribulation period. The great "sign" we believe to be a summary of Israel's history and the general features of this sign in Heaven are found in Genesis 37, where another Son of Jacob's house was persecuted and like the "Man-Child" exalted to a throne.

"Behold, I have dreamed a dream and, behold, the
**Sun**
and the **moon**
and the eleven **stars**
made obeisance unto me" (Gen. 37:9).

Jacob made interpretation of the dream to the effect that it signified the nation of which he was the head for said he:

"Shall I and thy mother and thy brethren indeed come to bow down ourselves to thee to the earth?" (vs. 10).

We are constrained to use these signs and symbols as they were first used—to signify the nation Israel.

This is not the first instance in the Holy Scriptures where Israel is compared to a woman. At the head of chapter 54 of the Scofield Bible is the caption—

**"Israel the Restored Wife of Jehovah"**

These are significant words and should not be considered lightly. At the opening of this chapter we have mention of "travail with child" as at Revelation 12.

"Sing, O barren, thou that didst not bear; break forth into singing, and cry aloud, thou that didst not travail with child: for more are the children of the desolate than the children of the married wife, saith the Lord" (Is. 54 1)

And again:

"Thou shalt not remember the reproach of thy **widowhood** any more" (vs. 4).

And again:

"For thy Maker is **thine husband**" (vs. 5).
"The Lord hath called thee as a **woman forsaken**" (vs. 6).
"How is she become a widow!" (Lam. 1:1).

See also important verses bearing on this subject—Isaiah 48; Jeremiah 3; Luke 18.

This woman bore a "man-child" and from the first announcement, at Genesis 3:15, that a woman should bear a child that would bruise the "serpent's head," the "dragon" has stood ready to devour the child. Some one has significantly said: "The reason Satan hates **the first three** chapters of Genesis and **the last three** of Revelation is because in the **first three** chapters of the Bible his sentence is **pronounced** and in the **last three** chapters of the Bible his sentence is **executed.**"

The record of Divine revelation from Genesis to Revelation is the tragedy of the dragon attempting to devour the woman's "manchild," but never coming to triumph!

This "sign" at chapter 12, is a summary of this conflict and an historical review of it.

At the birth of the first woman's "man-child," the dragon stood ready to devour him. Abel was slain by his brother. A murderous attempt upon the first-born commenced then, and **continued down to the Cross!** The first child was murdered and by his brother. Christ, the "man-child," was murdered and by His brethren after the flesh.

The source and secret of Cain's hatred is made known to us by the Apostle John, and sure enough, it was the "old dragon" who was the instigator and originator! See I John 3:12. Cain was of **"that evil one."**

God "appointed another." Eve called his name **Seth.** He was "another seed" taking the place of Abel whom Cain slew.

But the "old dragon" awaited the Seth line and stood ready to devour them and upon a corrupt and violent world God brought a judgment of flood and in Shem, according to the flesh, the "man-child" was caught up, in the ark and carried over the waters of judgment and out of death! Surely the dragon was ready to "devour."

Then came Abraham and Sarah his wife, who was barren. God miraculously gave them the "man-child" Isaac and in Isaac the seed was called (see Heb. 11:17). In type, Isaac passed through death but was caught up in resurrection, back to his father's bosom and love.

The dragon now waits to devour the man-child of the Messianic line. The struggle cf Jacob is an evidence of this as also is that of Joseph who was taken from a pit and taken up to a throne.

Moses escaped the wrath of the adversary and was preserved when the edict had gone forth to slay the man-child.

In the days of Ahab and Jezebel, the royal line was reduced to one child Joash, and the dragon awaited to devour him but he was borne away to the throne and the woman's man-child was safe.

In the day of Isaiah the Prophet another attempt was made to devour a man-child when Israel entered an alliance with Rezin, the king of Syria, against Judah and attempted to place Tabeal on the throne of Judah and overthrow the purpose of God in enthroning the man-child of the House of David and the woman's seed on the throne of the Dynasty of David! It was there the promise of the Virgin Birth is clearly foretold.

At last **the woman** brings forth the **man-child!** The long promised is now performed! Time became "full" and God was faithful and the virgin bore the "man-child."

It is said that every mother in America whose son went "over there" and died in France and was laid in an unknown grave, cherishes the hope that that unknown and honored soldier buried with such pomp and pretense may be her son.

It is said that every woman in Israel had a secret hope that she might be the hand-maiden of the Lord and the mother of the promised man-child, the woman's seed.

The words of Jesus are significant indeed and worthy of meditation;

> "A woman when she is in travail hath sorrow, because her hour is come; but as soon as she is delivered of the child, she remembereth no more the anguish, for joy that a **MAN** is born into the world" (John 16:21).

Mary was the chosen virgin and she forgot her anguish for the joy that a man was born into the world.

He was the God-man—the "man Christ Jesus." He was the woman's man-child the dragon would seek to devour!

In Galatians 4:4, 5—we have a brief statement for the great event of the incarnation when the woman brought forth her **"man-child."**

1. **The Prophecy Performed**—"When the fulness of time was come,"
2. **The Performer**—"God,"
3. **The Person**—"sent forth His Son,"
4. **The Process**—"made of a woman,"
5. **The Period**—"made under the Law,"
6. **The Purpose**—"to redeem them that were under the Law."

This involves the earthly life of Christ from His cradle to the Cross and from the Cross to the throne.

This verse is a summary of all events from the time the "woman brought forth her man-child," until He is "caught up to God and to His throne."

Was the "dragon," standing "ready to devour" the man-child? He was. A decree went forth to destroy all the babes under two years of age. The net was laid in vain for Christ! (see Matt. 2:13). The "dragon" attempted the slaying of Christ when He had come to years and to the threshold of His ministry by challenging Him to cast Himself down from the pinnacle of the Temple. There was no success (see Matt. 4:6).

The dragon infuriated the people of Nazareth to take Christ out and throw Him over the brow of the hill and leave His mangled body among the stones at its base! Anything to keep Christ from going to the Cross a voluntary offering unto God for the sins of the whole world.

He stirred up enmity and hatred, he stirred up storms and seas, he fed the hatred of the Pharisees and the rulers, but to no avail! The man-child shall not fail until He is "caught up to God and to His throne"! Christ **could not** and **cannot** fail under **any circumstances!** There is not an extreme of the universe that can overthrow Him or overcome Him! He can not fail! There is no crisis where there is a Christ! Amen and Amen!!

Then the "man-child," the woman's seed, went to the Cross, but this Cross was not only His death but His Cross **was the death of death!!** He, like David, who used the sword of Goliath with which to slay Goliath, took death, the weapon of Satan, and with death destroyed him who had the power of death! Praise God!

Then they sealed Him in a tomb! But what are tombs to the Triumphant One! What are underground prisons of the dead to One Who had the keys? Death could not hold Him! The grave was not the victor but He was Victor over the grave!

He came up from the grave in resurrection and went up to Heaven in ascension! He was "caught up" to God and to His throne! A great company saw Him go! He was taken up. Five hundred saw Him go! He went up to the throne of God! The dragon did not **"devour Him!"** He ever liveth and is at the right hand of the Majesty on high!

The woman's man-child is safe and the universe is safe in His Sovereign keeping!

Peter refers to this enmity and the extent of it when he says:

"The kings of the earth stood up, and the rulers were gathered together against the Lord, and against His Christ.

For of a truth against **Thy Holy Child,** Jesus, Whom Thou hast anointed, both Herod, and Pontius Pilate, with the Gentiles, and the people of Israel, were gathered together" (Acts 4:26, 27; also vs. 30).

But does this bring the conflict of the ages to an end? By no means, for now at the end of the age the conflict is renewed with the wrath of the dragon as the wrath of one who knows his time is short. The man-child will soon take the kingdom and reign—what will be the outcome?

Lesson Fifty-one

## MAN-CHILD AND THE DRAGON (Rev.12) Part 3

We saw in the former lecture, the woman's Man-child "caught up to God, and unto His throne." At the end of Christ's earthly life as at the beginning, there is a notable and miraculous manifestation. At the beginning of the Gospels, Christ has come down. At the close He has gone up. He came down in the miracle of the incarnation and has gone up in the miracle of the ascension. He came down beneath angels (for a "little while"), He has gone up far above angels for all time. Now that the Son from Israel's race has been caught up into Heaven this does not make an end of anti-Semitism—indeed, the woman is now the object of Satan's hatred, and in the tribulation days God will prepare a hiding-place for the nourishing of the faithful remnant. The "woman" who brought forth the Man-Child will be cared for in God's special manner.

In these days the 23d Psalm will be especially significant. It is a comfort to **any** now who read it, but it will be particularly consoling to the faithful remnant of Israel in the days of the great tribulation. The Bible is a timeless Book—and is for use of generations yet unborn. We desire in our selfishness to consume the Bible on ourselves, but this Book is a book greater than any one generation or any one dispensation.

In the days when the "Idol shepherd" is in the land, then the faithful remnant of Israel can sing;

**"The Lord (Jehovah) is my Shepherd."**

In the days when "want" is in the whole world of men this remnant can shout:

**"I shall not want."**

When all the green grass is burned up, fruit and field wasted under the blight and blast of the first trumpet judgment, then the remnant of Israel can cry:

**"He leadeth me in green pastures,"**

for God knows how to "prepare a table in the wilderness,"

When the waters are poisoned and turned to blood under the judgment of the second trumpet, the remnant can declare.

**"He leadeth me beside the still waters."**

When the whole world is under the conscription of the "Man of Sin" and the food stuff is under his control and no one can buy and none can sell without his mark, then the faithful remnant can declare,

**"Thou preparest a table before me in the presence of mine enemy."**

They shall enjoy a "full cup," indeed, a plentitude; it will be **"running over."**

When the whole world sits in the valley of the shadow of death and Armageddon draws near and the universal slaughter of that day, and fear is upon all men, this remnant will fear "no evil" the "Lord is with them" and His **"rod and staff will comfort them."**

God will hide His people till His indignation be past. He will say to them:

"Come, My people, enter thou into thy chambers, and shut thy doors about thee; hide thyself as it were for a little moment, until the indignation be overpast.

"For, behold, the Lord cometh out of His place to punish the inhabitants of the earth for their inquity" (Is. 26:20, 21).

Mr. Jas. Dunbar in his book entitled **"What Shall Be Done in the Dry"** suggests the hiding-place God has prepared and reserved for His people in the day when

His wrath is being spent on the nations of the earth. The "woman" will be "fed," cared for, for the two thousand, two hundred and three score days."

At this point war is seen in Heaven. It is a mighty warfare and perhaps a continuation of an old-time warfare. Says the seer:

"And there was war in Heaven; Michael and his angels fought against the dragon; and the dragon fought and his angels, and prevailed not; neither was their place found any more in Heaven" (Rev. 12:7, 8).

This war in Heaven reveals a change of tides. Instead of Satan waging war, it is of angelic origin. Michael takes the initiative. He opens war against the dragon and his angels. This is the hour for which Michael has long waited. He is the especially delegated guardian of Israel as may be seen in Daniel 12:1. Indeed there is but little doubt that this is the time which Daniel refers to in the 12th chapter of his prophecy. Chapter 12:1:

"And at that time shall Michael stand up, the great prince which standeth for the children of thy people; and there shall be a time of trouble, such as never was since there was a nation even to that same time: and at that time thy people shall be delivered, every one that shall be found written in the book."

This is the time in which Michael stands up among the princedoms of the angels. He has ever guarded Israel. He has never slumbered nor slept. At the time Satan contended for the body of Moses, the great leader and law-giver of Israel, Michael then stood up. He stood up against Satan, would have brought railing accusation against him had he not been prevented by the Lord. He stood at the grave of Moses contending for his body. See Jude 1:9.

This is the first time Michael is mentioned in the Book of Revelation, but we shall hear about him again in chapter 20. Here in chapter 12, he commences a work that is continued through the rest of the revelation and concluded at chapter 20. The purpose of this warfare is to drive Satan from his position in the Heavens. This time it is not Michael's rebuke, but the Lord's rebuke. The warfare will not cease until Satan is incarcerated in his prison house for a thousand years.

Satan's occupancy in the Heavens is not a new revelation in the Scriptures. To be sure, his position is not in the Heaven of heavens, but according to the last chapter of the Book of Ephesians, we learn of the wicked hosts in Heavenly places (see Eph. 6:12). They are intrenched in this sphere of the Heavenlies. The Church in the present dispensation experiences the hostility of these wicked spirits, but at the opening of this chapter we see Michael preparing to dislodge the enemy from the exalted position and thrust him down to earth.

Lesson Fifty-two

## MAN-CHILD AND THE DRAGON (Rev.12) Part 4

**And there was war in Heaven!** What a spectacle is this—a supernatural war in the upper world with angels, demons and the devil the contestants in the conflict! Surely this is dramatic and startling!

"Michael and his angels fought against the dragon, and the dragon fought and his angels" (12:7).

**Michael** the champion and Divinely appointed guardian of Israel (see Dan. 12:1). Now come to the woman's help and stages and wages a war in Heaven. The Angel-Helper now appears! Let us behold the results!

**The Dragon** is identified beyond doubt—he is "that old serpent the devil and Satan which deceiveth the whole world."

Many are surprised to find that Satan is on High and that he has a seat in the Heavens. Throughout the Scriptures he is seen either in Heaven or in earth. He originally held a high place. See Ezekiel 28:1-19. At this Scripture in Ezekiel his humiliation and casting down was forecast (see vs. 19). The regathering of Israel immediately follows as here in the Revelation (see vss. 25, 26).

In Job, chapters 1 and 2, the travels of Satan and the spheres which he enters may be seen, as also in I Chronicles 21 and I Kings 22.

In this conflict, which does not result in bloodshed or physical wound, the dragon **"is cast into the earth."** He is driven from the territory he has possessed. This was probably foretold by our Lord when He said—"I saw Satan as lightning fall from Heaven," though this may refer to his original fall.

Thus we see the usurper and squatter driven before the commander and generalissimo of angel warriors! What a scene this will present! But what a peril for the earth! Think of Satan and his army added to all the other tribulation features! It is little wonder that the Heavens were called upon to rejoice, and that a warning woe is issued in a proclamation—

"Woe to the inhabiters of the earth and of the sea! for the devil is come down unto you, having great wrath, because he knoweth that he hath but a short time" (vs. 12).

Notice that the sea and its inhabitants are warned along with the earth! We may expect a Satanic storming of the sea—indeed the first vision of chapter 13, takes us to the sea!

The time will be "short"—this must needs be for unless shortened no life would survive. **"Now"** or **"soon,"** "shortly" will come the salvation of our God and His Kingdom. Thy Kingdom come on earth, is about to be fulfilled. Yet a little while and another army will be seen descending from Heaven to the earth, it will be the army of the faithful and true—the Word of God—the Avenger of His people. See Revelation 19:11 to 16.

When the remnant of Israel returned from the captivity in Babylon Satan resisted their restoration as a nation. He withstood and contested. See Zechariah 3:2.

The restoration of Israel again to their land is about to be accomplished when God has finished with Babylon (see chaps. 17, 18) and here is the old enemy again in his hostility and wrath! His wrath will be of no avail, it will but bring praise to God! The Lamb Warrior and King will overcome and reign! He can not prevent the home-coming of Israel with songs in their hearts! He cannot prevent the establishment of the long-promised and expected Kingdom of Christ the Messiah and Heir of David's Dynasty!

Three years and a half is indeed a "short" time. He will wage a new and intensified war against the remnant, but God will allure them to the wilderness where He will "set them a table."

A wilderness sustained them once before and it will do it again. They were driven before a Pharaoh into the wilderness, but to be sustained and succored by God, Who will do this again. As in the days of Pharaoh, so here, the wilderness will be **but the way to the Land.**

Saith the Lord:

"Therefore behold, I allure her, and bring her into the wilderness, and speak comfortably unto her.

"And I will give her her vineyards from thence, and the valley of Achor for a door of hope; and she shall sing there, as in the days of her youth, and as in the day when she came up out of the land of Egypt" (Hos. 2:14, 15).

God will take care of the "woman" in the wilderness. He will bear them on eagle's wings (see verse 14, also God's past care of Israel in Deuteronomy 32:11 and 12).

During these days of the sojourn of the remnant in the wilderness, the **"enemy will come in like a flood,"** says the Revelator.

"And the serpent cast out of his mouth water as a flood after the woman, that he might carry her away of the flood" (vs. 15).

Isaiah may have had this event in his prophecy when he said (59:19):

**"When the enemy shall come in like a flood, the Spirit of the Lord shall lift up a standard against him,"** and this verse is followed by a prophecy of the advent of Christ which is so quoted and understood in Romans 11:26. Says the Prophet and also Paul:

"And the Redeemer shall come to Zion, and unto them that turn from transgression in Jacob" (Is. 59:20; see Rom. 11:26).

The Lord most certainly **lifts up a standard** or a defense against this flood-bringer for we read:

"And the earth helped the woman and the earth opened her mouth and swallowed up the flood which the dragon cast out of his mouth."

There was a flood which would have destroyed the royal line of seed, but God built an ark and Shem was safely carried over and in him the Jewish race and in that race according to the flesh, Christ (see Rom. 1:3). So again God will save the remnant of Israel from the enemy's flood!

Flee to the wilderness thou remnant of Israel; behold thou shalt meet the Lord thy God there, and He will companion with thee, while the "valley of the shadow of death" is the lot of the whole world of mankind.

"Flee from Judea" but for only a **"little while."** Soon the indignation will be over and in thy lot thou shalt stand.

Lesson Fifty-three

## BEASTS (Rev.13:1-8) Part 1

From the war in Heaven we now turn to the earth but to behold the results of the war in Heaven upon the earth.

The war in Heaven particularly concerned Israel. These two beasts concern the earth at large. This 13th chapter falls into two divisions each being concerned with one of the Beasts.

**I. THE MARINE BEAST**—(Out of the sea). Verses 1-10.

**II. THE MUNDANE BEAST.**—("Up out of the Earth"). Verses 11-18.

These two Beasts with the devil, who was cast down to earth in chapter 12, will bring upon the earth the tragedy of demonism and the reign of terror which was foretold at 12:12. It will be "woe" time for the world. The Beasts are "wild beasts." The word is **therion**—a "wild beast" or "beast of prey."

These days will be the days of Satan's supreme miracles, and surprise must not be expressed at any thing, Paul we are confident, is describing this time of the great tribulation when he says:

> "The working of Satan with **all power** and **signs** and **lying wonders.**
>
> And with all **deceivableness** of unrighteousness in them that perish; because they received not the love of the Truth, that they might be saved.
>
> And for this cause God shall send them strong delusion, that they should believe a lie:
>
> That they all might be damned who believed not the Truth, but had pleasure in unrighteousness." (II Thess. 2:9-11)

Satan will produce his masterpieces of deception and

delusion. He will mock God and mimic the miracles with his brief "all power."

God in the beginning called up birds out of the sea and wild beasts out of the land (see Gen. 1:20-24). What God did Satan will now attempt and perform. This will be a startling and strange miracle—it will astound the earth.

Like the witch of Endor who brought up a person at the call of Saul, so will Satan "bring up" a master end time delusion and demoniacal manifestation:

We shall look at these Beasts, each in their order considering first:

**I. THE MARINE BEAST**—("out of the sea"). Verses 1-10.

"And I stood upon the sand of the sea, and saw a beast rise up out of the sea, having
**seven heads** and
**ten horns,** and upon his horns
**ten crowns,** and upon his heads the
**name of blasphemy.**" (vs. 1).

We have here a person in whom all human government, worldly dominion, and all heads and successive powers are combined and united **in one.** He is the embodiment of political rule on the earth. The kingdoms of this world have become the kingdoms of this Beast out of the sea. We can but anticipate this Beast in chapter 13 where he is introduced, for in chapter 17 he will be seen in more general detail. In chapter 13 he is seen as the Generalissimo of all government. This Beast here is more than Rome or the fourth Beast of Daniel. There is here a confederation, a concentration in this one satanic supernatural and superhuman Beast. Beasts are seen in Daniel in human or mortal form but in the Revelation in the **superhuman and satanic.**

A description of this Marine Beast is striking in details.

"Like unto a **leopard.**"

"The feet of a **bear.**"

"The mouth of a **lion.**"

In the first verse we saw what **it had** and in verse 2 what it is like and in the two verses we have a **sevenfold** description. We shall see these seven under two divisions:

How the Beast Looked.

1. Ten **horns.**
2. Seven **heads.**
3. Ten diadems on heads.
4. Blasphemous titles on heads.

**Unto what the Beast was likened.**

5. A leopard in **general appearance.**
6. A bear's **feet.**
7. A lion's **mouth.**

It is full of spots and these are unchangeable spots. The leopard cannot change his spots.

He comes as the antagonist of the Lamb. It is to be the struggle of the **leopard and the lamb** from this time forth until the Lamb resigns. The lamb in contrast with this leopard is unspeakably distinguished as the leopard is in comparison with the lamb increasingly debased.

The leopard is full of spots; the lamb is "without spot or blemish."

The characteristics of the leopard as set forth in other Scriptures all combine and climax in this one like a leopard.

"A leopard shall watch over their cities; every one that goeth out thence shall be torn in pieces." (Jer. 5:6).

"As a leopard by the way will I observe them: I will meet them as a bear that is bereaved of her whelps, there will I devour them like a lion: the wild beast shall tear them." (Hos. 13; 7, 8).

In this passage we have the threefold designation of the wild beasts with the leopard, bear and lion, just as in the 13th of Revelation. These words of the Prophet are suggestive and significant,

"Their horses also are swifter than the leopards" (Hab. 1:8).

These passages throw light upon the character of this leopard—like the Beast from the sea. His nature and habits are revealed and all of his beastliness will be on full display before the tribulation days are brought to a close. Yet a little while and the Lamb will come down from His Throne and destroy the Beast that comes up out of the sea!

It will be also noticed that in presenting the likeness of the Beast out of the sea that the order is changed. There is a reverse to that found in Daniel 7. In Daniel there is the following order:

1. **The Lion.**
2. **The Bear.**
3. **The Leopard.**
4. **The Terrible Beast.**

But here it is the—

1. Beast Himself.
2. The Leopard.
3. The Bear.
4. The Lion.

Daniel at chapter 7 stood also by the sea and saw certain beasts arise therefrom (see Dan. 7:2). We are inclined to believe that both Daniel and John were beholding the same end time visions. A careful study of Daniel 7:7, 8, 19-27 will do the student much good. We are more inclined as the days pass, to the view that Daniel 7 and the Beast vision of the Prophet, belong to the **end time** rather than to the **all time** of Gentile "times" as covered and included in the image of Daniel 2. The Beasts of Daniel 7, in our judgment, will be better understood at the **end** and in the light of this first Beast out of the sea, than by any other interepretation.

The Marine Beast of Revelation 13, receives his authority from the dragon and the dragon is the devil as we have learned in chapter 12. The gift of the dragon to him is threefold:

1. The dragon gave him **his power.**
2. And **his throne.**
3. And **great authority.**

In these days of postmillennialism and modernism and rationalism it is quite smart to say that Satan has no **power, throne** or **authority.**

One leading high church official laughed at the idea that Satan should offer the kingdoms of this world to Jesus as reward for His worship, "Why," said he, "Satan did not have the kingdoms of this world to give." How ignorant was he and mistaken. He did have them, he offered them and the Son of Man refused them to await the time when the kingdoms of this world would be His. Here at Revelation the man of sin accepts from Satan what Christ **would not.**

He receives **power, throne,** and **authority.** What a world will this world be in such days! What an hour of lawlessness and lying! Thank God, we are not to be here at that period of time but will be yonder with our Lord! The man of sin, the first Beast, will accept what Christ has rejected and again we say **"Woe"** to the world! This hour was prophesied to come upon the world and it will. It is foretold in Revelation 3:10 and is described as the "Time to try all them that dwell upon the earth."

The devil, according to chapter 12, came down with great wrath and it must be spent upon a world ready for his final stroke before a long term of imprisonment.

In this study we can but introduce the first beast, in the following lectures we will consider his miraculous manifestation to deceive the whole world.

Miracles that will spring from satanic source will startle the world, which would have none of the true miracles of the Living and True God. Even as we write the world will believe anything science may claim and is ready to give credit to any phenomena, but not one Word of God in His Divine revelation will be acknowledged. Surely the age is ripening into these days foretold by John the seer on the Isle that is called Patmos.

Lesson Fifty-four

## BEASTS (Rev.13:1-8) Part 2

The **"Marine Beast,"** the beast "out of the sea" and the first beast of Revelation 13, was described in general detail in the former study. Everything is in readiness for his appearance. He is the person predicted in the prophecies. His portrait is foredrawn in Psalm 10, with the victory of Christ over him also in the forecast, **"that the man of the earth may no more oppress"** (vs. 10).

Israel as a nation enjoyed the visitation of the "Day-spring from on high." He came in His "Father's name," they would not "receive Him." Now one comes in **"his own name."** They will receive the deceiver. This was foretold by Christ and now it comes to pass. They would not receive the "Son of Man," but now they receive the **"man of sin."** The "man of sin" will combine in his person all the "sin of man." What Paul in Romans 3, in quotation from Psalm 10, and other Psalms and prophecies, describes as the "sin of man," now comes to its full and final manifestation in the "man of sin" (see Rom. 3:10-18).

Here in the first beast, the Marine Beast, we have a superhuman, diabolical and satanic creation. The "wicked generation" that rejected Christ at the beginning of the age now receives the "beast" at the end of the age. The mystery of inquity works to an age time climax. One came conceived and born of the Holy Spirit and they cried **"Crucify Him!"** Now one comes of a demon spirit and they cry, **"Crown him!"**

"The unclean spirit returns to the house from whence he came out, but

**not as he went out,** for he brings with himself **seven other spirits** more wicked than himself and they enter in and dwell there and the last state of that man is worse than the first."

This is our Lord's prediction in the parable of the "strong man." These tribulation days, during which this first beast appears; are doubtless the days Jesus had in mind when He uttered this parable and the full force of the interpretation is evident in the words, **"Even so shall it be also unto the wicked generation"** (see Matt. 12:43-45).

This "Beast" will accept what Christ rejected. Christ refused to receive at the hands of Satan the "kingdoms of the world" (see Matt. 4). Very dogmatic was the offer of Satan and very decisive was the refusal of Christ.

"And the devil taketh Him up into an exceeding high mountain, and sheweth Him all the kingdoms of the world in a moment of time.

"And the devil said unto Him, "All this power will I give Thee, and the glory of them; for that is delivered unto me; and to whomsoever I will I give it. If Thou therefore wilt worship me, all shall be Thine."

Satan as the "ruler of this age" now offers to the Beast, what Christ refused! He said he could give it to whom he would give it, and he performs his promise. Says John:

"And they worshipped the dragon which gave power unto the beast; and they worshipped the beast, saying; who is like unto the beast? who is able to make war with him?" (vs. 4).

"And all that dwell upon the earth shall worship him" (vs. 8).

Thus, through the medium of the beast, Satan becomes the object of world worship. The deification of Satan is accomplished and the desire of his rebellious heart is at last achieved. This was the cause of his original condemnation. He, doubtless, in the beginning turned praise from God and attempted to turn it unto himself. There is a reason why so many times in the Bible it says **Praise the Lord! "Oh, that men would praise the Lord!"** Praising the Lord is the most **un-Satan-like thing in the universe** and by nature not one of us will do it. It is never until we are new in Christ Jesus that we will praise the Lord. Instantly upon receiving Christ and the new life from above, the saved sinner cries, **"O praise the Lord."** No man ever breaks with Satan naturally. The old nature is of him and with him, but the new creature sends up praise to God in a testimony against Satan's original sin and in thanks for deliverance from the evil one!

Indeed, the mystery of inquity is great! Jesus knew what Satan meant when he said "Worship me and I will give it all to You" and this answer discloses and discovers the true character of Satan and his sin. **"Thou shalt worship the Lord thy God and Him only shalt thou serve"** (Matt. 4:10; Luke 4:8).

But now the beast receives all from Satan and Satan gives all to the beast. Satan has found his instrument. He makes full use of him. He is raised to the pinnacle of human pride, the height to which he sought to raise Christ and every one else in all the realm of human flesh and nature.

At last Satan is accomplishing what he desired to do in the beginning—**direct the worship of the whole world.** Indeed Satan is the god of this world and will fully reveal his power before the age comes to its end. Things are in a trend even now to devil worship, Satan has the world's worship to deliver unto whomsoever he will.

The student will note the power of Satan in this his last display of hatred against the Lord and His Anointed. Says the Apostle: "The dragon" (see Rev. 20:2).

1. Gave him his power.
2. And his seat.
3. And great authority. (vs. 2).

Man worships power and authority and in this beast, Satan's puppet for the hour of his purpose is the object of the world's admiration which is universally paid. Satan not only gives this beast his power and throne—his "seat." As the time is near when Christ the true David and King of God will take the throne of His father David, then it is the beast takes a throne of political sovereignty! This may be the throne the Psalmist had in mind when in Psalm 94:20 which he calls **"the throne of inquity."** This time may have also been in anticipation in 2:9 and 3:9, of this Book of Revelation.

This throne of Satan carries with it authority which means civil and legal power. This authority is but for a short period for **"All authority** is given unto Me in Heaven and in earth" said Jesus and He will soon take this authority and reign.

To sum up the facts concerning this first beast, the marine beast from the sea, we are bound to conclude:

**I. The Person of the Beast.** He is an actual person and not a principle for interpretation. He actually arises and appears (see vss. 1-3).

**II. The Political Prestige of the Beast.** He has an actual throne with political dominion extending to all kindreds, tongues and nations (see vs. 7).

**III. The Power of the Beast.** It is derived from Satan and is delegated. **Three** times John mentions the power of the beast (see vss. 2, 3, 7).

**IV. The Popularity of the Beast.** The whole world wonders after him (see vs. 3.) The world champions him and asks, Who is like unto him and who dares to meet him in military contest? He is exceedingly popular. He is the **"man of the hour."** His name is in everybody's mouth. He is the one theme of universal conversation (see vss. 3, 4, 8).

**V. The Period of the Reign of the Beast.** Power was given unto him to "continue" for a period of forty-two months—the last half of Daniel's prophetic week and for the time of the great tribulation.

**VI. The Persecutions of the Beast.** He is a persecutor. He could be nothing less. He is the great persecutor of Israel. He is an Anti-Semite. He makes war with the saints and this does not refer to the members of the Body of Christ, the Church, for the Church is not in this tribulation period. This doubtless refers to the faithful remnant of Israel as they have often been before the student in the Book of Revelation. The days of the beast will be days of sword, famine and peril. But those whose names are written in the Lamb's Book of Life, survive his persecutions. For all time God has been looking to this end time.

Lesson Fifty-five

## BEASTS (Rev.13:11-18) Part 3

In the first half of chapter 13 of the Book of Revelation, we beheld the uprising of the First Beast out of the sea which to identify and distinguish, we named the Marine Beast. We are now to consider the Second Beast or the beast from the earth—the Mundane Beast. The record of this Beast and his doings is found in verses 11 to 18. Each verse contains definite information concerning this beast and each verse also begins with "And." The Second "Beast" is also distinguished from the First Beast by the use of the title, "the Beast" which is always used of the **"First Beast."** The First Beast is predominant and pre-eminent in the Revelation, while the Second Beast is subordinate to and dependent upon the First. The Beast (the second) is called **"The False Prophet."** This at once throws much light on his character and his work. Three times he is designated as the **False Prophet,**—16:13; 19:20; 20:10. As the First Beast is the tool of Satan, so this Second Beast is the tool or instrument of the First Beast. The Second Beast is also a person as is the First Beast. These are not figures of speech, nor are they principles but **persons.**

As the "Man of Sin" or the First Beast is a person to be expected at the end of this age, so also is the Second Beast or the False Prophet. Christ foretold the coming of this Second Beast. See Matthew 24:24; Mark 13:22; Matthew 24:5, 11. Not only did Christ predict their appearance but in one sentence summarized the deceptive and delusive ministry and miraculous manifestations of these two when He said,

"And shall show great signs and wonders, insomuch if it were possible they would deceive the very elect."

Moses knew that at the end time such a Prophet would appear unto his people Israel to destroy and deceive them and gave due warning in advance. Said he:

"But the prophet, which shall presume to speak a word in My name, which I have not commanded him to speak, or that shall speak in the name of other gods, even that prophet shall die.

"And if thou shalt say in thine heart, How shall we know the word which the Lord hath not spoken?

"When a prophet speaketh in the name of the Lord, if the thing follow not, nor come to pass, that is the thing which the Lord hath not spoken, but the prophet hath spoken it presumptuously; thou shalt not be ashamed of him."

This second Beast is the last false prophet with whom Israel will have to do before the age comes to its end. The Lord sent them their True Prophet—they rejected Him. Moses told them clearly in advance that they reject Him not. Said he:

"The Lord thy God will raise up unto thee a **Prophet** from the midst of thee, of thy brethren, like unto me; unto Him ye shall hearken.

"I will raise up unto them a **Prophet** from among their brethren, like unto thee, and will put My words in His mouth; and He shall speak unto them all that I shall command Him.

"And it shall come to pass, that whosoever will not hearken unto My words which He shall speak in My name, I will require it of him."

The true Prophet Christ Who was rejected by them was raised up by God. This second Beast or false prophet is raised up by the devil—the dragon.

Christ the True Prophet was one of their "brethren." He was of the tribe of Judah and of the seed of David. This false prophet may come out of Gentile stock—indeed this is our conviction.

God put His Words in the mouth of Christ. He spake those things the Father commanded and was God's mouthpiece, but the false prophet "spake as a dragon" —that is as the devil impelled and commanded him. This second Beast has two horns and not **ten.** Ten horns undoubtedly denote dominion and two of **testimony** and in this case false testimony. Christ bore true witness, the second Beast, false witness. How could he speak otherwise, he is of the devil—"the dragon."

**Satan is subtle**—see Gen. 3:1.

**Satan is crafty**—see Gen. 49:17.

**Satan is deceitful**—see II Cor. 11:3.

The second Beast is an agent of the "dragon" and the "first Beast." **Eight** times is the expression used of the second Beast, that **"he causeth."** He has two horns "like a lamb" but he is of the dragon. There is no way to make a Christ out of an anti-christ. There is no way to make spiritual that which is natural. The second Beast or the **False Prophet** may be looked upon under the following aspects:

**I. His Description** (see vs. 11). He is "another beast," separate and apart from the first Beast but in alliance with him and under his authority. He had two horns like a lamb. He spake as a dragon.

**II. His Delegated Power** (see vs. 12). "He exerciseth all the power of the first Beast. He is but a delegate or a representative.

**III. He Directs Worship** (see vs. 12). Perhaps there was a time when Satan directed the praise of the universe. He was not Satan as now but an exalted creature. He attempted to turn the praise due to God unto himself and "fell into the condemnation of the devil." Here Satan uses the second Beast or the False Prophet to direct worship unto the First Beast, one who had been raised up from a death wound, a sort of a spectacular claim to resurrection or life from the dead.

Devil-worship is the ultimate before the age ends. It is sad to relate, but the facts are here stated and the extent to which it is carried is "the earth and they that dwell therein."

**IV. His Deceptions** (see vss. 13-15). "He deceiveth"

by means of miracles. The earth is always ready for signs and wonders and those things that startle the sight. The world walks by sight and not by faith. To this day the man or even minister who will put on the attempt at miracle and declare to give the deaf their hearing and blind their sight and lame their limbs, will draw great crowds and gather much attention. These things deplete the life of faith and fix attention upon signs and wonders rather than on the Living Lord at God's right hand. The highest Christian life, is not these things but a walk by faith and not by sight. He had power to do miracles in the sight of the Beast. His supreme miracle was not imitating Elijah in bringing down fire from Heaven, but in giving life to the image of the Beast. To create life is the attempt of science. This the modern delusion known as Christian Science, has attempted to do. It will be a master act of independence of God. It will be the stupendous miracle in imitation of the life which God gave Christ in His resurrection from the dead. He will force worship—men will worship the image of the Beast. As in the days when the Hebrew children were in Babylon so now.

Lesson Fifty-six

## BEASTS (Rev.13:11-18) Part 4

At verse 11 of the 13th chapter of Revelation we have the **description** of the Second Beast.

At verse 12, we behold his **delegated** power and the **direction** of universal worship committed to him. At verses 13 and 14, the **deceptions** that are practiced by him.

We shall further study the diabolical ministry of this second or Mundane Beast under three divisions.

**I. His Command to Universal Idolatry**—vss. 14, 15.

**II. His Commercial Control of the Earth**—vss. 16, 17.

**III. The Calculation of His Name Numerically**—vs. 18.

Each of these shall receive brief consideration.

**I. His Command to Universal Idolatry**—vss. 14, 15.

The world is always ready for the miracle-worker who can satisfy their sight and make no demand for faith. Christ the true and sent One of God came with the control and command over nature as its Lord and Despot, but immediately His work was attributed to the devil and they would not receive Him either for His Word or His works. The Prophet Isaiah foresaw and foretold this in the words found at the opening of the 53d chapter of his prophecy and quoted in John 12:38. They would not behold the revealed arm of the Lord and the miraculous ministry of Messiah. But now with the rest of the world, they will be deceived by the False Prophet. He is a Judas into whom Satan has entered.

He is energized by Satan. It would seem that he attempts the imitation of the miracles of the two witnesses and bring fire down from heaven thus deceiving the earth dwellers into thinking that his god is the God that answereth by fire. His god is the "dragon." Elijah on Mount Carmel gave this sign and proof and this is his imitator. Satan under permission of God, brought fire down from heaven on the personal effects of Job. This fire act appears to be one of Satan's "specials." This False Prophet is enabled by the devil to accomplish what the prophets of Baal could not do. This fire miracle is done "in the sight of men." This is its purpose. For a world that will not believe there will be plenty of "sight," but what they see will prove to be a "strong delusion."

But deeper grows the deception and delusion of the False Prophet. Christ is "the image of invisible God" and the False Prophet must create an image of his god —the god of this age. Such an image is made. It is the image of the First Beast. It must show itself "alive," for Christ the True Prophet showed Himself alive by many infallible proofs, **after His resurrection.** So the Beast that had suffered the wound of the sword must live. So he works a miracle by the power of Satan and the image **"lives"** and **"speaks."** O stupendous miracle! O devilish burlesque!

Then the False Prophet commands universal homage and worship and the whole world becomes idolatrous! John's words now become full of meaning—"Little children, it is the last hour"—"Antichrist cometh"—"Even now"—"Little children, keep yourselves from idols!

It is at this time that Satan puts forth his masterpiece of iniquity. He displays the boldest effrontery to God perhaps since his original sin and fall when he attempted to lift himself up into equality with God. He opens full defiance against God and shows this defiance in the face of the first commandment of a Holy God which is:

**"Thou shalt have no other gods before me."**

He sets up the image and declares it to be God and actually **causes and commands the whole world to idolatry!** There is another God beside "the **Lord your God."** It is the old satanic lie. It is of the devil! He sets up the image before God who has said:

"Thou shalt not make unto thee any graven image, or any likeness of any thing that is in heaven above, or that is in the earth beneath, or that is in the water under the earth.

"Thou shalt not bow down thyself to them, nor serve them" (Exod. 20:3-5).

This False Prophet brings the world to worship a graven image and bow down to it in open hostility and defiance of God. Who is God? What are His commandments? We shall have an image if we want it and bow down where we please. Who is God that we would obey Him?

The student may further consider the image of the Beast in Revelation 14:9, 11; 15:1; 16:2; 19:20; 20:4.

This forced worship is to bring the faithful remnant of Israel into the perplexity of the three Hebrew children and of Daniel, but this desire to bring them into idolatry fails as in the case of the above mentioned.

They are brought to their "wit's end" but not to God's protection for their preservation.

The 73d Psalm may be read, we verily believe in the light of these days when the image of the beast is worshiped. It is a graphic description of these idolatrous days. Notice the question the Psalmist asks in verse 11. See also what he says about understanding only after he had gone into the sanctuary. See verse 19 and ponder it! Hear the Psalmist cry:

**"O Lord, thou shalt despise their image,"** for so will the Lord.

Notice the significant words of the Psalmist, "I was a beast before thee."

Thus we have a little picture of these days when men have thrown off the restraint of God, for God has always been a restraint to men. They hate and despise law or authority. They are of the "wicked one" who is now in full control of the affairs of the earth.

**II. The Commercial Control of the Earth**—vss. 16, 17.

Not only does the False Prophet attempt to force worship on the earth and thus bring with the rest of mankind, the faithful remnant of Israel into idolatry, but he also gains commercial control and corrals the food stuff and may force the remnant to idolatry or starvation. He succeeds in producing a situation by which only those who have the mark of the beast upon them can buy or sell. He enters the trade marts and establishes the most stupendous boycott that has ever been known. He extends this embargo on food stuff to affect all classes.

The Record says:

"He causeth all, both small and great, rich and poor, free and bond to receive a mark in their foreheads. And that no man might buy or sell save he that had the mark, or the name of the beast, or the number of his name."

In these days the only men who will appear in the market place, at the chamber of commerce, will be the ones who have the mark of this beast on their foreheads. There can be no change or exchange apart from the permission of the False Prophet. There are three claims upon commerce as here stated:

1. "He that had the mark,
2. Or the name of the beast,
3. Or the number of his name" (vs. 17).

This condition will exceed famine. It is beyond the imagination to conceive. It will introduce a spy system that will stagger anything the world has ever known.

Living will be worse than death and even money will be useless and where the exchange will go, no one can guess. It will plunge the financial world into chaos. The monetary solidarity of the world will be imperiled and the credit of nations will crash. Money can not do anything in these days, though now there are those who think it will do everything.

Men will be branded or marked. They must have the official seal of the Beast. Those who will not brave the decree of the Beast must take the brand and there are those who prefer his seal to their starvation.

It will be a dark day but God will feed His own. He will know how to set a table in this wilderness. He can feed His own and prepare a table in the presence of their enemy. The 23d Psalm will have a wonderful meaning to this remnant of Israel in the days of the two Beasts. They can shout—"Jehovah is our Shepherd—we shall not want" nor shall they! Again we consider briefly:

**III. The Calculation of His Name Numerically—** vs. 18.

It is at this point we must remember that we are in the Book of Revelation and not the Book of speculation. It is here speculation has run wild. The extravagance of speculation has driven many from the study of the Book. We shall not attempt to translate the number of the Beast into the name of any man. This calculation we must leave to others. We do not believe there is indicated here **the name of any man who has been known to history.** The one whose calculation this will be the interpretation, is not an historical personage. He is **yet to come** and has not yet come. This person known as the First Beast, has not yet appeared upon the stage of history. He will appear during the tribulation days and after the Church, the Body of Christ is gone from the scenes of judgment. The seal, trumpet and vial judgments will not fall upon the Church which is neither Jew nor Gentile, bond nor free, male or female, **but upon Israel and nations.**

We cannot join with some others in seeking out a person of the past or the present upon whom the name and the number will meet in fulfillment of this prophecy. A great many names have been found in this enumeration by many expositors and we honor these expositors and are not worthy to be even mentioned among them, but we can not accept their findings. In our judgment the key to the understanding of this passage is to be found in the words—**"for it is the number of a man and his number is Six hundred, three score and six."**

**Seven** is the number of **spiritual perfection.** It is the complete number. Six is one **short** of seven and is man's number throughout the Bible for man comes short of the glory of God as six is short of seven. It is the number associated with sin. He was created on the **sixth** day. He came short of God's rest and must be made a new creature in Christ Jesus. Six became, as one has expressed it, the **"hall mark of man."**

Govet says: **"Six** is the half of the sacred twelve wanting one of God's perfect **seven** is the number of sin." Nebuchadnezzar's image was **sixty** cubits high and six cubits broad and with that image was associated the number 66 or two sixes while with this image of the Beast there are three sixes—a trinity of sixes—**666.**

When Christ died for sin and all the sin of the **world and the universe** was laid on Him and He was **"made sin,"** it was on the **sixth** hour and perhaps the **sixth day.** The number of the Beast is **six,** thrice repeated. It is the combined and allied sin of the **"dragon"** the devil, the **First Beast** and the **False Prophet!** The sin of man comes to a head in the man of sin. It is the mystery of iniquity that is here expressed in this number. It is sin at its triple climax and brief triumph.

Pastor Archibald Wright in a sermon preached at Newtownards First Presbyterian church, Ireland, said significantly:

"It is ever short of the perfect seven, showing that however the Beast king may attempt to show himself as God he will fail to deceive the elect. It may seem strange that the world with all its wisdom and culture could be so deceived by the Man of Sin and be led to worship such a character but **it all becomes clear when** we remember that **man by wisdom never knew God!"**

Behold the ignorance of the world in the crucifixion of Christ! Says Paul, "None of the princes of this world knew; for had they known it they would not have crucified the Lord of Glory." The Cross was from the human side a tragedy of the ignorance of a wise world. The world by wisdom at the Cross knew not God. Nor will the world at the coming by wisdom know God. Their wisdom will be their ignorance and they will enthrone the Man of Sin as God and again display their ignorance. Indeed "the foolishness of God is wiser than men and the weakness of God is stronger than men." Surely, "their foolish hearts were darkened."

The **dethronement** of God and the **deification** of man, Satan's man, is the world's intent. It will come to pass. It will be of but brief duration for the record tells of the great arrest:

"And the beast was taken, and with him the false prophet that wrought miracles before him, with which he deceived them that had the mark of the beast, and them that worshipped his image. They both **were cast alive** into a lake of fire burning with brimstone" (Rev. 19:20).

They will be joined a little later by the one in whose power they exercised their ministry. See Revelation 20:10. This is the final destination of this trinity of evil and iniquity. Thank God! Amen!!

Lesson Fifty-seven

## ONE HUNDRED FORTY-FOUR THOUSAND (Rev.14:1-5)

We now turn from the one "like a lamb" unto the Lamb Himself. We turn from the Beast to the blessed and from those who bear the mark of the Beast, to those who have **"the Father's name on their foreheads."** We turn from the seal of the Beast to the seal of the Lamb. We turn from earth unto Heaven, though it be but for a little while, for yet the judgments of the Seven Vials must be poured out upon the earth. We now turn to God's Great Gross—"the one hundred and forty-four thousand."

They are seen with the Lamb on Mount Zion and they are known as the **"firstfruits unto God and to the Lamb."** James may have had this company in mind when he wrote to "the twelve tribes of Israel which were scattered abroad" (James 1:1), "that we should be a kind of firstfruits of His creatures" (James 1:18).

The Israelite who knows the Scriptures of the Old Testament, fully understands this company with the Lamb in the midst and the reference to the "firstfruits."

Among the calendar and feast days of Israel was one known as the feast of the first-fruits. On that day they brought a sheaf of the first-fruits of the harvest unto the priest. The record will be found in Leviticus 23.

"When ye be come into the land which I give unto you, and shall reap the harvest thereof, then ye shall bring a sheaf of the first-fruits of your harvest unto the priest:

And ye shall wave the sheaf before the Lord, to be accepted for you; on the morrow after the Sabbath shall the priest wave it.

And in the day when ye wave the sheaf ye shall **OFFER A HE-LAMB WITHOUT BLEMISH,** (R. V.) of the first year for a burnt offering unto the Lord."

So here on Mount Zion we see the first-fruits and the **Lamb** with them. It is the time when the harvest of the first-fruits will be celebrated. It is time for the vintage to be reaped. Soon the angels will be thrusting in the sharp sickles (see Rev. 14:18-20), for the "harvest is the end of the age" (Matt. 13:39).

With the harvest and feast of the first-fruits near its celebration we can now understand the Old Testament type of this time of triumph.

Now for voices to be lifted in the glad harvest songs. Now for the joy and behold the united voices ready for praise. Now for the songs of victory!

"And I heard the
**Voice** from Heaven, as the
**Voice** of many waters, and as the * *
**Voice** of a great thunder; and I heard the
**Voice** of harpers harping with their harps."

Then came the harvest song: A new song at **that!** We shall look upon this festive scene.

**I. THE SONG.** It is a new song. There had been a new song sung at chapter 5 but this is a second new song and apart from that one. The elders and the four living creatures sang that song (see 5:9). It has never been sung before—it is new!

**II. THE SITUATION.** This new song is sung **before the throne.** It is rendered before the place of majesty and sovereignty. When singers are invited to appear before the throne of a crowned head, it is an honor which is published wide-spread. This new song is sung before the **throne.** It is an imperial setting. This song is not only sung before the throne and the **Throne Sitter** but it is also sung before the throne servants and surrounders—"the four beasts and the elders" (vs. 3). What an august audience! What spectators!

**III. THE SINGERS.** No man could learn this song, but the one hundred and forty-four thousand. It was exclusively theirs. They had been redeemed from the earth. They only could sing such a song. They had been sealed to pass through the tribulation at chapter 7. They were the overcomers and promise had been faithfully made at 3:12 and now it is in this projected prophecy faithfully fulfilled! Through the great tribulation and the wrath of the beast they are now seen as having successfully passed. It is their song, it could not be others. It is their song of victory. It is the song of those who are the "first-fruits of the Lamb."

They have been kept from the abominations which have filled the earth. Like Noah they have been "pure in their generation." Throughout the tribulation period they have refused to partake of the idolatries and fornications of the multitudes.

They have been kept from the defilement of women. They are clean. Notice under the sixth trumpet judgment how fornication is one of the open sins against and in defiance of God and His judgments. This company were not in this sin. In their mouths was not the "Lie" (see II Thess. 2:11). They received not the Lie. These have a wonderful future. They are to "follow the Lamb whithersoever He goeth." They understand what He meant when He said, "Follow Me." They are a **purchased possession** and a **privileged people.** They were purchased from among men." They are a "first-fruit to God and the Lamb." They are chosen ahead of their nation and a pledge, a proof and a guarantee of the redemption of the rest for "if the first-fruit be holy, the lump also is holy" (Rom. 11:16). They are privileged with the presence of the Lamb. They follow, He leads. He leads them indeed to "green pastures and still waters."

Such is the reward of the remnant who like their Lord did no violence neither was any deceit in their mouth. He "did no sin, neither was guile found in His mouth" (I Peter 2:22). Thus Peter who wrote in his First Epistle we believe **especially** and **particularly** to this faithful remnant, exhorted them to clean mouths and sinless conduct, holding up the example of the Lord as incentive.

After this little projection of prophecy showing the end-time results, the Prophet now sees the final scenes of judgments. The angels will appear one after the other in rapid succession. The scenes are to shift rapidly from this time forward with now and then a brief glimpse into Heaven to encourage and embolden as this one has done.

Lesson Fifty-eight

## SIX ANGELS AND SON OF MAN (Rev.14:6-20)

It must be remembered that we are yet between the sounding of the **Seventh Trumpet** (see 11:15) and the pouring forth of the **First vial** (see 16:2). Within the parenthetical portion covering the chapters from 12:1 to 15:8, is, among other matters this sort of a **preliminary preparation** to the last of the three series of judgments, the judgments of the **Seven Vials.**

We are to behold **seven persons;** six angels and the **Son of Man,** but the **Son of Man** is "in the midst." This is the order:

**I. The First Angel**—vss. 6, 7.

**II. The Second Angel**—vs. 8.

**III. The Third Angel**—vs. 9-13.

**IV. The Son of Man**—vs. 14.

**V. The Fourth Angel**—vss. 15, 16.

**VI. The Fifth Angel**—vs. 17.

**VII. The Sixth Angel**—vs. 18-20.

But **one** of the angels is **numbered** and it is the third angel" (see vs. 9). The other five are designated as **"another angel."** See this at verses 6, 8, 15, 17 and 18.

**Three** of these angels are **heralds. Three** of them are **harvesters.**

We shall consider them under these two aspects of their angelic ministry. The order of events is as follows:

**THE ANGEL HERALDS**—14:6-13.

1. **The First Angel**—vs. 6, 7.
2. **The Second Angel**—vs. 8.
3. **The Third Angel**—vs. 9-13.
4. **THE SON OF MAN**—vs. 14.

**THE ANGEL HARVESTERS**—14:15-18.

5. **The Fourth Angel**—vss. 15, 16.
6. **The Fifth Angel**—vs. 17.
7. **The Sixth Angel**—vs. 18.

**THE HERALD ANGELS** will be first considered. They each had a **proclamation.** They are the angelic heralds in this dark hour of the earth.

**I. THE FIRST ANGEL HERALD**—vs. 6.

He was seen flying in the midst of Heaven. His proclamation or preaching was to "them that dwell on the earth" and of course not to the Church of God, the Body of Christ, for the Church is not in this tribulation period. This we have discussed fully in former studies.

The ministry of this angel is universal. He makes known his message to

"Every nation,
and kindred,
and tongue,
and people."

There is committed to his heraldic ministry **"The Everlasting Gospel."** This is a phase of "God News" or "Gospel" that has never yet been published or proclaimed. The word Gospel means "good news" or "God news." There are many aspects of God's good news. They have each had their due time and season. There is

1. The Gospel of the Kingdom.
2. The Gospel of God.
3. The Gospel of the Grace of God.

4. The Gospel of the Glory.
5. The Everlasting Gospel.

Each of these are distinct and different aspects of the Good News which God would have published. We are not privileged here to enter details of characteristic differences. To this angel was committed the "Everlasting Gospel." This is the only Gospel or Good News that is not committed to men. It is the only committal of any aspect of the Gospel unto an angel. This "everlasting Gospel" is proclaimed by a herald angel in the very midst of the apocalyptic judgments. It follows the judgments of the **Seven Seals,** the **Seven Trumpets** and precedes the judgments of the **Seven Vials.**

There is no word in this "Everlasting Gospel" about "grace" or "Blood" or "forgiveness" or "redemption." There is no exhortation to worship a Redeemer but a simple command to fear God as a Creator. There is no exhortation to repentance—it is just

"fear God and give glory to Him for the hour of His judgment is come: and worship Him that made heaven and earth and the sea and the fountains of water."

There is no "grace" preached in this hour. The offer of grace has been withdrawn and is withheld. It is the fear of God as a Creator that is proclaimed by this angel. It is a touch of mercy in the midst of judgment. Christ as the Creator is acknowledged. This has before been noted and mentioned in this Book. See 4:11. Now that heaven, earth, sea and fountains of water are under His judgments, it is not strange that attention is called to the Creator. The sum of the whole matter is "fear God" and worship Him as Creator.

## II. THE SECOND ANGEL HERALD

makes his proclamation which is a declaration concerning **Babylon.**

"Babylon is fallen, is fallen, that great city, because she made all nations drink of the wine of the wrath of her fornication." (vs. 8).

This is preliminary and preparatory announcement—for the fall of Babylon is to be taken up in chapters 17 and 18. This is anticipatory and a sort of a table of contents or a preface to the events that must shortly follow. Babylon is not mentioned in the Book of Revelation until now. With this publication the second angel is silent but to be succeeded by

## III. THE THIRD ANGEL HERALD,

whose proclamation is a denunciation and is directed against the Beast of chapter 13. Then follow six verses of this denunciation. This is one of the severest of all denunciatory Scriptures. The loud voice of the angel herald is most solemn as well as severe. The Beast is at the height of his popularity and power. All that we read of his methods in chapter 13, is now in exercise. The whole world is in a state of wonder and admiration of the Beast. He is fully manifest in his miracles and his signs and his wonders. It is at this time God commands the third angel to proclaim. Behold the proclamation from the High Court of Heaven as cried by this angel:

> "If any man worship the Beast and his image and receive his mark in his forehead, or in his hand,
>
> "The same shall drink of the wine of the wrath of God, which is poured out without mixture into the cup of His indignation; and he shall be tormented with fire and brimstone in the presence of the holy angels and in the presence of the Lamb;
>
> "and the smoke of their torment ascendeth up for ever and ever; and they have no rest day nor night, who worship the Beast and his image and whosoever receiveth the mark of his name" (vs. 9-11).

Who can imagine the full meaning and the import of this malediction contained in the proclamation of this third angel? To drink the wine of God's wrath which will be served in a cup of indignation and without the slightest dilution, for it is to be served "without mixture" or dilution—what can it all mean?

And then to be "tormented with fire and brimstone"

in the presence of such spectators! **The holy angels and the Lamb!** With smoke ascending for ever and ever without rest during the day nor the successive nights! How terrible these judgments but God has spoken! Notice the order:

I. **The Persons Included**—"any man" who worships the Beast or receives his mark (see vs. 9).

II. **The Punishment Inflicted**—The punishment is most severe and consists of:

1. The Intoxication—"Drink of the wine of God's wrath."
2. The Indignation—"into the cup of His indignation."
3. The Tormentation—"Tormented with fire and brimstone."
4. The Humiliation—"in the presence of the holy angels and the Lamb."
5. The Duration—"the smoke of their torment ascendeth up for ever and ever."
6. The Continuation—"no rest day nor night."

Thus we behold the seventy of the third herald angel's pronouncement and it is a forecast of the judgment that actually occur in the chapters which are before us and under the Seven Vials that are yet to be poured out.

And it is little wonder that following this malediction there is immediately a benediction. Hear the **benediction** on the dark background of the **malediction** of this herald angel—behold the beatitude of the tribulation days—a Heavenly beatitude—a "blessed" in the midst of promised wrath! After the denunication, now hear the consolation! Hear the voice of the Spirit from Heaven!

**"Blessed are the dead which die in the Lord from henceforth; yea saith the Spirit, that they may rest from their labors; and their works do follow them." (vs. 13).**

No rest for the Beast worshipers, but rest to the faithful ones of the remnant of Israel in these days of the Beast and his power. "**From henceforth** means from that time. If any desire to use this Scripture as an **application** in the present time, they may, but the **interpretation** has to do with **that time.** It is held out as a special source of strength to those who hold out against the Beast and who would rather die than receive his mark or his name. Who can imagine what this will mean to the suffering ones in the dreadful days of the tribulation? There is a special beatitude of benediction pronounced upon them to steady, stay and secure them in that day. They will be "faithful unto death" and God who never lets a sparrow fall without His notice, will not let one of these fall from that time forward without His special care and remembrance. Oh, blessed beatitude, blessed benediction!

We have seen the three **Herald Angels**; there are yet the three **Angels of the Harvest** and also the **Lord of the Harvest,** for at verse 14 there is a "little apocalypse" and the "son of Man" is seen with a sharp sickle in His hand. It is harvest time—and the Harvest Angels are ready.

Lesson Fifty-nine

## GOD'S WRATH AND HIS WINEPRESS (Rev.14:14-20)

In our former study of chapter 14, we found Six Angels in preparation for the Judgment of the Seven Vials. Three of these Angels we designated as the **Herald Angels** (see vss. 6-13), three of them the **Harvest Angels** (see vss. 15-20). Between the Herald Angels and the Harvest Angels we behold the **"Son of Man in the midst."** Just a glimpse of Him is given unto us at verse 14.

"And I looked and behold a white cloud and upon the cloud one sat like unto the Son of man, having on his head a golden crown, and in his hand a sharp sickle" (vs. 14).

It is "harvest time." **The Son of Man** and each of the **Harvest Angels** have sickles.

The **"Son of Man"** is seen in the parable of Matthew 13 as the **"Sower"** here the Son of Man is seen as the **Reaper.** He is the **Husbandman** in the Gospels but the **Harvester** in the Revelation.

"He that soweth the good seed is the Son of man;

"The field is the world; the good seed are the children of the kingdom; but the tares are the children of the wicked one;

"The enemy that sowed them is the devil; the **harvest is the end of the age** (R. V.); and the **reapers are the angels."**

"As therefore the tares are gathered and **burned in the fire**; so shall it be at the **end of this age.**

"The Son of man shall send forth his angels, and they shall gather out of his kingdom all things that offend, and them that do inquity;

"And shall cast them into a furnace of fire: there shall be wailing and gnashing of teeth.

"Then shall the righteous shine forth as the sun in the kingdom of their Father" (Matt. 13:37-43).

This parable and this portion of Revelation are in prophetic harmony. The parable is the **prophecy,** this portion of Revelation is the **fulfillment.**

The end of the age has come. The tares have been sown. The Son of Man sits as the Harvester and commands His angels! Soon the offending ones and those that do inquity will come under the swift judgment of His hand. The great separation begins. The harvest of the earth is **ripe** (see Joel 3:13) and the harvesters are **ready.**

One of the Herald Angels (see 14:8) had announced the fall of Babylon and Jeremiah the Prophet spoke of this hour which has now come. Said Jeremiah:

"The daughter of Babylon is like a threshing floor; it is time to thresh her; yet a little while, and the time of her harvest shall come."

It has **come.** "Immediately he sendeth the sickle, because the harvest is come" (Mark 4:29). Said Joel: **"Put in the sickle for the harvest is ripe"** and the sickle is thrust in! Behold the angel reapers even as He said!!

## BEHOLD THE SON OF MAN!

Once no place to lay His head, now look upon that head! This is the last time He is called the Son of Man in the New Testament, see where He was first called the Son of Man in the New Testament.

The first use of the title Son of Man is found in the 8th Psalm, and the 8th Psalm has for its subject the dominion the Son of Man is about to take! As David sees Him in the 21st Psalm so here. David said, "Thou settest a crown of pure gold on His head" (Ps. 21:3) and soon He will be seen coming with many crowns on His head (see Rev. 19:12).

"All judgment is committed to the Son of Man" (see John 5:27). The "seventieth week" of Daniel is the end of the age time. The faithful remnant of Israel and the "workers of inquity" are together. They must be separated. This is the time—it is the "End of the Age." The cup of iniquity is full. The "press is full and the fats overflow," says Joel. **"Their wickedness is great,"** so great that it is God's time to remove the offense. The workers of inquity must be burned with fire and the righteous must shine in the Kingdom of their Father. Soon this will all be accomplished! Hasten, O Lord, to the harvest! Thrust in the sickle, ye angelic harvesters! Consider these angels who are the executors of judgment under the Son of Man. See 14:15-20.

Notice a few things in particular. **Three** angels. The **first** of the three (see vs. 15) came out from the temple which is in Heaven but no mention is made of a sickle. He specifically mentions the harvest of the earth.

The **second** of the three, came out of the temple which is in Heaven, having a sharp sickle but no utterance is his (see vs. 16).

The **third** of the three came out from the **altar** (see vs. 18). He especially mentions the vintage and gathers the "vine of the earth."

The vine of the earth is first introduced to us in a memorable song—**The Song of Moses** (see Deut. 32). It was a song written for a witness against Israel (see Deut. 31:19). It was written for them that "when many troubles had befallen" the nation, then this song would be a witness against them (see Deut. 31:21). Speaking of the nations God said:

> "For their vine is of the vine of Sodom, and of the fields of Gomorrah: their grapes are grapes of gall, their clusters are bitter. Their wine is the poison of dragons, and the cruel venom of asps" (Deut. 32:32, 33).

This is the vintage to be gathered and cast into the great winepress of the wrath of God which is perhaps Armageddon! What a winepress and what wrath! It is trodden without the city where so long the Gentiles or nations trod down Israel. This seems to be a premature announcement at Armageddon and perhaps the same event was in the mind of Isaiah when he wrote chapter 63:1-6.

Oh, what a day—the day of the Lamb's wrath! Who will be able to stand? The angels are now ready so also are the **vials.** We shall see them poured out upon the earth. God sustain us to think on these things which will actually take place upon the earth. Those who are in Christ Jesus will not come into these judgments.—Let us praise the Lord for exemption through the Blood of redemption!

Lesson Sixty

## SEVEN ANGELS, GOLDEN VIALS AND PLAGUES (Rev.15)

This is one of the most dramatic scenes in all the Book of Revelation! John, when he saw it ahead of its time, called it "great and marvelous" (vs. 1) and such it is. It is a chapter of unusual awe and significance. It is, the immediate pause or separation, or perhaps a preface to the last of the judgments—the Vials of God's Wrath.

This chapter, as one may see at a glance, may be simply divided as follows:

I. **The Sign in Heaven**—vs. 1.

II. **The Sea of Glass**—vs. 2.

III. **The Singers and Their Victory**—vs. 2.

IV. **The Song and Its Theme**—vss. 3, 4.

V. **The Seven Angels**—vss. 5, 6.

VI. **The Seven Golden Vials**—vss. 6, 7.

VII. **The Seven Last Plagues**—vs. 8.

We shall consider this chapter under these seven divisions.

### I. THE SIGN IN HEAVEN—vs. 1.

At chapter 12, we have the first "sign"—the sign of the **sun-clothed woman.** See 12:1.

At chapter 12:3 we have "another sign in Heaven."

At the opening of this chapter 15, we have what John calls **"another sign in Heaven."** It was to the seer a "great and marvelous sign" and to read over the chapter the wonder, majesty and marvel of the scene of this sign, one agrees with John's description, though his words mean more than we can conceive. "Seven Angels" have "the seven last plagues." (The word "seven" occurs eight times in this chapter.) There are a good many **"last"** things in the Book of Revelation and this is the last of the plagues, with these judgment comes to its end. But the fiery fury of these last seven vials—who can know? The cup of God's wrath is full; it must now be poured out! They appear in succession in the next chapter and follow the Seventh Trumpet, for this Trumpet expands into the Seven Vials.

Perhaps this event was in the mind of the Lord when He said to Moses:

"Before all thy people I will do marvels, such as have not been done in all the earth, nor in any nation; and all the people among which thou art shall see the work of the Lord; for it is a terrible thing that I will do with thee" (Exod. 34:10).

Here are the "terrible things" about to occur in God's controversy with the nations because of His people Israel. This is the **third** sign and three, seems to be associated with signs in the Scriptures.

**Three** signs were given to Moses.
**Three** signs were given to Gideon.
**Three** signs were given to Saul.
**Three** signs were given to Elijah.
**Three** signs here in the Revelation.

## II. THE SEA OF GLASS—vs. 2.

John says; "I saw as it were, a sea of glass mingled with fire." It looked glassy but was not of glass. Who that travel, have not seen a glassy sea with a sheen of glaze as if it had been polished?

This glassy sea was mingled with fire. At the pouring out of the second vial upon the sea it became as the blood of a dead man (see Rev. 16:3).

The glassy sea, fire mingled, carries our minds back

to the Exodus and a "Red Sea" where there was another song and at which singing Moses was present (see Exod. 15:1 and Rev. 15:3).

It is into the Red Sea of flame the Pharaoh of these great tribulation days, the Beast, the Man of Sin and his allies must enter, and like Pharaoh and his hosts, they will not pass. Just a little later we behold the beast, the false prophet in a sea or lake of fire. See 19:20. This lake of fire is seen again at 20:14, 15, and then immediately—"no more sea" (Rev. 21:1).

### III. THE SINGERS AND THEIR VICTORY—vs. 2.

These singers by the sea are designated by John as

"Them that had gotten the victory over the beast, and over his image, and over his mark, and over the number of his name" (vs. 2).

What a company of overcomers are here! They had "gotten the victory." It is but little wonder such encouragement was held out to overcomers in the 2d and 3d chapters of the Revelation, for the battle has been with

1. The Beast.
2. His Image.
3. His Mark.
4. The Number of His Name.

They had been successful over them all. They were tribulation days non-conformists and refused to come under the power of the Beast or worship his image. They kept company with Daniel and the Hebrew children in a furnace fired by the Beast who was inspired by the Devil and seven times heated by Satanic fury. They would not receive his mark and through all the famine which this mark had produced, they got the victory! They had not taken the number of his name for commercial advantage and without this, they have come through and have gotten the victory and are now ready to sing and shout at the sea of glass. (Well, praise the Lord!) See them **stand.** They **stand** now because they **stood.** Behold them with the harps of God! What minstrels and musicians are these! It was a song of victory, for theirs indeed was the victorious life! But does not God keep His every promise? Is He not true? Did He not promise to give "hidden manna" to the overcomer (see Rev. 2:17), so why should they need the mark of the beast as a commercial charm, when God set a table in the wilderness? See them stand on the sea in a miracle and make music and sing!

Hear these harpers and their Heavenly holy harmony! This is indeed a "song in the night," a song in the darkest night the world has ever known, but near the daybreak of the brightest day the world has ever seen. Surely He gives His people songs in the night!

Let us next consider

## IV. THE SONG AND ITS THEME—vss. 3, 4.

They **"sing the song of Moses the servant of God, and the song of the Lamb"** (vs. 3). This great anthem swells from the singers' hearts!

Personally we do not believe this song of Moses the servant of God has reference to Exodus 15. There is only one song in the Scriptures called the Song of Moses. The Song at chapter 15 of the Book of Exodus is a song Moses sang with the children of Israel. But there is a song called distinctly the song of Moses. See (Deut. 31:19, 21, 22).

**The Song of Moses is Deuteronomy 32.** Deuteronomy 32 is what Franz Delitzsch has called it—**"The compendium of all Prophecy."**

It begins with the "Most High" making choice of Israel (see vss. 8, 9) and the **deliverance of Israel from** Egypt (see vss. 10, 11, 12). This is followed by the conquest of the land when Israel rode on the high places of the earth (see vss. 13, 14), but Israel "waxed **fat**" and there follows in this song the record of their **failure** (see vss. 15 to 19) and the hiding of Jehovah's face from them (see vs. 20) and the national judgment which followed. We next behold the judgments of God on them (see vss. 22-27) with the great end-time judgments also and a summary of the Apocalypse (see vss. 29-42). This is followed by their great deliverance when the Lord takes up the controversy of His people (see vss. 41, 42), which issues in a stanza of rejoicing:

"Rejoice, O ye nations, with His people; for He will avenge the blood of His servants, and will render vengeance to His adversaries, and will be merciful unto His **land** and to His **people**" (vs. 43).

This is the song of Moses and at this time in the Book of Revelation, just preceding the execution of the last of the judgments when He will render vengeance to His adversaries, the song is sung by the singers above described.

This "Song" is indeed a witness, just as God had said —a witness for the **latter days** (see Deut. 31:29).

The Song of the Lamb is supplied here and the words which are august and wonderful—

"Great and marvelous are Thy works, Lord God Almighty; just and true are Thy ways, Thou King of Saints, Who shall not fear thee, O Lord, and glorify Thy name? for Thou only art holy; for all nations shall come and worship before Thee; for Thy judgments are made manifest" (vss. 3, 4).

What a note of praise of His glorious Person and His glorious power with which to begin these last seven terrible judgments!

Read with this Jeremiah 10:7; Psalm 102:13-22; Micah 7:16, 17; Psalm 86:9-12.

The glad millennial days are in view in this song. The time when all nations will worship Him is in the forecast here and will be in fulfillment soon. See Isaiah 66:15, 16, 23; Zechariah 14:16, 17; Psalm 86:8, 9 and many other Scriptures.

But now to the seven angels.

### V. THE SEVEN ANGELS—vss. 1, 6, 7, 8.

These seven judgment angels are now before us. Theirs is a solemn service. They are selected to execute the severest of God's plagues. Chapter 16 reveals their dramatic actions as the administrators of God's wrath and fury! Till then we must withhold comment. A description of the appearance of these angels will be found in verse 7. They are clothed in pure white linen and their "breasts are girded with golden girdles."

### VI. THE SEVEN GOLDEN VIALS—vss. 6, 7.

One of the four Living Creatures committed to the seven angels seven golden vials. These vessels of precious metals held a strange brew, they were filled with the "wrath of God." Men who will not drink of the cup of salvation must drink of this cup now full. Chapter 16 will begin the pouring out of this wrath.

### VII. THE SEVEN LAST PLAGUES—vs. 8.

A little glimpse into the temple has been given at verse 5. There it was opened. Here a smoke issues therefrom and no man is able to enter the temple till the seven last plagues of the seven angels were fulfilled. At the opening of the Tabernacle by Moses there was a cloud. See Exodus 40:34-36. When Solomon opened the Temple, there was a cloud (see I Kings 8:10, 11). There was no smoke in these instances. Here there is smoke. It is God's hour of judgment and it seems no intercession will be made, it is **all retribution** for the season of the duration of the Seven Vials.

"How great and terrible are thy judgments, O Lord," soon they will be in full force and fury!

Lesson Sixty-one

## GREAT DAY OF HIS WRATH (Rev.16:1-7) Part 1

We have come to the last series of judgments to fall upon the earth—the judgments of the **Seven Vials.** Three chapters of the Book of Revelation are devoted to these vials. Following these last seven judgments, is the return and reign of Christ. The "Judge of the whole earth" will be personally present, and indeed, even now, the "Judge standeth before the door" (James 5:9).

The time covered by the Seven Vials, chapters 16, 17, and 18, is the "great day of His wrath" or the "great tribulation."

According to the Revised Version, the word "great" occurs **eleven** times in chapter 16, **two** times in chapter 17, and **nine** times in chapter 18. The oft occurrence of the word "great," is not without much significance.

These three chapters (16, 17 and 18) deal with the following:

Chapter 16—**The Great Judgments of the Seven Vials.**
Chapter 17—**The Great Whore Is Judged.**
Chapter 18—**The Great City Is Judged.**

In chapter 16, which we are now to consider, the word "great" appears in the following verses:

**"Great voice"** (vs. 1).
**"Great heat"** (vs. 9).
**"Great river"** (vs. 12).
**"Great day"** (vs. 14).
**"Great voice"** (vs. 17).
**"Great earthquake"** (vs. 18).

**"Great an earthquake"** (vs. 18).
**"Great city"** (vs. 19).
**"Great Babylon"** (vs. 19).
**"Great hail"** (vs. 21).
**"Great plague"** (vs. 21).

A world that demands "great" events and things, will get them now, but not for pleasure, but rather for displeasure. The pouring out of the seven vials by the seven angels, divides this chapter into its seven divisions:

**THE ORDER, OBJECT AND OUTCOME**
**of the**
**JUDGMENTS OF THE SEVEN VIALS** (see Rev. 16)

The Order— The Object—
**The First Vial** (vss. 1, 2)—"Upon the earth"
—The Outcome—
"Grievous sore upon the men."
**The Second Vial** (vs. 3) —"Upon the sea"
"Became as blood."
**The Third Vial** (vss. 4-7)—"Upon the rivers and fountains"
"They became blood."
**The Fourth Vial** (vss. 8, 9)—"Upon the sun"
"Scorching great heat."
**The Fifth Vial** (vss. 10, 11)—"Upon the seat of the Beast"
"Darkness and pain."
**The Sixth Vial** (vss. 12-16)— "Upon the great river Euphrates"
"Waters dried up."
**The Seventh Vial** (vss. 17-21)—"Into the air"
"Great earthquake."

"And I heard a great voice out of the temple saying to the seven angels, Go your ways, and pour out the vials of the wrath of God upon the earth" (vs. 1).

The **great** voice of command is heard by the angels who exist to do His commandments. They each move to their appointed task and sphere. "Go your ways," saith the great voice. Each had his way and his work. They each bear a strange receptacle—a vial of "God's fury" or "wrath." This is the strongest brew ever poured out. The cup of human iniquity is full, so also the vials of God's wrath.

One would think that the judgments on Egypt were being re-enacted, and indeed they are. This is in the forecast at Exodus 34:10; Isaiah 11:16.

**The First Plague upon Egypt** resulted in the waters turning to blood.

At the pouring of the **second** and **third** vials of Revelation the **waters became blood** (see Exod. 7:18; Rev. 16:2).

**The Second Plague upon Egypt** resulted in the appearance of **frogs.**

At the pouring out of the **sixth** vial, is the appearance of **frogs** (see Exod. 8:2; Rev. 16:13).

**The Sixth Plague upon Egypt** produced boils.

The **first** vial of Revelation results in the same (see Exod. 9:8; Rev. 16:2).

**The Seventh Plague upon Egypt** was hail.

The **seventh** vial of Revelation results in the same (see Exod. 9:22; Rev. 16:21).

**The Ninth Plague upon Egypt** was darkness.

The **fifth** vial of Revelation results in the same (see Exod. 10:21; Rev. 16:10).

A careful study of these vial judgments will reveal that six out of the seven vials, have their counterpart in the judgments upon the Egyptians. It is only the

**fourth vial** of Revelation that has no corresponding judgment upon the Egyptians.

Thus it will be seen that once again God is going to say to the end time "Oppressor" and "Pharaoh" of His people—,**"Let My people Israel go."**

This is to be the deliverance of which Isaiah speaks as the **"second time"** (see Is. 11:11, 16).

**The First Vial Poured**—vs. 2. The **object** of this vial was the **"earth."** The **outcome** of this vial, a grievous sore upon men. These men, however, are particularly designated—"men which had the mark of the beast, and upon them which worshipped his image." This series of judgments, it will be noticed, is visited particularly upon the Beast and his worshipers. Thus is this terrible oblation of wrath "poured out." How could it be otherwise? The Beast has exalted himself "as God"—has lifted up his defiance against the Living God. It is an unbelievable sight. Jeremiah was right when he said:

> "The kings of the earth, and all the inhabitants of the world, would not have believed that the adversary and the enemy should have entered into the gates of Jerusalem" (Lam. 4:12).

But they have, to the astonishment of heaven and earth! The Lord must accomplish His fury. He will again pour out His fierce anger (see Lam. 2:11). The 79th Psalm well describes this scene. It is as if this portion of the Book of Revelation was written in advance, and indeed this is what it is. **"Pour out Thy wrath,"** cries the Psalmist. Here the imprecatory prayer is answered by the speedy and successive outpouring of the seven vials.

This plague is not a new one in the earth. Satan used this sort of an affliction upon Job (see Job 2:7, 8). A judgment of similar nature fell upon Miriam (see Num. 12:10). These things are spoken of in Deuteronomy 28:15, 27, 35; Leviticus 26:16.

In Egypt the plagues were sent upon the people because of the golden calf and its image (see Exod. 32:35). Here these judgments are sent because of the image of the Beast. God will smite idolatry. He is a jealous God. Remember Exodus 20:3, 4.

**The Second Vial Poured**—vs. 3. The **object** of this vial is the sea and the **outcome** of it, death to the living things in the sea. With the second vial as with the second trumpet (see Rev. 8:8), the judgment falls on the sea and the sea-dwellers. The extent of the judgment is far greater under the vial, as only one-third of life in the sea was affected by the trumpet affliction. This judgment will greatly affect transportation, as ships attempt to plow through a sea of blood and rotting, stinking fish filling the air with disease, death and pestilence! And besides this, under the fourth vial, there is to be a terrible "scorching heat" which will add to the stench and scourge of the sea.

Thank God, as members of the Body of Christ, we will not be in this judgment. **We are promised exemption by the Blood of redemption!**

In Egypt God turned their water into blood, so here also. Says the Psalmist, in referring to Egyptian history, "He turned their waters into blood, and slew their fish" (Ps. 105:29). Saith Jehovah: "I dry up the sea, * * their fish **stinketh,** * * and dieth for thirst" (Is. 50:2). You may see a little prophetic vision of this Apocalyptic judgment at the opening of Nahum. See Nahum 1:2-14. Here mention is made of a number of the vials (see vss. 4, 5, 8, 14). How many fishermen and seamen will be left without employment by reason of this second vial? This will be a severe blow at commerce. With a scorching sun above and a stinking sea beneath what pestilential vapors will fill the earth! Men who will not have God's mercy and grace, **must take His judgment and wrath.**

**The Third Vial Poured**—vss. 4-7. The **object** of the judgment is the rivers and the fountains. The **outcome** is waters turned to blood. This plague of the third vial, covering verses 4 to 7, may be divided as follows:

1. **The Vial**—"the third angel poured out his vial" (vs. 4).
2. **The Visitation**—"upon the rivers and fountains; and they became blood" (vs. 4).
3. **The Voice of the Angel in Justification**—"Thou art righteous" (vs. 5).
4. **The Voice from the Altar in Vindication**—"True and great are thy judgments" (vs. 7).

This third vial is visited upon the same physical sphere as was the third trumpet—the rivers and the fountains. Then, one-third of them were made **bitter,** here all of them are made **blood.**

The "angel of the waters" speaks forth in justification of God and in his speech the reward of the wicked is disclosed and the recompense of God declared. "Thou art righteous, O Lord," said the angel. **"They have shed the blood of saints and prophets,"** and is it not written that "whatsoever a man soweth, that shall he also reap"? They shed blood, shall they not now sup blood? Did they not shed the blood of the two witnesses in chapter 11? Is it not time for God to remember, requite and reward? Does the great Avenger forget to avenge His people? Read Deuteronomy 32:

> **"For I lift up my hand to heaven, and I say, I live for ever (comp. 16:5). If I whet my glittering sword, and mine hand take hold on judgment; I will render vengeance to mine enemies, and will reward them that hate me.**
>
> **I will make mine arrows drunk with blood and my sword shall devour flesh; and that with the blood of the slain and of the captives, from the beginning of revenges upon the enemy.**
>
> **Rejoice, O ye nations, with his people: for he will avenge the blood of his servants, and will be merciful unto his land, and to his people" (Deut. 32: 40-43).**

From the beginning of the world, there has been a scarlet stream of the blood of the slain saints and prophets of God. Christ refers to this in a severe indictment and covers a wide period of time when He says: "From the blood of righteous Abel unto the blood of Zacharias son of Barachias, whom ye slew between the Temple and the altar." Read Matthew 23:34, 35.

That was also a startling prophecy in John 16:2. Read also Luke 11:47-51.

God is always justified in what He does or He would not be God. His acts are always "righteous and true."

As severe as these judgments may appear, one can but say, **Amen, Hallelujah!!** "Righteous Thou art." "Because Thou judgest thus, Thou art Holy!" It is the holiness of God that brings judgment. Indeed, it is **the holiness of God** that is the basis of all government and law and order in the universe. If God should wink at sin, then a world of sin would never know forgiveness for sin. God does not condone sin; He **condemns sin. Even when He found it on His own Son.** The "angel of the waters" and the "voice from the temple" are both right—God is justified and vindicated in all His judgments.

Lesson Sixty-two

## GREAT DAY OF HIS WRATH (Rev.16:8,9) Part 2

**THE FOURTH VIAL** is now poured out. It is poured out upon the **sun.** Says John:

"And the fourth angel poured out his vial upon the sun; and power was given unto him to scorch men with fire.

And men were scorched with great heat and blasphemed the name of God, which hath power over these plagues: and they repented not to give him glory" (16:8, 9).

During the visitation of the judgments of the Trumpets, as recorded in chapters 8 and 9, there was an order which is followed somewhat in the judgments of the Vials. Under the Trumpets, things agricultural, aquatic and astronomical, were judged. Here the second and third vial judgment is visited upon **things aquatic.** The fourth vial is poured upon things **astronomical,** or the sun. Under the trumpet judgment, the light and heat of the sun were **reduced,** here the heat of the sun is **increased.**

For many long centuries God has made His sun to rise on the good and evil alike, but not in these days of the great tribulation, for it now rises on the evil to scorch them. When a day of intense heat has prevailed, turning the congested city into an oven seven times heated, the death-toll is always large. This will be a thousand times increased in these days when under the fourth vial, the sun scorches men with fire. There will be sun-strokes and suffocations as when flames create a great heat.

This, with the dead things in the sea, as seen under the second vial (see vss. 4, 5) will create an awful condition for those who are suffering from the boils brought about on the first vial (see vs. 2). The sun which can shine can now scorch. If the sun beat on the head of Jonah till he fainted and he wished he could die, what then will this be?

This may be the sign in the sun of which Christ spoke in Luke when He said: "And there shall be signs in the sun." (Luke 21:25)

Malachi spoke of a day coming

"That shall burn as an oven; and all the proud, yea and all that do wickedly, shall be stubble" (Mal. 4:1).

Could not Isaiah have had this time also in mind when he wrote 24:6 and 42:25?

The faithful remnant of Israel will not be touched by this heat. They will be in the midst of this furnace as the three Hebrew children in the fiery furnace; "Upon whose bodies the fire had no power, nor was an hair of their head singed, neither were their coats changed, nor the smell of fire had passed on them" (Dan. 3:27). Upon the major part of the nation which will pass through this judgment, it will be even as Moses has spoken:

"They shall be burnt with hunger, and devoured with burning heat" (Deut. 32:24).

From this darkness and distress let us turn for a moment back the pages of the Book of Revelation to the 7th chapter where is seen a great multiude who, having escaped this stroke of judgment, it is said of them: **"The sun shall not light on them nor any heat"** (7:16). Let us turn forward also the Book of Revelation to the time when it is said: **"And the city had no need of the sun."** This will comfort us to go forward with these unparalleled judgments.

But from this sun-scorching judgment, we must turn to yet others for this fourth vial judgment did not bring repentance or remorse to those upon whom it fell, but rather defiance and blasphemy. The judgments of God will not bring men to repentance—the human heart is a state of enmity against God.

**THE FIFTH VIALS**—vss. 10, 11.

"And the fifth angel poured out his vial upon the seat of the beast; and his kingdom was full of darkness; and they gnawed their tongues for pain,

"And blasphemed the God of heaven because of their pains and their sores, and repented not of their deeds" (vss. 10, 11).

Under this fifth vial, assault is made upon the Beast, the first Beast of chapter 13. The judgment here is one of darkness—**neither the sun or the moon!** Thick darkness was on the land of Egypt three days. No one arose out of their place for three days. The dominion of the Beast's kingdom is "full of darkness." Without doubt Joel has foretold this day in his prophecy:

"For the day of the Lord cometh, for it is nigh at hand;

"A day of darkness and of gloominess, a day of clouds and of thick darkness" (Joel 2:1, 2).

"The sun shall be turned into darkness" (Joel 2:31).

The awful darkness does not bring repentance. They charge God with their pains and their boils, for men always place blame on God for their own sins. So here it is true also. While they blaspheme they **"gnaw their tongues."** When in great pain folk have been heard to say, "I just bit my lips and stood it." Here they bite the tongue in the agony of pain. How much like the fifth trumpet judgment to this one! Compare them (see chap. 9:1-3).

But through all this the remnant of Israel, the One Hundred and Forty-four Thousand, are safe. As the children of Israel had light in the Egyptian darkness, so this remnant has light. They have been sealed and secured to survive this tribulation period. The Prophet Isaiah drew a series of contrasts which we think had these days in mind. He shows the favor of the remnant against the dark background of the sufferings of those who are under the judgments of that hour and time.

"Behold, my servant shall eat,

but ye shall be hungry:
Behold, my servants shall drink,
but ye shall be thirsty;
Behold, my servants shall rejoice,
but ye shall be ashamed:
Behold, my servants shall sing for joy of heart,
but ye shall cry for sorrow of heart, and shall howl for vexation of spirit (Is. 65:13, 14).

And the reason for this discrimination is found at Isaiah 65:12. Let these things be pondered. God knows how to care for His own. In the day of trouble He is the God of resources! Then follows

**THE SIXTH VIAL**—vss. 12-16. The object was the river of Euphrates. The sixth trumpet was associated with the river Euphrates and so also this sixth vial. At the sounding of the sixth trumpet a strange cavalry were liberated to slay many. Here an army is gathered and marshaled to Armageddon.

This river is actually the river Euphrates. Why should we attempt to make it mean anything else for if it means anything else **it may mean anything else** and no **interpretation will ever be reached.**

The first mention of the Euphrates river is found in Genesis 2:14. It is mentioned as one of the "four rivers" and was a literal and actual river, why then does not John mention an actual river also? **He does.** The Lord made a covenant with Abraham concerning a land, the boundaries of which included the river Euphrates (see Gen. 15:18). In this Book of Revelation the struggle is against the people of this covenant and concerning this land, therefore why think it strange that the Euphrates appears again and is mentioned? It would be strange if it were not mentioned. The Euphrates is mentioned in other places at Deuteronomy 11:24; Joshua 1:4; II Samuel 8:3. Jeremiah went and hid in the hole of a rock at the Euphrates river (see Jer. 13:1-8). There is a prophecy in Isaiah which is doubtless concerning the river Euphrates (see Is. 11:15). The river over which He shakes His hand is in our judgment the Euphrates.

As in other places the actual river is meant, then this **is not the exception.**

It is indeed a "great river." It is 1,800 miles long and as wide as 3,600 feet and very deep.

It is not too long, too wide or too deep to be "dried up" when God is ready to use it. Let it be known that the author of this article **believes God, and that it is and will be ever as He has spoken!**

When this judgment fell on the river Euphrates it was to dry up its waters as a preparation for certain kings known as the **"Kings of the East."** They are coming! Zechariah also mentions this congress and coming of kings and also the drying up of the river. See Zechariah 10:10, 11. These kings may be designated as the "Kings of the Sunrising." They are the Kings of the East. In Egypt God held up and back the waters to let His people Israel out from their enemies. But here, He dries up the waters that the enemies of Israel may get into them. It is but the death trap which is set and a snare for those who would ensnare.

This sixth vial contains three great facts to be fixed in the student's mind:

**I. The Drying Up of the River Euphrates**—vs. 12.

**II. The Demon Spirits Issuing from the Dragon, Beast and False Prophet**—vs. 13.

**III. The Day of God Almighty and Its Nearness**—vs. 14.

Demon spirits like frogs will work miracles. Thousands will be attracted and attached to them. The world is always waiting for a "miracle man." Signs and wonders will be indeed a deceptive lure to those who never walked by faith. It is sad today to see the number of Christians who **must "see" to believe rather than believe to see.** The kings of the earth will come. It will be a mobilization by the means of these miracles. The false miracles will be used to call them to battle. It will be the battle of God Almighty for this is His battle name.

In the Hebrew tongue the name of this place is Armageddon. It is in Palestine and not in Europe. The Greek is Harmageddon which means the "Mount of Megiddo." Wonderful events and great battles have occurred there in the past. Read Judges 5:19; II Kings 23:29; II Chronicles 35:22-25; Zechariah 12:11. On this great plain of Esdraelon this conflict will be staged. This is the first announcement of the battle. It will be described in chapter 19:11-18.

Is it any wonder that in the midst of the description of the events occurring under the sixth vial, the Spirit of God hesitates to exhort and assure and promise. See this wonderful interpolation:

"**Behold**, I come as a thief.
**Blessed** is he that watcheth, and
Keepeth his garments, lest he
Walk naked, and they see his shame" (vs. 15).

Notice the **"Behold"** and the **"Blessed."** These words will bear wonderful encouragement and strength to the little remnant of Israel in the days when the Dragon, the Beast and the False Prophet are in their power and despotism. These words will mean unspeakably more to them than we can now understand. It is a tribulation exhortation. It is unto the remnant of Israel for the Church is not in this judgment, for the Church is God's "new creation" and there is no judgment due to the "new creation" nor will there ever be in all time and eternity. These judgments are on the earth and the earth dwellers, and the Church the Body of Christ is a

Heavenly Body. God has never seen the Church on earth but always beholds the Church as raised and seated with Christ, and at His right hand entirely outside the age, for the Church has been delivered from this "present evil age."

Lesson Sixty-three

## GREAT DAY OF HIS WRATH (Rev.16:17-21) Part 3

**THE SEVENTH VIAL IS POURED OUT!** Says the Revelation: see 16:17-21.

This is the **twenty-first** judgment. It is the last vial of the last series of judgments. Once again the Temple appears as it has at the close of the seal and trumpet judgments. The Temple comes into view for the **last time,** for in the new heavens and earth there will be no Temple. Says John, **"I saw no temple therein for the Lord God Almighty and the Lamb are the temple of it."** Out of this Temple many voices are heard praising Christ at the opening of the 19th chapter and then the Temple scenes are over.

At the hill of Calvary there was heard a voice crying: **"It is finished!"** It was the finish of a purchase a redeeming transaction. It was the finish cf the atoning and ransoming work which the Son of God accomplished. It was the "It is finished," of our salvation. But here the voice, **"It is done,"** indicates the end of the age is at hand; the hour of the Son of Man has come; the hour for the final judgment has arrived and soon the **King** will take the Kingdom and all that offend shall be cast out. It is done—the last vial of the last judgment is poured out, and chronologically we are brought up to the events of chapter 19:11, where we behold the coming Christ. The descriptive details of the fall of Babylon in chapters 17 and 18 are an interpolation—a sort of an explanatory clause introduced into the subject. The voice that bid the vials be poured out, declares the judgment act at its close. It is the voice of the God of the Temple.

It is a terrible hour!

Lightenings,
Voices,
Thunders,
Earthquakes.

A time of terrible electric storms. Flashing lightnings, rolling thunder and great voices! Consternation and terror fall upon all! The "heavens are angry" indeed and the earth trembles when shaken by great earthquakes exceeding anything the world has ever yet known. It is the time of which the writer to the Hebrews has spoken. As a nation they refused "Him that speaketh." "In times past," says the author of the letter specifically to Hebrews, "God spake unto our fathers in the Prophets, hath in the end of these days (the end of the days of the Law and the Prophets) in His Son." "How shall we escape," says the writer, "if we neglect so great a salvation?" "For if they escaped not who refused Him that spake on earth, much more shall not we (Hebrews) escape, if we turn away from Him that speaketh from Heaven: whose voice then shook the earth: but now He hath promised, saying,

"Yet once more I shake not the earth only, but also Heaven" (Heb. 12:25, 26).

This is a quotation from the Prophet Haggai as found in 2:6 and 7 of his prophecy. The Prophet includes the sea and the dry land also. This is without doubt the same event of which John in the Revelation under the seventh vial, and the writer of the Hebrews refer. It will be interesting to note that at the close, or rather the conclusion of this passage, in both Haggai and Hebrews, Christ and the Kingdom immediately appear. See Haggai 2:7: "And the desire of all nations shall come."

See Hebrews 12:28: "Wherefore we receiving a Kingdom." This is also true in the Revelation.

There have been many earthquakes; but never one like this.

There was a most remarkable earthquake in the twenty-seventh year of the reign of Uzziah, the king of Judah. Both Amos and Zechariah mention this earthquake as outstanding. Says Amos in referring to it: **"Two years before the earthquake"** (Amos 1:1). Says Zechariah in mentioning it: **"Ye shall flee, like as you fled from before the earthquake in the days of Uzziah king of Judah"** (Zech. 14:5). Josephus says of this particular earthquake that **"it was so violent as to divide a mountain in halves, which lay to the west of Jerusalem, and moved one part of it from its place four furlongs or five hundred paces."**

As great an earthquake as was this in Uzziah's days, the earthquake under the seventh vial will exceed it, it will be, says John, **"such as was not since men were upon the earth"** (16:18).

At the time of our Lord's crucifixion there was an earthquake. Matthew 27:51 records it. Many have been of the opinion that this earthquake was perceived by all the world. It must have been severe for the Temple gates were shaken and the vail in the Temple torn or rent. It was so terrible that it deeply impressed the centurion who thought it was to acknowledge the injustice of Christ's condemnation (see Matt. 27:54).

But this earthquake under the seventh vial is greater.

There was an earthquake in Philippi when Paul and Silas were imprisoned (see Acts 16); there was an earthquake under the sixth seal (see chap. 6), and an earthquake at the slaughter of the Two Witnesses (see chap. 11), but this is the greatest of all and is foretold by Ezekiel and fulfilled in the Revelation. Says Ezekiel:

**"Surely in that day there shall be a great shaking in the land of Israel; so that the fishes of the sea, and the fowls of the heaven, and the beast of the field, and all creeping things that creep upon the earth, and all the men that are upon the face of the earth, shall shake at my presence, and the mountains shall be thrown down, and the steep places shall fall, and every wall shall fall to the ground" (Ezek. 38:19, 20; see also Hag. 2:21, 22).**

So great was this earthquake that Babylon was divided into three portions. Other cities were affected, for says the Record, **"And the cities of the nations** (Gentiles) **fell."** This is evidently a reference to the cities of the confederated nations or allies of Babylon. They fell also. It is indeed such an earthquake as men on the earth have never known.

**"Babylon comes up for remembrance."** God never forgets. Chapter 14:8, gave us an indication of this hour and prepared the mind for this event. It has now come. The next two chapters will give us detail of this fall of Babylon. God holds a cup in His hand. It has a strange and strong brew—it is the **"cup of His wrath."** It contains the **"wine of His fierceness."** Babylon must drink as she has made drunk. It is a cup of fury! He will not let the cup pass from Babylon. She must drink the cup of God's wrath!

Along with other features of this judgment of the seventh vial there is reported the sinking of islands and mountains. They are gone from the places the geographical surveys have located and tabulated them. There are hundreds of islands in the Adriatic sea and associated seas, but they are all gone now! Mountains have disappeared. Surely God is shaking the earth! The maps of physical geography bear false witness, for the mountains and islands are no longer where indicated. In chapter 6:14, they were **moved,** here they **flee.** And with all this a great hail follows. The Egyptian hail was literal and so is this. These hail stones are very large. Their weight is the weight of a talent. This is one hundred and fourteen pounds troy weight. (A talent in Greece was about fifty-six pounds.) A Roman Catapult threw stones the weight of a talent by means of an engine prepared for the same. Can God send down prodigious hailstones upon the earth when He is ready? He can and He will for He **will fulfill every word John has foretold.** They may be the product of the reduced heat and light of the sun and moon, as seen under the fourth trumpet (see Rev. 8:12).

Lesson Sixty-four

## THE HARLOT AND THE BEAST (Rev.17) Part 1

**"Come hither,"** at chapter 4:1 and with this voice of command John is granted a vision in Heaven. Again and the command of one of the seven angels: **"Come hither"** and John beholds the judgment of "the great whore that sitteth upon many waters" (17:1). Following this John heard once again this command for we read; "And there came unto me one of the seven angels which had the seven vials full of the seven last plagues, and talked with me, saying, **Come hither,"** I will shew thee the Bride, the Lamb's wife" (21:9). But before we see the "Bride, the Lamb's Wife" we must see the whore, the harlot, the illegitimate paramour of the nations.

Before we shall be vouchsafed the vision of a new Jerusalem, we must behold an old Babylon. We must behold a woman and a beast before we behold a Bride and a Lamb.

Judgment must come to an end before blessings begin. The **"Come hither,"** of 17:1 is pre-millennial. The **"Come hither,"** of 21:9, is post-millennial. Before we reach the glory of the Bride and the Lamb, many things must transpire. We introduced this last "come hither" to keep up the anticipation and expectation of the student for dark indeed is the period into which we are now entering at chapter 17. It is the judgment of

### The Harlot Woman and the Scarlet Beast

This 17th chapter with the 18th is perhaps the most conspicuous prophecy in the Book. Over these chapters there has been much controversy and many contentions have arisen. We cannot settle these nor shall we attempt to do so. We will say, however, that we believe that these chapters with the others of Revelation are all **future.** They have to do in our judgment, with the days of the tribulation after the Church, the Body of Christ has been removed.

The events recorded in these chapters we believe are **prophecy to be fulfilled** and **not history that has been or is being fulfilled.** With those who hold a viewpoint which differs we have deep regard and respect and love, but we are held firm in our conviction that the prophecies of the Book of Revelation are future. They are **yet to be fulfilled** and are **not yet history.**

Chapter 17 may be divided into two great divisions which we believe will simplify the study of the chapter:

**I. WHAT THE ANGEL SHEWED JOHN EXCITING HIS ADMIRATION**—vss. 1-6.

**II. WHAT THE ANGEL SAID TO JOHN BY WAY OF EXPLANATION**—vss. 7-18.

What John **saw** will first come under our consideration and then what the angel **said.** In the light of the angels explanation we may arrive at interpretation. This is a Divinely-given vision. We must have a Divinely-given interpretation. Whatever liberties men may take at the application of these words we shall leave to their own responsibility and in our minds it is a serious thing to make application apart from true interpretation. Interpretation is **primary,** application is **secondary.** It is difficult for our minds to grasp the real magnitude of these Apocalyptic judgments and without doubt these visions will be better understood in the days when these judgments are occurring in the earth, but we do not have to wait for these days to understand for God has made this last Book a **revelation** and not concealment. We must also remember that Scripture is best known by Scripture and in the study of the Bible we may always cry: **O God! In Thy light we see light."**

**I. What the Angel Shewed John Exciting His Admiration**—vss. 1-6.

What the angel **shewed** John (see vs. 1-6) is interpreted by what the angel **said** to John. This does not leave us to **interpret** the vision but to **believe** it. The Book of Revelation is never without its own interpretation. It is always to be taken literal unless **otherwise stated.** When the Spirit of God designates a "sign" as at chapter 12:1, 2, or supplies the symbol and the figure of speech as He does here and **explains what it means,** or if the Spirit of God speaks, as He does at 8:8, and says, **"as it were,"** then we know to interpret symbolically or figuratively. He has never left us without the key to interpretation, for the Bible is a sufficient key to the understanding of the Bible. The Bible is sufficient for the Bible. No book outside of the Book is required.

**The Bible is the best commentary on the Bible!**

We shall present a few parallel passages that we may give illustration and thus come to the interpretation. For instance; **What is meant by the "whore" the "woman" of verses 1 and 3?**

| WHAT JOHN SAW | WHAT THE ANGEL SAID |
|---|---|
| "I will show unto thee the judgment of the **great whore**—vs. 1. I saw a **woman** sit"—vs. 3. | "And the woman which thou sawest is that great city which reigneth over the kings of the earth"—vs. 18. |

Here we have God's own explanation and therefore

**true interpretation.** We dare not introduce anything as the meaning here for God has plainly spoken.

Again; some may ask, **What are the "many waters" mentioned here?** The text itself will furnish the full explanation and we display them for comparison.

| WHAT JOHN SAW | WHAT THE ANGEL SAID |
|---|---|
| "Come hither; I will shew unto thee the judgment of the great whore that sitteth upon **many waters**"—vs. 1. | "And he saith unto me, The **waters** which thou sawest, where the whore sitteth, are peoples, and multitudes, and nations, and tongues"—vs. 15. |

Here we have God's explanation and we need not go astray. Nor must we introduce into this Scripture anything contrary to what is written. The angel is the best interpreter and we must abide by this. We must yet further consider the various figures of speech used in this chapter.

**Who or what is the "scarlet beast" according to the angel?**

| WHAT JOHN SAW | WHAT THE ANGEL SAID |
|---|---|
| "I saw a woman sit upon a scarlet coloured beast"—vs. 3. | "The beast that thou sawest was, and is not; and shall ascend out of the bottomless pit, and go into perdition"—vs. 8. |

Here is yet further light and these things must be pondered. Again there is light on some details of the beast. He has seven **heads** and **ten horns.** What do they mean or signify?

| WHAT JOHN SAW | WHAT THE ANGEL SAID |
|---|---|
| "Beast * * having seven heads"—vs. 3.<br>"The beast that carrieth her, which hath seven heads and ten horns"—vs. 7. | "The seven heads (represent) seven mountains, and they are (or represent) seven kings"—vs. 9, 10.<br>"The ten horns which thou sawest are ten kings, which have received no kingdom as yet; but receive power as kings one hour with the beast"—vs. 12. |

Thus we behold what infinite pains the Spirit of God has taken to explain the meaning of each figure. It is not what we read **in** the Book of Revelation that is confusing, it is what we read **into** the Book of Revelation.

We are now ready for the interpretation of the vision and coming to the time when the "mystery of iniquity" has come to its fullness and the Babylon which had its rise in Genesis, has had its run and now comes to its ruin. This is the judgment of the **seventh vial** continued and when it is finished the King of kings and the Lord of lords will appear. Armageddon will follow, after which the reign of David's Son and Lord and the earth filled with millennial blessedness!

Lesson Sixty-five

## THE HARLOT AND THE BEAST (Rev.17) Part 2

When God gave unto John the vision of a woman, He explained what He meant. "The woman which thou sawest is that great city, which reigneth over the kings of the earth" (vs. 18). We cannot call therefore a city a "system" or a "religion." We have no authority or right to change a symbol to some other significance when God has plainly spoken. If this process were followed there would be no end to such a method and there would be continuous confusion. We believe the city referred to here is Babylon and not Rome or Jerusalem. Upon the forehead of the woman this was plainly written. The Revised Version in the margin spells the word "mystery" in small letters, indicating that the word mystery is not a part of the title. This is thought by many to be the correct reading and also that the word "great" does not form a part cf this name, but rather is a description and Divine interpretation of it. The secret symbol on her forehead was

**"BABYLON THE GREAT**

**the mother of harlots and abominations of the earth."** There are many teachers who are our superiors who attempt tc make this to be Rome and the Roman Papacy, including, of course, the Pope and the entire Papal system. We do not so understand this and while we respect those who differ, we steadfastly stand by our convictions. We would respectfully request those who think otherwise to withhold their correspondence for we have gone over the subject not a little. We are aware of the awful abominations of Romanism and are also certain that Romanism is Babylonianism and that the idolatry of Babylon has been carried into Rome. This, Hyslop has shown in his remarkable book, entitled, "The Two Babylons." We believe Babylon to be the mother of Rome and also that the Scriptures teach the rebuilding of Babylon. With this viewpoint many choice and cultured teachers disagree. We do not intend to throw the matter into controversy at this point.

Babylon from the beginning has been the fountainhead of all idolatry. Rome had its source and spring in this fountainhead and for this reason there is such a strong resemblance between the mother and her child. Perhaps, the mystery of inquity referred to in II Thessalonians 2:7 is a reference to this. This city was founded by Nimrod. Babylon was his city as we learn at Genesis 10:10. Cain's city before the flood was doubtless the same sort and kind. After the flood Babylon became the seat of demon abnormalities, half human, superhuman and demon. When we read in the Scriptures of Nephilim or of Rephaim and of Anakim they are no doubt demon products. There are the Titans of the Greeks and Ishtar, Isis, Ashtoreth and the abominations of other nations. We all know that these abominations and idolatries existed long before Rome. In the Old Testament we read of idolatry in the worship of Moloch and of Remphan and of Chium. See Acts 7:43 and Amos 5:25, 26. We read of the abominations of Zidonians and of Chemosh and of the abominations of the Moabites and of Milcon and not least the abomination of the children of Ammon which were introduced by Solomon (see I Kings 11:5; II Kings 23:11). These abominations were all prior to the abominations o. Rome. Rome is one of the abominations to be classified with the others. You must go back to the land of Shinar. The Babylon of Nebuchadnezzar days does not date far enough back. Some derive the name of Babylon from the name of the principle idol which was Belus. Nimrod called the city Bab-el. This seems to be derived from Babah-gate which seems to be lifted up in contest and contrast with Bethel, The House of God. Many interpret the statement that Nimrod was a "mighty hunter" as meaning that he was a mighty rebel before the Lord. This city was the seat and the source of all idolatry of which Rome is the **follower** and not the **founder.** Let us remember that thousands of years before Rome, idolatries and abominations filled the earth. When we come to study Romanism we find all of the manifestations of idolatry in full display. It is the fruit of Babylon the source from which Rome is sustained.

Verse 6 declares that this great city is drenched with the blood of saints and the blood of the martyrs of Jesus and when he saw this he was caused to "greatly wonder." By the spirit of God he was permitted to look in advance into the martyrdoms which will take place during the time of tribulation covered by the Book of Revelation. Read also chapter 13:7; Daniel 7:21; 11:7; and 12:1, 7. These things were foreknown and foretold by the Psalmist as well as by the Prophet John. This terrible massacre was doubtless in the mind of the Psalmist when he said:

> "O God, keep not Thou silence:
> Hold not Thy peace, and be not still, O God.
> For, lo, Thine enemies make a tumult:
> And they that hate Thee have lifted up the head.
> They take crafty counsel against Thy people,
> And consult together against Thy hidden ones.
> They have said, Come, and let us cut them off from being a nation;
> That the name of Israel may be no more in rememberance."

Here is the greatest persecution that Israel has yet known, planned and promoted. It is a great anti-

Semitic persecution. Its purpose is to blot Israel out of national existence. We are conscious in fact that Rome has put to death many martyrs but there were many martyrs put to death before Rome existed. The spirit that exists in Rome existed before Rome. In the days to come after the removal of the Church, which is the Body of Christ, under the directions of the Beast the Man of Sin, terrible persecutions will arise. Babylon will have in her many martyrs and just as John saw it. It will be a most terrific assault. Psalm 79, verses 1-3 show us these martyrs with blood like water and with none to bury the dead. See also Psalm 9:10; 44:22; 104:5. The days to come are to be bloody days and Babylon will furnish her quota of the slain. John saw this and foretold it. He was not looking back into history and upon the past, but out into prophecy and the future. The Bible may be read together into one harmonious whole. The Babylon which commences in Genesis is the Babylon which continues through the rest of the Scriptures and concludes in the Book of Revelation. In Genesis, Babylon is founded, in Revelation it is fallen.

Lesson Sixty-six

## THE HARLOT AND THE BEAST (Rev.17) Part 3

The Beast, the Seven Heads and the Ten Horns, now come under our consideration. These singular persons of prophecy challenge us to careful meditation.

The Beast is described in this chapter three times as the one, **"who was," and "is not," and "yet is."** See verses 8, (2 times) and 11. It is a summary of the past, present and the future of the Beast.

**I. His Past.** He **"was"** and is, seen first, at the opening of chapter 13. This is the Beast as we see him during the first half of this prophetic week—in his first manifestation. The student may return to Revelation 13, and review the facts and refresh the memory. At chapter 13:3, we learn that he received a "deadly wound," he was assassinated—wounded to death and died. This explains the words, **"is not."**

**II. His Future.** He is about to "ascend out of the bottomless" pit. He **"yet is."** There will be a superhuman manifestation. He will be "healed" (Rev. 13:3). This healing and revival from death will cause the whole world to wonder after him. Just the thing desired to accomplish the dominical design.

He **"ascended"** out of the Abyss (see 13:1). He will **"go into perdition"** (see Rev. 19:20, and 20:10). See also John 17:12.

The only ones who will not "wonder" after and seek and patronize this Beast, are those whose names are written in the Book of Life "from the foundation of the world" (vs. 8).

With the revival of the Beast to the wonderment of the world comes a confederation of kings who are associated with the Beast in the end time persecution and closing days of the "Times of the Gentiles." We cannot speculate as to these kings, but this one thing is evident, they have **"one mind and give their power and strength to the Beast."** This will be the most colossal and gigantic confederation and alliance the world has ever seen. The words of the 2nd Psalm will take a full meaning:

"Why do the nations rage, and the people imagine a vain thing? The kings of the earth set themselves, and rulers take counsel together against the Lord and his anointed, saying, Come let us break their bands asunder, and cast their cords from us."

Look upon these words a moment. First, we have **"nations,"** then **"peoples,"** next **"kings of the earth,"** then **"rulers,"** all taking **"counsel."** The Beast is the one who counsels them. He is in **supreme command.** They have **"one mind"** and give national strength and political power to the Beast. At Revelation 17:15, we have practically the same enumeration; "peoples, multitudes, nations and tongues:" It is a universal confederation under the one head—the Beast.

This may be seen in another phase of prophecy at Psalm 83:

"They that hate **Thee** have lifted up the head (the Beast). They have taken crafty counsel against Thy People" (vss. 2, 3). Does not the Beast and his confederates make war against the Lamb? See Revelation 17:14. The hatred is to "Thee" and the counsel against **"Thy People."** The Psalmist is in full harmony with the Seer of the Apocalypse. Psalm 110, shows the enemies of Christ being subjected to Him or made His "footstool." It is strange then that we should have a picture prophecy by the Psalmist of the Lord.

"Striking through kings in the day of his wrath" (see Ps. 110:5).

He is seen at Ps. 110:6, judging among nations with many "dead bodies." We see also the Beast receiving the **"wound"** and then as the "head over many countries," **"lift up the head."**

**John** and **David** saw the same confederation, the same "head" over the countries in the confederation, and the judgment of the Lord upon the "head" and the confederates (read Ps. 110:6, 7).

At verse 12 (chap. 17), ten kings receive power to reign "one hour with the Beast." Who they are now we do not know. It will be known at the time of the Beast. Theirs will be but a **brief reign.** These are gathered together for a battle that is fought in chapter 19. Armageddon will create a new "valley of the kings" but their dead bodies will be food for birds of prey (see 19:21).

"The Lamb shall overcome them." The confederation is folly. **"The Lord shall * * vex them in His sore displeasure"** (Ps. 2).

The agreement or confederation which the kings make with the Beast is under the **over-rule** of God. He puts it into their hearts, awaiting the fulfillment of His own purpose (see vs. 17). How God does make the **"wrath of man to praise Him."** He can take a Pharaoh, a Herod or a Beast, and cause them to work **out His own will!**

The whore is yet due the hate of the confederated kings. When the chapter opens, she sits in "purple and scarlet color, decked with gold and precious stones, and pearls, having a golden cup in her hand." See 17:4. But she is "drunk with the blood of saints and the blood of the martyrs of Jesus" (see vs. 6). This **honor** at verse 16, has turned to **hate.** They strip her of her garments and gold and glory and make her desolate and naked. Her flesh is roasted.

This woman is a "great city." The "great city" will

come before us in our next study. The fall of Babylon is near and with Babylon the Beast and his confederation. Soon we shall hear the cry; **"Alas! alas, that great city!"** (chap. 18:10).

God will make short work of it.

In the stead of the kingdom of the Beast and his throne, **the throne of our God** and **His Christ must succeed.** Behold the vision which God has given the Psalmist of the days when "**a King rules in righteousness.**" It will strengthen our hearts for the horror and the terror we must confront in chapters 18, 19. Read, and rejoice, and pray for the return to reign! (See Psalm 72).

Lesson Sixty-seven

## FALL OF BABYLON (Rev.18)

Now for the last stroke of the successive judgments. God will "cut it short" in righteousness and make a "quick work" of it.

The **Babylon,** which we saw arise in **Genesis,** now falls in **Revelation.** Babylon **commenced** in Genesis, **continued** through all the Scriptures, comes to **conclusion** here in Revelation.

This Fall of Babylon is one of the last acts in the **"Divine Drama of Judgment,"** which began at Chapter 6. It occurs under the **Seventh** or last **Vial.**

This is a **prophecy** of Babylon. It does not record things that have gone into **history** but are yet to be fulfilled in history. Whatever has been the past history of Babylon, does not exhaust **this prophecy.** We believe that the great prophecies concerning Babylon are foretold of the **Babylon of this chapter.** The fall of Babylon as described here is apart from anything Babylon has yet known.

The prophecy of Isaiah and as recorded in chapter 13:9, 12, requires this chapter to fulfill them.

There is a cry in Jeremiah the Prophet, which if compared with this of chapter 18:6, 10, 21, will be found to harmonize. **"Babylon is taken,"** says Jeremiah. **"Babylon is fallen,"** says John. John and Jeremiah saw the same Babylon. See further, Jeremiah 50:28, 40, 41, 46. See Jeremiah 25:12, also 51:3, 6, 26, 27, 29, 43. Says Jeremiah, **"Babylon is suddenly fallen"** (51:8). Says

John, **"Alas, alas, that great city Babylon, that mighty city! for in one hour is thy judgment come."** They see the same city **and the same judgment.**

Babylon was never destroyed "suddenly," it will be here at the time foretold by chapter 18.

"Arabs" do "pitch their" tents on the site of the Babylon that was, but they will not on the site of the Babylon that is here destroyed.

It is not the "abode of dragons," but this, the rebuilt Babylon, after this judgment has passed upon it, will be even as God has spoken.

There are a few things in the chapter to notice in particular. The judgment is **sudden.** At verse 8 we are told that her plagues will come in **"one day."** These plagues are: "death, mourning, famine and fire." They came to Japan with such rapidity and in **one day** as a past terrible catastrophe revealed.

The period time known as **"one hour"** is mentioned **three times.** See verses 10, 17, 19.

**At verse 10,** the **kings of the earth,** the kings we saw **in** chapter 17 look upon her ruins to lament and cry, "that great city, mighty city, in **one hour** is thy judgment come."

**At verse 16, the merchants** who have greatly profited in her, take up the lament because commerce has suffered, "In **one hour** so great riches is come to nought."

**At verse 19** they wail again because of the destruction of maritime facilities. They have come to naught and their lament is, in **one hour** is she made desolate."

The lamentation **"Alas, alas!"** occurs **two times.** See verses 10 and 16.

How could it be otherwise? This city, the seat of the world's commerce and culture, is also the seat of demonism and humanism.

"And he cried mightily with a strong voice, saying, Babylon the great is fallen, is fallen, and is become the habitation of devils, and the hold of every foul spirit, and a cage of every unclean and hateful bird.

For all nations have drunk of the wine of the wrath of her fornication, and the kings of the earth have committed fornication with her, and the merchants of the earth are waxed rich through the abundance of her delicacies."

Here we see:

1. **Babylon, the habitation of demons—**, "devils, foul spirits, unclean and hateful birds" (see vs. 2).

2. **The intoxication of the nations in association with Babylon—**, "drunk" (vs. 2).

3. **The fornication of the kings of the earth—**, "have committed fornication with her" (vs. 2).

4. **The association of merchants for financial gain—**, "waxed rich through her power and luxury" (see vs. 2).

Within this city of Babylon, at the time of this judgment, will be a company of the people God called **"My people."** They are not difficult to identify. They are not the Church, which is the Body of Christ. Most students will agree that the Church is out in these judgments but present with the Lord.

Who **"My people"** are here will be found in Jeremiah 50:4-9. See Jeremiah 51:45. They are a remnant of "His people," His own chosen nations which He will remove.

4 "And I heard another voice from heaven, saying, Come out of her, my people, that ye be not partakers of her sins, and that ye receive not of her plagues."

The cause for the calamity of Babylon is then stated: vss. 5-8.

1. **The Reach of Her Sins**—"unto heaven" (vs. 5).

2. **The Reward of Her Iniquity"**—"reward her double" (see vs. 6).

3. **The Retort of Babylon**—"I sit a queen * * see no sorrow" (vs. 7).

4. **The Retribution upon Her**—"death, famine, fire" (see vs. 8).

As Abraham looked back upon Sodom and saw the "smoke of her burning," so here **three** classes look upon

Babylon and behold the "smoke of her burning" (vs. 9).

1. **The Mourning Kings** are seen at verses 9, 10.
2. **The Mourning Merchants** at verses 11-16.
3. **The Mourning Maritime Masters** at verses 17-19.

Then follows the command to **Rejoice!**

20 "Rejoice over her, thou heaven, and ye holy apostles and prophets; for God hath avenged you on her."

1. **The Angel and the Stone**—vs. 21.

He illulstrates the sudden judgment of Babylon in a pictorial action. He casts the stone into the sea, saying,

"Thus with violence shall that great city Babylon be thrown down, and shall be found no more at all."

See Jeremiah 51:63; Ezekiel 36:21.

2. **The Mirthless and Musicless City!**—vs. 22.

22 "And the voice of harpers and musicians, and of pipers, and trumpeters, shall be heard no more at all in thee; and no craftsman, of whatsoever craft he be, shall be found any more in thee; and the sound of a millstone shall be heard no more at all in thee;"

**Lonely, lightless,** and **forsaken** city!

23 "And the light of a candle shall shine no more at all in thee; and the voice of the bridegroom and of the bride shall be heard no more at all in thee: for thy merchants were the great men of the earth."

We shall hereafter turn to another city to hear harpers and musicians and pipers. We shall hereafter turn to another city to see a light greater than that of a candle and where we shall hear the voice of a bride and a bridegroom! It will be a city **"whose builder and maker is God." It is the City of Revelation 21.**

God, turn our eyes from the ruin of Babylon to the revelation of the New Jerusalem! From the city of man to the City of God!

Lesson Sixty-eight

## VOICES IN HEAVEN (Rev.19:1-10)

After looking upon Babylon and the destruction of this great city we are now attracted by a voice and a vision in Heaven. We approach the **climax** and the **crisis** of the Book. We are to see "Heaven opened" and the **White Horse Rider** traveling in the "greatness of His strength." There is here a portion of a chapter of praise preceding the closing events of the age and the Advent of Christ to begin the Millennial or Kingdom age.

There is **sevenfold praise** in verses 1 to 6.

**I. Much People in Heaven** (vs. 1). **Alleluia!**

**II. The Four and Twenty Elders** (vs. 4). **Alleluia!**

**III. The Four Beasts** (vs. 4). **Amen, Alleluia!**

**IV. The Voice Out of the Throne** (vs. 5). **Praise our God!"**

**V. The Voice of a Great Multitude** (vs. 6).

**VI. Voice of Many Waters** (vs. 6). **Alleluia!**

**VII. Voice of Mighty Thunderings** (vs. 6).

This chapter may be divided into two divisions;

**I. ALLELUIA AND AMEN (Voices in Heaven)**—Vss. 1-10.

**II. ADVENT AND ARMAGEDDON (Vision on the Earth)**—Vss. 11-21.

We shall first consider verses 1-10 or division number **One.**

**I. "ALLELUIA" AND "AMEN" (The Voices in Heaven)**—Vss. 1-10.

This is a portion of preparatory praise in expectation and anticipation of the immediate manifestation of the Lord from Heaven.

In chapter 18 the voice was crying on **earth, "Alas! Alas!"** (18:16), but at the opening of this chapter it is a "great voice of much people **in Heaven"** saying' "Alleluia!" **Four** times they say, **"Alleluia!"** (vss. 1, 3, 4, 6). The word **"Hallelujah"** is a compound Hebrew word which may be pronounced, **hallelu-jah** and means **"Praise-ye-jah."** The time to "Praise the Lord" has come. The word Hallelujah, ("Alleluia," in the Greek) occurs **four times seven,** or **twenty-eight** times in the Bible. **Twenty-four** of these occurrences are in the Old Testament and the remaining **four are in this Book of Revelation.** It shows two things; (1) The Book of Revelation is a **judgment Book** and (2) it deals with Old Testament prophecies, namely, the **King** and His **Kingdom** for the **earth.**

The word **Hallelujah** occurs in the Bible for the first time at **Psalm 104:35.**

This Psalm closes with the words—"Praise ye **THE LORD"** (vs. 35). This is the Hebrew for **"Hallelujah."**

It is here connected and associated with the Divine judgment of the wicked and their overthrow, as is also the first **Alleluia** of the New Testament: Rev. 19:1. Indeed verse 35 of this 104th Psalm is a summary for the 19th chapter of Revelation,

> "Let sinners be consumed out of the earth,
> And let the wicked be no more.
> Bless thou the Lord, O my soul.
> Praise ye **THE LORD."**

See Ps. 111:1; 112:1; 113:1; 146:1; 148:1; 150:1. (See the margin of Bible.) The word **"Hallelujah"** is a study in itself and is used in **judgment only.**

The **first two** times the word **"Alleluia"** is used, it is in **rejoicing** over an event that **is past.**

The **next two times** the word **"Alleluia"** is used, is in **rejoicing** over an event that **is to come.**

Verses 1 to 3 look upon the fallen Babylon of chapters 17 and 18. **"Alleluia."**

"He hath judged the great whore, which did corrupt the earth with her fornication, and hath avenged the blood of His servants at her hand." **"Alleluia."**

This is a retrospective glance with praise to God for the events of the past. **"Babylon is fallen,"** and this is the **cause** of rejoicing.

Verses 4 to 10 look forward, not backward, to the **"Marriage of the Lamb"** and the readiness of **"the Bride,"** is the cause of the use of the word **"Alleluia,"** in verses 4 and 6. "Let us be glad and rejoice," for thus it always is at a **marriage and a marraige feast.**

In the Babylon which had just fallen, and as recorded in chapters 18 and 19, there was "no voice of the bridegroom and of the bride" anywhere heard in it (see 18:23), but now again, a **marriage** and a **marriage supper** is planned (see vss. 7-9), and instead of a harlot Babylon, a holy Bride; instead of a woman in **scarlet,** a wife in **white linen.** How great the change from the desolation of Babylon to the anticipation of a marriage!

There are Four things about this **Marriage of the Lamb** and its announcement, we call to attention:

**I. THE PROCLAMATION**—vss. 6, 7. **"Be glad" —"Rejoice"—"Give honour to Him."**

There was a **former call to a wedding.** See Matt. 22:2-7. But they would not come—they did not "rejoice." They gave no honor, but here there is no miscarriage of the marriage plans. Those now "bidden are worthy." The event is ready. The virgins of Matt. 25:10 are ready to enter in. Praise the Lord!

**II. THE PREPARATION**—vs. 7. **"His wife hath made herself ready."**

There is also a parable which tells of a wedding feast where there were guests without garments, but not so here—the wife is **"ready."** See Matt. 22:11. There are no "speechless guests" here for all are **voicing their rejoicing** (see vss. 4-9).

**III. THE DECORATION**—vs. 8. **"Arrayed in fine linen."**

"Fine linen clean and white." The counsel to the Laodicean assembly included the necessity of **"white rainment"** for clothing (Rev. 3:18). The meaning of the white linen is explained to be the righteousness of the saints, a **rewarded righteousness.**

**IV. THE INVITATION**—vs. 9. **"Blessed are they which are called."**

The five wise virgins "were ready" and went with him into the marriage. So here the invitation has gone out and they are now ready to go in. The word **"blessed"** occurs **seven** times in the Book of Revelation and this is the forth occurrence. This is another one of the many beatitudes and benedictions that intersperse this Book of maledictions. In the midst of many **"woes"** the word **"blessed"** comes with benediction. Here is the reward and recompense of the "Overcomers"—God has kept His Word and fulfills every promise.

We next hear the **attestation** of the angel—**"These are the true sayings of God"** (vs. 9). The veracity of the words of this Book are often **attested** (see also 21:5 and 22:6). The angel messenger knew the authenticity and the infallibility of these words, if the fallen sons of Adam do reject them.

Then follows the **adoration** and **prostration** of John. **"He fell down before his feet to worship him."** The angel would not receive worship. This could not be. **"Worship God"** is the instruction found here. At the opening of the Revelation, John fell at the feet of the risen and glorified Lord, and fell at His feet as one dead, but before **"His feet,"** only not an angel's, for an angel is but a **creature,** but Christ is the **Creator** of all angels and all else! For this reason the angel's **exhortation, "See thou do it not"** (vs. 10). Both of them were serving John's brethren, how could servant worship servant? This is the import of the angel's rebuke.

Lesson Sixty-nine

## A KING ON EARTH (Rev.19:11-16)

Now for the **WHITE HORSE RIDER** and the **White Horse Riders!**

"And I saw heaven opened, and behold a white horse; and he that sat upon him was called Faithful and True" (vs. 11).

"And the armies which were in heaven followed him upon white horses" (vs. 14).

Behold this spectacle and dramatic scene of the long-looked-for and longed-for, advent! The One who said, **"I will come,"** now **COMES.** It will be well for us to look upon the entire panorama that shall fill the heavens and startle the earth, before we attempt description. (Read vs. 11-21).

Here is the prophecy of many a Prophet coming to fulfillment! Here is the subject, the object, the goal, the gaze, of many prophets realized. This is the one event to which all creation moved and the present dispensation in its trend was reaching to this end! It is this for which all waited. It was for this, patience was exercised. It is in expectation of this that Habakkuk spoke in exhortation;

"Write the vision, and make it plain upon tables, that he may run that readeth it.

For the vision is for an appointed time, but at the end it shall speak, and not lie: though it tarry, wait for it; because it will surely come, it will not tarry" (Hab. 2:2, 3).

This is the promised advent, the return of the Lord, the great premillennial manifestation—the end of the dispensation and the beginning of a new one covering in period of time, a **thousand years!** We shall look first upon the **WHITE HORSE RIDER** and then upon the **White Horse Riders.**

The white horse rider of chapter 6 is not Christ. They can not be one and the same. The appearance of that white horse and its rider, was the beginning of a series of judgments which were foretold in Matthew 24:4-28, but the **White Horse Rider** of chapter 19, brings this series of terrible judgments to an end.

The white horse rider of chapter 6, had a **bow** (6:2). The **White Horse Rider** here at 19, has a sharp two-edged sword proceeding out of His mouth.

The white horse rider of chapter 6, rides on the **earth.** This **White Horse Rider** of chapter 19, comes from an open Heaven.

There is no name given the white horse rider of chapter 6, but the **White Horse Rider** of chapter 19, is named.

1. **He that sat upon him was called "Faithful and True"** (vs. 11).

2. **He had a name written, that no man knew, save Himself** (vs. 12).

3. **And His name is called the Word of God** (vs. 13).

4. **And He had on His vesture a name written, KING OF KINGS, AND LORD OF LORDS** (vs. 16).

He is identified by this fourfold name and all that is said about Him, and could be said about no other, as **Christ.** It is the longed-for and looked-for Messiah.

Christ rode once in procession upon the earth. How significant is the contrast!

Then, He rode on a colt the foal of an ass. See Zech. 9:9.

**Here on a white horse**—19:11.

Then He rode on an ass—Matt. 21:5.

**Here, on the white steed—a horse.**

Then, He came in humiliation.

**Here He comes in open manifestation.**

Then, but children shouted Him welcome.

**Here, He comes as a Sovereign and a Lord.**

As surely as He rode on an ass, so shall He ride on this **white horse.**

The Psalmist saw this advent and spoke of the events here mentioned. Said he;

"Gird thy sword upon thy thigh, O most mighty,
Gird thyself with glory and majesty.
And in thy majesty ride forth prosperously because of truth and meekness and righteousness;
And thy right hand shall teach thee terrible things.
Thy throne, O God, is for ever and ever:
The sceptre of thy kingdom is a right sceptre" (Ps. 45:3-6).

This as if the entire scene of Revelation 19, had been spread in panorama before the Psalmist's eyes, and indeed it was, for such is the uniform testimony of prophecy or, as Gaebelein puts it, the harmony of the prophetic Word."

When John saw Christ in Heaven he described Him as follows;

**CHRIST AS JOHN SAW HIM AMIDST THE CANDLESTICKS**

"Clothed with a garment down to the foot, and girt about the paps with a golden girdle. His head and his hairs were white like wool as white as snow; and his eyes were as a flame of fire; and his feet like unto fine brass, as if they burned in a furnace; and his voice as the sound of many waters. And he had in his right hand seven stars: and out of his mouth went a sharp twoedged sword: and his countenance was as the sun shineth in his strength" (Rev. 1:13-16).

**CHRIST AS JOHN SAW HIM ON THE WHITE HORSE**

"His eyes were as a flame of fire, and on his head were many crowns;

And he was clothed with a vesture dipped in blood: and his name is called The Word of God.

And out of his mouth goeth a sharp twoedged sword, that with it he should smite the nations: and he shall rule them with a rod of iron: and he treadeth the winepress of the fierceness and wrath of God Almighty.

And he hath on his vesture and on his thigh a name written, KING OF KINGS, AND LORD OF LORDS" (Rev. 19:12-16).

In the first vision He is **retained in Heaven** (Acts 3:21) and the second He is seen **returning to the earth.** In the first vision He is **concealed**; in the second He is **revealed.** In the first He is in the **exaltation of the**

**resurrection**; in the second, He is in the **manifestation of the revelation.** In one He is seen in the place of **advocacy** in the other, coming in the glory of the **advent.** In the first vision, John fell in **prostration** (1:17) and in the second, in **adoration** (19:10). In the first vision He is **rejected** from the earth; in the second He comes to **rule** the earth.

## TWO GREAT SCRIPTURES

are introduced here in this passage—one from the prophecy of **Isaiah,** and the other from the **Psalms.** They are both Scriptures that have to do with the advent and the wrath of the Lamb. It is at this place that the **"great day of His wrath"** of which John spoke at chapter 6:17 has **"come."** The company that John saw at 6:15, are here also. See the comparison;

| REVELATION 6:15 | REVELATION 19:18 |
|---|---|
| "And the kings of the earth, and great men, and the rich men, chief captains, mighty men, bondmen, and freemen." | "The flesh of kings, captains, mighty men, flesh of all men, both free and bond, and small and great." |

The first Scripture introduced in this scene is **ISAIAH 63:1-6.**

It is the day of the **Vengeance of Our God.** It is the opening again of the Book which Christ closed at Nazareth. He closed the Book then at Isaiah 61:2, where it reads,

**"To proclaim the acceptable year of the Lord"** (61:2; compare with Luke 4:19).

The next statement reads;

**"And the day of vengeance of our God."**

This is the "day" now ready for fulfillment. The Prophet Isaiah is once again introduced. This time it is at chapter 63 and to this prophecy verse 13 refers, also verse 15, where He **"treadeth the winepress alone."** See Isaiah 63:1-6.

The work of a kinsman was not only to **redeem** but to

**avenge.** Here is the great **Avenger** with His blood sprinkled garments. Here He treads the **winepress alone!**

There is also introduced here the **SECOND PSALM** (see Ps. 2:9 and Rev. 19:15). This Second Psalm is in full harmony with chapter 19, and indeed deals with this very period and judgment.

This Psalm describes the **Confederation of the Nations** (vss. 1-3) and the **Retribution of Messiah** (vss. 4-9) and the **Subjugation of the Nations** (vss. 10-12).

Thus we see the converging of the great prophecies about this event and advent. The long promised is now speedily accomplished. He cuts it short in righteousness. He comes with the **Rod** to **Rule.** He is the **Shepherd Sovereign.**

Followed by white horse rider (vs. 14) He presents the greatest spectacle the universe has ever seen. What a scene of militant militarism! It is **Jude 1:14 and 15** at last! Elijah at Dotham saw a great spectacle when his eyes were opened, but nothing like this scene where Heaven is opened. White horses, how many no one knows. The "**armies of Heaven**" they are called. Ten thousand times ten thousand and thousands of thousands. It beggars human description and imagination!

Lesson Seventy

## ADVENT OF THE AVENGER (Rev.19:17-20:3)

The "day of His wrath has come!" Lo, the "dread Avenger" comes in the long-expected advent. The events move in rapid succession, behold them. See vss. 17-21.

### I. THE CLARION CALL FOR THE CARRION BIRDS—vss. 17, 18.

This call is issued from the sun and to the fowls. It is a call for carrion birds—flesh-eating birds. They are called to a supper which is known as the **"great supper of the Great God."** This scene was foretold also by Ezekiel in fullness of detail except in Ezekiel the beasts are called also. (Ezek. 39:17-22).

This cry from the sun for the birds is immediately answered. The flying creatures come at the command. Genesis 1:20, shows their creation and the sphere of their existence, and now in the Revelation they are called to assist in the judgment of God. What a scene it will be!

They come to devour the carcases of the slain. They are the scavengers of the battlefield.

**The two suppers,** one found earlier in Revelation 19, present strange contrast. One is the **Supper of the Lamb** (vss. 7-9), the other is the **Supper of the Great God.** One is all joy, the other all judgment. Next follows the record of:

**II. THE CONFEDERACY OVERTHROWN—** vss. 19-21.

The **"Beast"** (of chap. 13) is found in confederation with the **kings** of which chapter 17 had spoken. With him also was the **False Prophet** (chap. 13:11-17).

These were taken. The entire confederacy is overcome and overthrown. The arrest is made and the culprit is seized. It is a notable arrest. It is the crush of the rebellion and only one of the trio still remains at large. Soon he also will be apprehended and imprisoned.

They are brought to instant judgment. They need no trial, God cuts it short in righteousness. They are cast alive into a lake of fire which burneth with brimstone. They are superhuman beings dealt with by God. The **Beast** and his supporter, the **False Prophet,** are judged together as they deceived together. God's judgments are **righteous and true.** If any desire to take issue with these things, they must deal with the Author of the Book that states these things. We believe them to be true (see further, Rev. 20:10, concerning these two). The armies that were with them and the kings are slain. The birds deal with the flesh of the slain.

**III. THE CHAINING OF SATAN**—20:1-3.

There is yet one of the trio of evil yet untaken. It is the one who energized and manipulated the other two. He is the real culprit of all the ages. He gave his power to the Beast and the False Prophet, but could not save them when Deuteronomy 32:40-42 is fulfilled. Moses prophesied it, here it is performed for the last verses of chapter 19 show its accomplishment.

"For I lift up my hand to heaven, and say, I live for ever.

If I whet my glittering sword, and mine hand take hold on judgment; I will render vengeance on mine enemies, and will reward them that hate me.

I will make mine arrows drunk with blood, and my sword shall devour flesh; and that with the blood of the slain and of the captives, from the beginning of revenges upon the enemy" (Deut. 32:40-42).

There is yet one who is not captive. Here is the arrest as John saw it, and as it shall be accomplished:

And I saw an angel come down from heaven, having the key of the bottomless pit and a great chain in his hand.
And he laid hold on the dragon, that old serpent, which is the Devil, and Satan, and bound him a thousand years,
And cast him into the bottomless pit, and shut him up, and set a seal upon him, that he should deceive the nations no more, till the thousand years should be fulfilled: and after that he must be loosed a little season (20:1-3).

He will be seized and bound. This will be the most startling event of the underworld ever known. The duration of the imprisonment will be 1,000 years. As to his identity we are not left in doubt—it is the old serpent the **Devil** and **Satan.** The chains that have been upon those he deceived (II Peter 2:4; Jude 1:6) are now his. He will be placed in the Abyss or the bottomless pit. He will no longer be active as I Peter 5:8 describes him. See also Job 1:7. A thousand years later he will be taken from the Abyss and placed in the lake of fire with the Beast and False Prophet (see Rev. 20:10).

These things are a reality—Satan is a person, the Abyss is a place and the binding of Satan is actual and the writer stands in awe of these things and faints not at believing them.

Lesson Seventy-one

## A THRONE: THE END OF JUDGMENTS (Rev.20)

Until now the events of the Book of Revelation have been **premillennial**—that is, **events occurring before the millennial Reign of Christ.** With this chapter (20), we see things: **premillennial,** (the arrest and imprisonment of Satan, vss. 1, 2) **millennial,** (the reign with Christ a thousand years, vss. 3-6), **postmillennial** (the events after the thousand years, vss. 7-15).

This makes simple and plain the contents of the chapter. We shall see these under separate divisions:

### I. EVENTS PRECEDING THE MILLENNIUM—Vss. 1, 2.

The arrest and incarceration of Satan is told in few words but they are sufficient. The term of the sentence covers **one thousand years** which is the meaning of the word "millennium" and the English for the Latin words meaning **a "thousand annums".** Having deceived the nations throughout national history, he is now placed where he cannot longer practice his deceiving art. The reason for his imprisonment is stated; **"That he should deceive the nations no more."** This is the charge against him and the cause of his arrest and imprisonment. If one could tell the nations today they were being deceived by Satan, they would resent it. They believe their diplomacy to be more discerning and their statesmen--ship to be above this, but the facts remain the same. He is **subtle** enough for statesmanship and **deceiving** enough for diplomacy.

The arresting angel we know not. This is not the book of **speculation** but the Book of **Revelation.** God has withheld this from us and we seek to speak only where He has spoken.

Today he goeth about as a **"roaring lion,"** such liberty shall not be his for the thousand years' period foretold in this chapter. Such a prison as this has been mentioned at other places in Scripture (see I Peter 3:18, 19; II Peter 2:4; Jude 1:6). This will be the most sensational arrest and the most notable prisoner ever taken!

What a wonderful world it will be without Satan to tempt and buffet and deceive!

"There will be no tempter then" will be a reality. But how futile and faulty are words to describe or depict! These are the days of which the Prophets have spoken! They are the days of the "regeneration" and "pacification" of the world. "Thy Kingdom" has **"come."** The will of God is **"done."** It is the rule of Heaven on earth or the **"Kingdom of Heaven."** It is **"His day,"** the days of the **"Son of Man."** O hasten the day!

## II. EVENTS OCCURRING DURING THE MILLENNIUM—vss. 3-6.

In this chapter we have the thousand-year period mentioned **six times.** This is the duration of the millennial reign of Christ. This will complete the week of seven prophetic days a thousand years each! The thousand years mentioned here are the days of the earth's Sabbatization. These are the days foretold and forecast. This is the "rest" that remains for the people of God. This is the time of the occupation of the Davidic throne. There is no detail here for this has all been considered in other Scriptures, such as II Samuel 7; Isaiah 9 and 11; Psalm 2. It is to this throne Luke 1:32, 33 refers. It was to this throne Matthew 25:31 refers. In chapter

19 we have the **return,** here in chapter 20, we have the **reign.** It is of this reign, during this thousand years of which our Lord in Luke 22:29, 30 speaks. There will be **"thrones"** and by these thrones the twelve tribes of Israel will be judged. This accounts for the words—**"and I saw thrones."**

**The Lord will be King.** The earth will have its Divine Dictator. See Zechariah 14:19. Of this great event all the Prophets have spoken. See Isaiah 24:23; Isaiah 9:7; Jeremiah 3:17; 23:5. It will be a day of universal adoration and coronation! See Micah 4:7; Ezekiel 43:7 and a hundred kindred Scriptures. What the Prophets from Moses forward described in much detail is here summarized in one phrase—**"the thousand years."** It is called **"the thousand year**s" as a definite period and known as such.

The cry is raised now and then that pre-millennialists base the doctrine of the reign of Christ upon the earth upon **"the one single and solitary passage of Scripture."** One passage would be sufficient. If God spoke **once** it would be enough. But the fact is that there is no such thing as a single and solitary verse of Scripture. It is a unit and each Scripture demands the others and this is the case here. The thousand years mentioned six times here has been the theme of all the writers and its realization here was in anticipation throughout the Old and New Testament writings.

Many wonderful changes will take place. Time fails us at this point. See such Scriptures as Psalm 67:6; Isaiah 32:1; Isaiah 29:18, 19; 33:6; 33:24; 65:20-23.

## III. EVENTS OCCURRING AT THE CLOSE OF THE MILLENNIUM—vss. 7-15.

These events are as follows:

1. **The Loosing of Satan**—vs. 7.

2. **The Deceiving of the Nations**—vs. 8.
3. **The Mobilization of the Nations**—vs. 8.
4. **The Besiegement of the Holy City**—vs. 9.
5. **The Devouring Fire Falling from Heaven**—vs. 9
6. **Satan Cast into the Lake of Fire**—vs. 10.
7. **Satan's Punishment and the Period**—vs. 10.
8. **The White Throne Established**—vs. 11.
9. **The Throne Sitter**—vs. 11.
10. **The Books**—vs. 12.
11. **The Judgment**—vs. 12.
12. **The Judged**—vs. 12.
13. **The Sea and Death and Hell Yields Prisoners**—vs. 14.
14. **The disposition of Death and Hell**—vs. 14.
15. **The Final Judgment Act**—vs. 15.

This chapter concludes all judgments for ever for there is nothing else to judge or no one else. Here we see **Satan's Final Rebellion.** He will never again lift himself against God. All misrule put down for ever. All rebellion is for ever at an end! Christ must reign until I Corinthians 15:25 and 26 is fulfilled!

"All enemies under His feet," is a little glimpse at the victorious end. Psalm 110:1 will come to literal and actual fulfillment!

Lesson Seventy-two

## POST-MILLENIAL ORDER (Rev.21-22) Part 1

We hear so much of the "land of the beginning again." It is at Revelation twenty-one that we are really at the beginning again. It is here that all things are new. The former things have passed away. The heavens and earth of Genesis 1:1 are no longer in sight. It is now that the new heavens and earth of Revelation 21:1 come into view. We can as we reach this point of the Revelation commence to understand the difference between the temporal and the eternal. For seven thousand years the present heaven and earth have been seen but the heaven and earth of Revelation 21 has but been in promise and prospect. Paul said, "The things which are seen are **temporal** but the things which are not seen are **eternal."** At the close of Revelation twenty, we are through with the things that are seen. A week of millenniums has measured man's probation and occupation of the heavens and earth which are now. Man had his six days of work, each day a thousand years. Man had his Sabbath day extending over the term of a thousand years. This duration and probation is now at an end. There will be found things that are new. The old creation will be laid aside like an outworn garment. It has been folded up as a vesture. The Divine conflagration and purgation of which Peter and the Prophets have spoken, is accomplished. The Divine dispensations measured into human epochs, have come to a close. There are no words to express the emotion that one feels as he looks back from Revelation twenty-one, upon the record of the past which we find one of **sin, sorrow, suffering, death, disease**, dissolution, decay and destruction. One hears the centuries of sighing and crying and looks upon the dying and the diseased. Like the panorama of the past there is spread before our eyes the Satanic strife and struggle which began prior to the advent of man, on the earth and which strife continued until we reached the close of Revelation twenty where Satanic strife and struggle was forever put down. We cannot recall the tale of the ages which are all now history. The Messianic contest and conflict, which was waged throughout all dispensations need not be recalled at this point. Upon these things we have pondered and wondered in our former studies. We are now to turn from the tragedy of sin to the triumph of grace. We are now to turn from the record of ruin to behold the full result of redemption. We are now to behold a heaven and an earth wherein dwelleth righteousness. It is impossible to speak without deep feeling of a world which has been the stage upon which has been enacted the sad record of sin. What shall we say as we look back and see an Eden, a deluge, a Babel, an Abraham and his sons, Moses, Joshua, the Davidic kingdom, its disruption and corruption, then Christ in the flesh, the **Cross,** the empty tomb, the resurrection, ascension, the apocalyptic judgments, the thousand years reign and the white throne and its results! These are all past. Behold these words;

"And I saw a new heaven and a new earth: for the first heaven and the first earth were passed away; and there was no more sea."

All that this means we can never know until we shall know as we are known. We see these things but through a glass darkly. Everything is new at this point. It is what Govett says "A new epoch begins." There is a new creation in honor of the last Adam just as there was a creation prepared for the first. There will be a new heaven, a new atmosphere, new stars but no sea. Distillation, evaporation and condensation will not be required to maintain the equation of things.

There will be no need of the sun. There will be a new and a Divine order unlike anything in the past and beyond the human mind to conceive. It is all too great for the mind of man. What prophet Isaiah foresaw, God now fulfills. Isaiah has two times referred to the events recorded in this chapter.

"For, behold, I create new heavens and a new earth: and the former shall not be remembered, nor come into mind" (Is. 65:17).

"For as the new heavens and the new earth, which I will make, shall remain before me, saith the Lord, so shall your seed and your name remain" (66:22).

What the prophet Isaiah saw, John also saw. Peter also was concerned with this event and spoke of these things. (See II Peter 3:5-13). This is as we stated at the opening, the place of beginning again. It is called by some the eternal state and this we believe to be true. It will be a Divinely and eternally fixed condition. There will be no variableness, no changing. Throughout the past change and decay in all around we see but here never again disorder, change or chaos. The trail of the serpent shall never mark or mar this fair creation. We are standing as it were at a mountain's peak, looking a landscape over. What we shall see will beggar human language to express.

Lesson Seventy-three

## POST-MILLENIAL ORDER (Rev.21-22) Part 2

For many chapters in the study of this Book, we have seen **pre-millennial disorder** except for the thousand years, the duration of Christ's reign. We now come to **The Post-Millennial Order** into which order confusion will never again come.

The disturber of things has gone to his incarceration and final destination! This is fully told at the close of chapter twenty. It will never be told again but will pass out of mind forever.

The old has been laid aside, the garment was outworn. The new is now inaugurated. The days of the old earth are now fulfilled. We now behold a **new heaven and a new earth.** We have seen two "heavens and earth," now we come to the third and **final.**

### THE THREE HEAVENS AND EARTH OF SCRIPTURE

**First**

**I. THE HEAVEN AND EARTH OF GENESIS 1:1**—II Peter 3:5.

**II. THE HEAVENS AND EARTH OF GENESIS 1:3 to 31**—II Peter 3:7.

**III. THE HEAVENS AND EARTH OF REVELATION 21:1**—II Peter 3:13.

The heavens and earth that **"were"** and **"are"** are now passed away. The new heaven and the new earth comes to view. The earth that **now is** is not the earth that **was** nor the earth that **is** to be.

How wonderful it is to turn to the "new"! The waxing old of the present, may be everywhere seen. The new is unseen and from this time on we are not longer to look upon the things that are seen for they are temporal. These things are **eternal.** We have come to the eternal state at the opening of chapter 21.

This chapter is concerned with two visions;

The First Vision; **New Heaven and New Earth**—21:1-8.

The Second Vision; **The Bride the Lamb's Wife**—21:9-27.

We shall look upon this chapter under these two divisions.

**The First Vision; THE NEW HEAVEN AND THE NEW EARTH**—21:1-8.

The **"new era"** and the **"new world"** of which men have so glibly spoken comes only at Revelation 21:1. Until then all things are of the old creation. The millennial period is a time of renewal and release but it is staged upon and over the old creation. Here all things are **"new."** The former things have passed away.

It will be interesting to notice the things that are "minus" or missing in the new order.

1. **No More Sea** (vs. 1).
2. **No More Death** (vs. 4).
3. **No More Sorrow** (vs. 4).
4. **No More Crying** (vs. 4).
5. **No More Pain** (vs. 4).
6. **No More Temple** (vs. 22).
7. **No More Sun** (vs. 23).
8. **No More Moon** (vs. 23).
9. **No More Night** (vs. 25).
10. **No More Abominations** (vs. 27).

**Five** of these "No mores" are mentioned under the **first vision** (21:1-8), and **five** mentioned under the **second vision** (21:9-27). The Book of **Romans** which is the

"Court Room" of the Bible is the Book of the **"much mores."** (See Rom. 5:9, 10, 15, 17, 20; 9:22; 11:12, 24.) There are **seven** "much mores" in Romans. In the Book of Revelation which is the "Throne Room of the Bible," there are **ten** "no mores." It is no longer **"much more"** but thank God it is **"no more."** The number **ten** is said to denote **ordinal perfection.** It is the combination of three which signifies Divine perfection, with number **seven,** which signifies **spiritual perfection.**

These things are the minus and missing things in the new order.

**There will be a new order** for the equation of temperature and the former system of evaporation, condensation and evaporation in which the sea played its part, will no longer maintain.

**There will be a new order** and creation into which death will never enter and therefore, none of the things which have come as the result of death, which is the result of sin, will longer maintain. Without sin, then "no death," and with no death, "no sorrow," and without sorrow "no crying." There will be "no pain" for all the things mentioned are the bringers of pain. How quickly we have written and you have read these words! How little we understand the eternal import of this brief statement which for ever sets aside all the former things. Is it little wonder the word **Behold!** as an exclamation and an exultation, appears two times in this chapter! This is the second occurrence and quotation of Isaiah 49:10. (See 7:16, 17).

"They shall not hunger nor thirst; neither shall the heat nor sun smite them."

God keeps His Word with His Prophets. By this we see also the far-flung projection of Isaiah's prophecies. They reach to the visions of the New Heaven and earth. Indeed the last chapter of Isaiah contains the same vision as the last chapter of the Bible. See Isaiah 66:22.

"For as the **new heavens** and the **new earth** which I will make shall **remain** before Me, saith the Lord, so shall your seed and your name remain."

See also Isaiah 25:7, 8; 35:10.

With this **first vision** there was a **"voice."** What was said is found at verses 3 and 4.

This voice is followed by the words of the **Throne Sitter** (vs. 5) who gives a **dictation** (write vs. 5) in which we see, first

**A Benediction.**

"I am Alpha and Omega, the Beginning and the End. I will give unto him that is athirst of the fountain of the water of life freely. He that overcometh shall inherit all things. I will be His God and He shall be My Son." (vss. 5-7).

**A Malediction.**

"But the fearful and the unbelieving and the abominable, and murderers and whoremongers and sorcerers, and idolaters, and all liars, shall have their part in the lake of fire which burneth with fire and brimstone; which is the second death."

The angel which we saw with the seven last plagues, at chapters 15 and 16, now appears to unveil the **second vision** (9-27).

This vision may be divided as follows:

I. **The Mountain Vision**—vss. 9-14.

II. **The Measurements of the City**—vss. 15-17.

III. **The Materials Used in the City**—vss. 17-21.

IV. **The Missing or No More Things**—vss. 22-26.

Let us behold;

## I. THE MOUNTAIN VISION—vss. 9-14.

When we stood at the threshold of Revelation we beheld the Vision of an **Ascended Christ.** Here it is the Vision of a **Descended City.** A city **coming down from God.** It is not a city **built up** by men. This city, like every other good and perfect gift, "cometh down from above." It is not an **evolution** as are the cities of men. It is an **involution,** it comes down from God. Other cities have for their builder and maker, men. This is the God built city. It is the long looked for city. It has been a common saying in a world like this, that God made the country and man made the city. In this case it is no longer true. This is the city God has made.

Abraham looked for it and all of the Hebrew heroes and heroines longed for it (Heb. 11:13-16).

The name of the city is the **Holy Jerusalem.** We have seen the earthly Jerusalem, this is the Heavenly (21:10).

**The Illumination** (vss. 11 and 23, 25). The provision of God for the lighting of the city. This will bear much consideration. The artificial forever gone. The very light of God of which God is light, will illumine this city.

**The Commemoration** (vss. 12-14). There are twelve gates. Each gate is a memorial gate. The names of the twelve tribes of Israel are on the gates. A name for a gate. This is God's commemoration. He will forever establish His memorial for Israel. **He never forgets.** (See Is. 49:15, 16).

## II. THE MEASUREMENTS OF THE CITY—vss. 15-17.

The measurement of the city was made by the angel with the golden reed. The **city gates** and **walls** were all measured. It was a perfect cube of 12000 furlongs (vs. 16). In the Temple, the Holy of Holies was a perfect cube of twenty cubits.

## III. THE MATERIAL USED IN THE CITY—vss. 17-21.

It was "pure gold." It was so pure and free from alloy and dross that it was clear like crystal. No refiner on earth could so refine gold as it is refined in this **Golden City of the Glorious God!**

**The Foundation** should be viewed with the illumination and the commemoration. All precious stones. Read the record as John reports the vision (vss. 19-21). This is the city that **"hath foundations."**

**The Ornamentation** is beyond human speech to portray. Compare in your study the **twelve stones** with those in the breast-plate of Aaron. Here are the stones for ornamentation and their order—

1. **Jasper.**
2. **Sapphire.**
3. **Chalcedony.**
4. **Emerald.**
5. **Sardonyx.**
6. **Sardius.**
7. **Chrysolyte.**
8. **Beryl.**
9. **Topaz.**
10. **Chrysophrasus.**
11. **Jacinth.**
12. **Amethyst.**

With jewel set gates and foundations, and with streets of pure gold is this city and we who are in Christ shall see it with our own eyes! What sights and scenes await us!

## IV. THE MISSING OR "NO MORE" THINGS—vss. *22-26.*

There was no Temple. No more need of sacrifice. No more need for access. No more need for oblations. No more need for a building. God and the Lamb is the Sanctuary and the meeting place.

No **sun** in the day time. No **moon** at night. The Light is Shekinah glory of God and the Lamb. The Light of the World is the Light of the new earth. There will be no darkness. The darkness has all fled away!

No gates to shut at night for there is no night. There is nothing in the dark for there is none. No gate-keepers in this city of God. Nations come and go and with them no abomination is forever known. There are no words but with our pen we acknowledge our penury and poverty as we speak. The vision overwhelms! To such a city as this we are forward bent. We also want to confess "no continuing city here."

O Golden City of the Glorious God, we long for your descent! Come down from God!

We thank God with unbared head, and broken spirit. Lord, the vision is too great for us. It is like unto Thee!

Lesson Seventy-four

## POST-MILLENIAL VISIONS (Rev.21-22)

The first five verses of chapter 22, in our judgment, continue chapter 21, where we beheld the City of God with its **foundation,** its **ornamentation,** its **commemoration** and its **illumination.** Now we shall see the **river** resulting in fertilization and vegetation and in association with the new creation.

When we opened the Bible, we found there a river went out of Eden to water the garden and from thence it was parted, and became into four heads (Gen. 2:10).

Now the four rivers have come into the one, the "river of Water of Life" (Rev. 22:1). The water was transparent. Its spring and source was from the **"Throne of God and of the Lamb."** For a thousand years the earth had known the throne of the great Priest-King of Zechariah 6:13. All thrones now give place (for I Corinthians 15:24-26 has now been accomplished) to this throne of God and the Lamb. God is "all in all" (for now I Corinthians 15:28 is an accomplished fact) and for that reason the Lamb takes the second place and it is called "the Throne of **GOD** and the **Lamb."** In Millennial days the river of Ezekiel proceeded from the Temple and was associated with the altar (Ezek. 47:1-11), the place of **sacrifice,** but here it proceeds from the **Throne,** the place of **Sovereignty.**

At the near opening of the Book of Revelation, at chapter 4, we saw a throne—a rainbow-circled throne which was doubtless set for the judgment of the wicked living on the earth. At chapter 20, we saw a throne which was established for the judgment of the wicked living. This throne, the throne of God and the Lamb, is not a judgment throne. There is nothing or no one to judge for there will be never again any one or any thing that "defileth" or "worketh abomination, or maketh a lie" (21:27). This throne is for majesty and glory and honor. **It is the throne of God and the Lamb.** It is the place of their **Presence** and the seat of their **Sovereignty!**

In the midst of the Street of the City and on either side of the river there was the Tree of Life. When the Bible opens we see there the Tree of Life. It is in the midst of the garden. Here it is in the midst of the street. There is no **seculsion** or no **exclusion.** It yields health or haleness for the nations. There is no sickness or death here. The former things have all passed away. See 21:4.

There is no more curse. It belonged to the old creation and not to the new. It was associated with the **former** heavens and earth, not with the **final** heavens and earth.

**Service**—"and His servants shall serve Him."

**Sight**—"and they shall see His face."

**Sealed**—"His name shall be on their foreheads." See vs. 3.

**"No night,"** therefore no need for illumination—the candle or the sun no longer required. There will never come a candle lighting time. There will be no sunrise, no sunset. No day, no night—just one continuous land of Light and the Lamb. God is light and He will be the Light of this endless age. What all this means we know not except we are conscious that volumes are compressed to one word or to one verse. The scientific signification of these things would stagger men if they knew. It is the new order entirely outside the old order which man has systematized scientifically to express his little information. These things infinitely transcend anything we ever thought or could think.

For ever and ever is the Divine scope—there is nothing left for the human to say.

The consummation of Divine revelation is too high for us to reach or too distant for us to comprehend in the present. God hasten to fulfill our hope for the future!

Lesson Seventy-five

## CONCLUSION (Rev.22:6-21)

We now come to the **Conclusion** (22:6-21).

At the **opening** of the Book it was "things which must shortly come to pass" (1:1) and now at the **close** of the Book it is the "things which must shortly be done." See 22:6.

At the **opening** of the Book God had "sent His angel" (1:1) and at the close once again it is written: "God sent His angel" (22:6).

At the **opening** of the Book this angel was sent to "His servant John" and at the close it is again "His servants." See 1:1 and 22:6.

At the **opening** of the Book Christ is the Faithful and True One (3:14) and now at the close of the Book these sayings as was the Person of Christ are "faithful and true" (22:6). When the Book **opened** it was entitled a prophecy (1:3) and now as it closes it is called the prophecy of this Book (22:7).

At the **opening** of the Book there is a beatitude and now at the **close** there is another—at the opening, blessed are they that **"hear, read** and **keep"** (1:3); here at the close it is "blessed is he that **keepeth"** (22:7).

When the Book is **introduced** to us it is, **"Behold He cometh,"** and when it is **concluded, "Surely I come quickly."** See 1:7; 22:20.

At the **opening** of the Book there is the testimony—**"I am the Alpha and Omega"** (1:11) and at the **close** again we read: **"I am Alpha and Omega"** (22:13).

At the **opening** of the Book John fell down in prostration (1:17) and at the **close** he falls down in **adoration** (22:8).

There was an **"even so"** at the **opening** and an **"even**

**so"** at the **close** of the Book. See 1:7; 22:20. Both times this "even so" is used following the announcement of His Coming.

When Daniel closes his prophecy it is with the Divine instruction: **"Go thy way, for the words are closed up and sealed till the time of the end"** (Dan. 12:9).

When John closes his prophecy it is with the Divine instruction:

**"Seal not the sayings of the prophecy of the Book for the time is at hand"** (Rev. 22:10).

What Daniel **foretold,** Revelation **fulfilled.** Daniel saw "the end from the beginning" and John saw the beginning of the end.

At the **opening** of the Book John "saw" these things (1:2) and at the **close** the testimony of John corroborates this. See Rev. 1:2 and 22:16.

At the **opening** of the Book John told of the things which were **hereafter** but at the **close** the time is at hand (1:19; 22:10).

At the **opening** of the Book the Lord Himself speaks unto John (1:17, 18). At the close of the Book the Lord Himself speaks to John (22:16).

In chapters 2 and 3 the churches are addressed (seven of them) and in chapter 22, the churches are again mentioned as the recipients of this message. See chaps. 2 and 3, and 22:16.

At verse 14 there is the last beatitude or **"Blessed"** of the Book. This is the **fiftieth** and last occurrence of the word in the New Testament.

**Five** denotes "Divine grace." The Greek word for "grace" has **five** letters. **Ten** denotes ordinal perfection and here is **five** times **ten** or **fifty.** At last the benediction of God has come. **"Blessed"** is all and everything. Two times the word **"blessed"** is used in this concluding portion. See vss. 7 and 14.

When our Lord Himself speaks He uses a **botanical,** a **genealogical** and an **astronomical** figure of speech in the titles He chooses (vs. 16).

**THE BOTANICAL FIGURE. I am the "Root."** He is the "Root out of dry ground" of Isaiah 53:2. He was the "tender plant" here mentioned. He is the One mentioned in Isaiah 11:1. **"There shall come forth a rod out of the stem of Jesse and a Branch shall grow out of his roots."** Under the figure of the Root He is associated with the earth. He is the **"plant of renown"**—the **"Rose of Sharon."**

**THE GENEALOGICAL FIGURE. "The offspring of David."** Here the genus is put for the species. See Acts 17:28. His generation is declared. David was the **first** human name mentioned in the New Testament writings (Matt. 1:1) and now the **last** human name mentioned (22:16). This is the **third** time the word **David** is used in this Book. See 3:7; 5:5; 22:16.

1. **He that hath the key of David** (3:7).
2. **The Lion of the tribe of Judah, the Root of David** (5:5).
3. **I am the Root and Offspring of David.**

It is not strange or singular that this reference to David is introduced in the Revelation, as it is the Book in which all the conditions of the **Davidic Covenant** (II Sam. 7) are fulfilled. Revelation is the Book in which we see the **confirmation** of the covenant and the **occupation** of David's throne.

**THE ASTRONOMICAL FIGURE. "The Bright and Morning Star."** This stellar figure takes us back to Numbers 24:17.

**"I shall see Him, but not now; I shall behold Him, but not nigh: There shall come a Star out of Jacob, and a Sceptre shall rise out of Israel."**

The **"not now"** of Numbers is **"now"** in Revelation.

The **"not nigh"** of Numbers is the "nigh" in Revelation.

The Star that "shall" come has come and the Scepter that "shall rise" has arisen.

The Bright and Morning Star has arisen! The Scepter is now in the ruling hand of God! The morning quickly breaks when

**"The Sun of Righteousness"**

arises with healing in His wings! (Mal. 4:2). "The Star shall come out of Jacob." God is as good as His Word and the Word is as good as God!

Then follows the **universal cry for His Coming** (vs. 17).

1. **The Spirit says "Come"** (vs. 17).
2. **The Bride says "Come"** (vs. 17).
3. **Him that heareth says "Come"** (vs. 17).
4. **John says "Come"** (vs. 20).

Then follows the **universal cry to come to the Waters:**

1. **Let him that is athirst come.**
2. **Let whosoever will come** (vs. 17).

The Water of Life (22:1, 2) is open to all who may freely come.

Before the last benediction of the Book there comes the maledictions. In this final malediction God makes use of the figures of mathematics employing **addition** and **subtraction.** You can not **add** to God's Word or subtract from God's Word. This is the solemn and serious statement. You may attempt to do it but only with this curse and malediction:

**"God shall add to him the plagues written in this Book."**

**God shall take his part:**

1. **"Out of the Book of Life.**

**2. Out of the Holy City.**

**3. From the things written in this Book"** (vss. 18 19).

Let those who deny the authority and veracity of this Book beware. This is indeed a solemn warning and malediction. God's Word will positively not admit of **addition** or subtraction. God's Word is **perfect** and from perfection there cannot be **addition** or **subtraction!** Ponder these things.

**"SURELY I COME QUICKLY"**—vs. 20.

This is the last utterance of our Lord. His testimony is completed. This is the **seventh** and last warning of our Lord concerning His Coming in the Book of Revelation. It is not only the one subject of the Revelation but of the Bible from Genesis to Revelation. This is the Book of **"the power and Coming of our Lord Jesus Christ."**

## THE BENEDICTION

**"The grace of our Lord Jesus Christ be with you all. Amen."**

And it has been grace and will be grace, till the judgments of this Book shall commence. God is still showing Grace to this age and world. How long, O Lord?

# SUGGESTIVE AND SIGNIFICANT NOTES

## NAMES OF CHRIST USED IN THE BOOK OF REVELATION AND THE NUMBER OF TIMES USED

The Faithful Witness (1); The First Begotten of the dead (1); The Prince of the kings of the earth (1); Alpha and Omega (4); The Beginning and the Ending (1); The First and the Last (3); One like unto the Son of man (2); He that liveth and was dead and is alive for evermore (1); He that hath the keys of hell and of death (1); He that holdeth the seven stars in His right hand and that walketh in the midst of the seven golden candlesticks (1); He which hath a sharp sword with two edges (1); The Son of God who hath His eyes like unto a flame of fire and His feet like fine brass (1); He which searcheth the reins and hearts (1); The Morning Star (1); He that hath the seven Spirits of God and the seven stars (1); He that is holy, He that is true, He that hath the key of David, He that openeth and no man shutteth, and shutteth and no man openeth (1); The Amen, the Faithful and True Witness, the Beginning of the creation of God (1); The Lion of the tribe of Judah (1); The Root of David (1); A or the Lamb (28); God's Christ (2); Faithful and True (1); Word of God (1); King of nations (1); Root and offspring of David (1); The Bright and Morning Star (1); Lord Jesus (1).

## NEW TESTAMENT BOOKS IN WHICH OLD TESTAMENT QUOTATIONS ARE PROMINENT

**Ninety-two** Old Testament quotations in **Matthew.**

**One hundred and two** Old Testament quotations in **Hebrews.**

**Two hundred and eighty-five** Old Testament quotations in **Revelation.**

These figures do not include repetition of quotations or allusions, but separate quotations. The Book of Revelation is rooted in the Old Testament with three times more quotations than any other New Testament Book.

The Book of Revelation is significantly stamped with the number Seven. Seven Churches. Seven Spirits. Seven Golden Candle-sticks. Seven Stars. Seven Lamps. Seven Seals. Seven Horns. Seven Eyes. Seven Angels. Seven Trumpets. Seven Thunders. Seven Heads. Seven Crowns. Seven Last Plagues. Seven Golden Vials. Seven Mountains. Seven Kings. Seven New Things.

The relation of the Book of Revelation to the Book of Genesis is most interesting. What begins in Genesis ends in Revelation. The following is taken from "the Companion Bible." (Oxford Press.)

| GENESIS | REVELATION |
|---|---|
| 1. Genesis, the Book of the beginning. | 1. Revelation, the Book of the end. |
| 2. The earth created (1:1). | 2. The earth passed away (21:1). |
| 3. Satan's first rebellion. | 3. Satan's final rebellion (20:3, 7-10). |
| 4. Sun, moon and stars for earth's government (1:14-16). | 4. Sun, moon, and stars, connected with earth's judgment (6:13; 8:12; 16:8). |
| 5. Sun to govern the day (1:16). | 5. No need of the sun (21:23). |
| 6. Darkness called night (1:5). | 6. "No night there" (22:5). |
| 7. Waters called seas (1:10). | 7. "No more sea" (21:1). |
| 8. A river for earth's blessing (2:10-14). | 8. A river for the new earth (22:1, 2). |
| 9. Man in God's image (1:26). | 9. Man headed by one in Satan's image (13). |
| 10. Entrance of sin (3). | 10. Development and end of sin (21; 22). |
| 11. Curse pronounced (3:14, 17). | 11. "No more curse" (22:3). |
| 12. Death entered (3:19). | 12. "No more death" (21:4). |
| 13. Cherubim, first mentioned in connection with man (3:24). | 13. Cherubim, finally mentioned in connection with man (4:6). |
| 14. Man driven out from Eden (3:24). | 14. Man restored (22). |
| 15. Tree of Life guarded (3:24). | 15. "Right to the Tree of Life" (22:14). |
| 16. Sorrow and suffering enter (3:17). | 16. No more sorrow (21:4). |
| 17. Man's religion, art, and science, resorted to for enjoyment, apart from God (4). | 17. Man's religion, luxury, art, and science in their full glory, judged and destroyed by God (18). |
| 18. Nimrod, a great rebel and king, and hidden anti-god, the founder of Babylon (10:8, 9). | 18. The beast, the great rebel, a king, and manifested anti-god, the reviver of Babylon (13-18). |
| 19. A flood from God to destroy an evil generation (6-9). | 19. A flood from Satan to destroy an elect generation (12). |

| | |
|---|---|
| 20. The bow, the token of God's covenant with the earth (9:13). | 20. The bow, betokening God's remembrance of His covenant with the earth (4:3; 10:1). |
| 21. Sodom and Egypt, the place of corruption and temptation (13; 19). | 21. Sodom and Egypt again: spiritually representing Jerusalem (11:8). |
| 22. A confederacy against Abraham's people overthrown (14). | 22. A confederacy against Abraham's seed overthrown (12). |
| 23. Marriage of first Adam (2:18-23). | 23. Marriage of last Adam (19). |
| 24. A bride sought for Abraham's son (Isaac) and found (24). | 24. A Bride made ready and brought to Abraham's Son (19:9). See Matthew 1:1. |
| 25. Two angels acting for God on behalf of His people (19). | 25. Two witnesses acting for God on behalf of His people (11). |
| 26. A promised seed to possess the gate of his enemies (22:17). | 26. The promised Seed coming into possession (11:18). |
| 27. Man's dominion ceased and Satan's begun (3:24). | 27. Satan's dominion ended, and man's restored (22). |
| 28. The old serpent causing sin, suffering, and death (3:1). | 28. The old serpent bound for 1,000 years (20:1-3). |
| 29. The doom of the old serpent pronounced (3:15). | 29. The doom on the old serpent executed (20:10). |
| 30. Sun, moon, and stars, associated with Israel (37:9). | 30. Sun, moon, and stars, associated again with Israel (12). |

The Book of Revelation is the Book of the "**Lamb.**"

**Twenty-eight times** the Lamb is mentioned. See 5:6, 8, 12, 13; 6:1, 16; 7:9, 10, 14, 17; 12:11; 13:8, 11; 14:1, 4, 10; 15:3; 17:14; 19:7, 9; 21:9, 14, 22, 23, 27; 22:1, 3.

The Book of Revelation is also the Book of the "throne." It is the "throne room" of the Bible. Trace the foollowing: 1:4; 3:21; 4:2-6, 9, 10; 5:1, 6, 11, 13; 6:16; 7:9, 10, 11, 15, 17; 8:3; 12:5; 14:3, 5; 16:17; 19:5; 20:4, 11; 21:5; 22:1, 3.

What a key to the character and contents of this Book is the use of these two words!